The Electorate Reconsidered

D1602507

SAGE FOCUS EDITIONS

The Electorate Reconsidered

edited by
John C. Pierce and
John L. Sullivan

SAGE PUBLICATIONS   Beverly Hills   London

For information address:

SAGE Publications, Inc.
275 South Beverly Drive
Beverly Hills, California 90212

SAGE Publications Ltd
28 Banner Street
London ECIY 8QE, England

Printed in the United States of America

Library of Congress Cataloging in Publication Data

Main entry under title:

The Electorate Reconsidered.

    (Sage focus editions)
    Bibliography: p.
    1. Elections—United States—Addresses, essays, lectures. 2. Voting—United States—Addresses, essays, lectures. 3. Public opinion—United States—Addresses, essays, lectures. 4. United States—Politics and government—1945–   —Addresses, essays, lectures. I. Pierce, John C. II. Sullivan, John L., 1945–   III. Series.
JK 1968 1980 .E4   324'.0973   79–28415
ISBN 0–8039–1342–7
ISBN 0–8039–1343–5 pbk.

FIRST PRINTING

CONTENTS

ABOUT THE EDITORS AND CONTRIBUTORS

Edward G. Carmines is Assistant Professor of Political Science at Indiana University.

Pamela Johnston Conover is Assistant Professor of Political Science at the University of Kentucky.

Stanley Feldman is Assistant Professor of Political Science at Brown University.

Morris P. Fiorina is Professor in the Division of Humanities and Social Science at the California Institute of Technology.

Paul R. Hagner is Assistant Professor of Political Science at Washington State University.

Marjorie Randon Hershey is Associate Professor of Political Science at Indiana University.

Jonathon M. Hurwitz is a doctoral student in Political Science at the University of Minnesota.

George E. Marcus is Associate Professor of Political Science at Williams College.

John P. McIver is a doctoral student in Political Science at Indiana University.

Mark A. Peffley is a doctoral student in Political Science at the University of Minnesota.

John R. Petrocik is Associate Professor of Political Science at the University of California, Los Angeles.

John C. Pierce is Professor of Political Science at Washington State University.

James E. Piereson is Assistant Professor of Political Science at the University of Pennsylvania.

W. Phillips Shively is Professor of Political Science at the University of Minnesota.

James A. Stimson is Associate Professor of Political Science at Florida State University.

John L. Sullivan is Associate Professor of Political Science at the University of Minnesota.

Herbert F. Weisberg is Professor of Political Science at Ohio State University.

Christine B. Williams is Assistant Professor of Political Science at Mt. Holyoke College.

ACKNOWLEDGEMENTS

As in most projects of this nature, the editors accumulated many debts. We wish to acknowledge the indispensable contributions of Dell Day, Joyce Lynd, Cynthia Avery, and Bonnie Milligan, each of whom typed a portion of the manuscript. Pierce is grateful to the E. O. Holland Fund for financial assistance at the early stages of the book. We wish to thank the authors of the book's chapters. Deadlines for outlines, drafts, and revisions were met with uncommon regularity. Finally, we wish to acknowledge our gratitude to the community of scholars whose persistent and critical examination of the American electorate led to this book and the broader literature it represents.

PART I: INTRODUCTION

1

AN OVERVIEW OF THE AMERICAN ELECTORATE

John C. Pierce
John L. Sullivan

Three decades ago there surfaced what has been called a revolution in the study of the American electorate, a revolution based in the systematic or "scientific" analysis of public opinion and political behavior (Dahl, 1961; Eulau, 1963). The roots of this "behavioral" approach to the study of politics extend much deeper than the late 1940s or the early 1950s. Yet, in that postwar period there emerged a burgeoning storehouse of behavioral studies.

Out of the behavioral literature there developed a widely accepted picture of the American electorate, a picture almost uniformly unflattering when juxtaposed with the normative model of the ideal democratic citizen. In one early and major study, *Voting*, the authors concluded that: "Individual voters today seem unable to satisfy the requirements for a democratic system of government outlined by political theorists" (Berelson et al., 1954: 312). In the eyes of many, the series of landmark studies produced by the scholars at the Survey Research Center of the University of Michigan (Campbell et al., 1960; Campbell et al., 1966; Converse, 1964) appeared to reinforce the pejorative view of the electorate. In the company of several other important works (e.g., Lipset, 1960; McClosky, 1964), the Michigan studies produced what has since been called the "traditional" view of the American electorate. Indeed, this view has found a home both in the basic textbooks and in the scholarly literature.

The posthumous publication of V. O. Key's *The Responsible Electorate* (1966) seems an appropriate watershed for a reconsideration of this traditional view. Following Key's affirmation of the rationality of the electorate ("voters are not fools"), there appeared a new wave of studies loosely called "revisionist" (Asher, 1976). Although the revisionist studies contain reconsiderations of many aspects of the electorate, they cohere more in their shared questioning of the traditional literature than in the kinds of new answers they provide. Even so, the reconsiderations of the electorate generally provide a more positive picture, one that emphasizes the public's fundamental rationality and fitness for an active role in a democratic political process. Reconsiderations of the electorate continue. Yet, perhaps inevitably, the revisionist studies themselves have engendered their own flock of critics.

This book reflects some of the many currents present in the study of the American electorate. The following chapters explore distinct elements of the public's political beliefs and behavior. At the same time, no orthodoxy has been imposed on the contributions. Although each chapter provides an overview of previous research, the approaches differ considerably in building on those overviews. Some chapters document changes in the electorate; others offer new ways to look at old problems; and still others define new problems to examine.

THE RECONSIDERED ELECTORATE: A SUMMARY

The reconsiderations of the American electorate cover almost every aspect of its political character. Yet, the reasons for the reconsiderations vary rather widely. Moreover, there is substantial disagreement about many of the new findings. Indeed, there are revisions of the revisions. This section provides a brief overview of the most important changes in the scholarly view of the American public.

POLITICAL THINKING

The traditional view of the quality of the electorate's political thinking was rather unflattering. The majority of the public was thought to be unable to think about, and evaluate, politics in a sophisticated way (Campbell et al., 1960). Similarly, the public's beliefs on various issues of public policy were not consistent with each other, and many expressions on those issues were thought to be only random, reflecting no true attitude (Converse, 1964).

Reconsiderations of the electorate challenge this negative view. Several studies show an increase in the number of ideologues since the mid-1950s (Field and Anderson, 1969; Pierce, 1970; Nie et al., 1976). There also occurred an apparent increase in the consistency of the public's beliefs across different issues (Bennett, 1973; Nie and Andersen, 1974). The generality of the initial findings about belief system consistency has been challenged on various grounds (Luttbeg, 1968; Lipsitz, 1970). Similarly, methodological criticisms have been directed at the argument that the public expresses political opinions only randomly (Achen, 1975; Pierce and Rose, 1974). Overall, the reconsiderations of the public's political thinking suggest an electorate more closely matching the "democratic norm."

POLITICAL CULTURE

The American electorate of the early 1960s was widely depicted as trustful, efficacious, and intolerant. That is, the public exhibited support for the political system and felt their participation in politics would make some difference (Campbell et al., 1960; Almond and Verba, 1963). On the other hand, while the public would give support to general democratic principles of tolerance (e.g., freedom of speech), that tolerance dissipated when it came to applying those principles to specific unpopular groups, such as communists (McClosky, 1964; Prothro and Grigg, 1960; Stouffer, 1955). Political leaders, however, were more likely to support this application of democratic principles.

Recent years have witnessed a fundamental disruption of the traditional American political culture. Across the entire American electorate there has been a precipitous decline in the public's political trust (Miller, 1974), although there is some dispute about whether the change reflects a reaction to incumbents or a fundamental alienation from the political system (Citrin, 1974; Citrin et al., 1975). Likewise, the American electorate no longer feels as politically efficacious as it once did (Converse, 1972; Inglehart, 1977; Flanigan and Zingale, 1979). Several studies report that the electorate has become more tolerant, that it has increased its support for the application of democratic principles to groups that are unpopular or nonconformist (Lawrence, 1976; Davis, 1975; Nunn et al., 1978).

POLITICAL LEARNING

The traditional view of political learning in the American electorate concentrated on the socialization of support—the way people acquire the dominant norms of their relevant social and political environment (Hyman, 1959; Sigel, 1970). The substantive emphasis of the traditional view was on the early development of positive or benevolent perceptions of the political system and of political authorities, a process called "idealization" (Easton and Dennis, 1965; Greenstein, 1960). Similarly, very young children appeared to acquire orientations to partisan politics (Greenstein, 1965), usually in a form reflecting that held by their parents (Converse and Dupeux, 1962). Indeed, the family, supplemented by the public schools, was assumed to play a paramount role in transmitting appropriate political beliefs (Davies, 1965).

In recent years many changes have occurred in the study of political learning. No longer is the sole focus the development of support for the political system; the subject has been expanded to include the learning of any political orientation. There is a sensitivity to potential variations in political learning among different subcultures in the United States (e.g., Jaros et al., 1968; Engstrom, 1970; Garcia, 1973). There is an increasing emphasis on individual characteristics that produce differences in political learning (Harvey and Harvey, 1970; Knutson, 1973). There is speculation that the family is not as important as it once was, or that perhaps its importance was overestimated. There is an increasing emphasis on the mass media, especially television, as agents of political learning (Chaffee et al., 1977; Becker et al., 1975; McCleod and O'Keefe, 1972). And the children of the early and middle 1970s were much less likely than their counterparts of a decade earlier to believe that public officials and government could be trusted (Arterton, 1974; Dennis and Webster, 1975).

PARTY SUPPORT

Political parties play a central role in the traditional view of the American electorate (Campbell et al., 1960: 120–167; Flanigan and Zingale, 1979: 51–74). Most Americans considered themselves to be members of one of the two major political parties. The electorate used the party labels of candidates as voting cues. Party identification was handed down from generation to generation within families and contributed to the stability of the two party system.

Political parties apparently no longer hold their favored status in the American electorate (Pomper, 1975; Nie et al., 1976; Ladd and Hadley, 1978). The number of independents has increased, as has the amount of ticket-splitting (DeVries and Tarrance, 1972). Voters are more likely to make their choices on the grounds of candidates' issue positions or personal attributes, whereas party affiliation had been the dominant concern (Pomper, 1975). People are more likely to articulate negative attributes when commenting about the parties (Nie et al., 1976), and they are less likely to believe that political parties can be trusted, or to think that parties are important to the political system (Dennis, 1975). These negative orientations are the most prevalent among the youngest generation (Abramson, 1974; Converse, 1976). In sum, there has been a considerable drop in party support in the American electorate and that dissatisfaction gives every indication of persisting for some time.

THE ISSUE AGENDA

The traditional view of the electorate suggested that public concern with political issues was weak and that the public had little control over, and interest in, the content and structure of the political agenda—the policy questions on which decisions must be made. Moreover, the dominant issues of any concern to the public dealt mainly with social welfare—the role of the government in providing social welfare programs to the public (Campbell et al., 1960; Dawson, 1973).

Beginning in the early 1960s, the public's issue concerns changed. Different types of issues became important, surpassing or clouding the New Deal divisions. Civil rights dominated the middle 1960s. Widespread public opposition to, and protest of, the war in Vietnam developed. Support for the protection of the environment surfaced, culminating in "Earth Day." There developed what Miller and Levitin (1976) have called the "New Politics"— conflicts and political coalitions based in differences over issues new to the political agenda. Similar contentions are found elsewhere (Raine, 1975; Scammon and Wattenberg, 1970; Phillips, 1969), although the labels differ somewhat (e.g., "the social issue"). More recently, there is speculation that the public's issue concerns may have narrowed considerably, that there is now a "single issue" mentality. Many believe that only a single issue should dominate the agenda, and there is widespread disagreement as to what that issue should be.

PRESIDENTIAL VOTE CHOICE

The traditional view of why someone voted for a particular presidential candidate centered on the demographic correlates of vote choice (Berelson et al., 1954) and the role of party identification (Campbell et al., 1960). These sociological and psychological models of the vote choice dominated for some time. The importance of individual beliefs about political issues was minimized. With most of the public identifying with a political party and with that identification usually leading to a vote for the party's candidate, presidential vote choices and presidential election outcomes were determined primarily by the distribution of party identification.

The revisionist view emphasizes the increased importance of political issues in individual vote decisions (RePass, 1971; Pomper, 1975; Miller et al., 1976; Nie et al., 1976). The electorate distinguishes more clearly between the policy positions of the two major parties (Pomper, 1972; Margolis, 1977), and is able to apply its own positions on those issues when evaluating party and candidate alternatives in elections. While some argue that the role of issues has been increasing, others suggest greater importance of evaluations of candidates' images (Popkin et al., 1976). In either case, the long-term force of party identification is less important.

THE MASS MEDIA

The influence of the mass media on the electorate's political beliefs and behavior has been examined in three generations of scholarly work (Nimmo, 1978: 382–391). The first generation emphasized the "hypodermic" effect of mass media communications to the public—some automatic effect as a result of exposure to the communication. The potential impact of the media was maximized. The second generation of studies minimized the direct impact of the media, suggesting that communications from the media were filtered through two intervening processes: opinion leaders (Katz and Lazarsfeld, 1955) and the individual's existing predispositions (Klapper, 1961). This second generation of studies comprised the major elements of the traditional view of the electorate, a view suggesting that the effects of the media are minimal.

The third generation of media studies, the current "reconsideration" of the role of mass media, again emphasizes the importance of communications in the electorate's actions. The electronic media have cut the costs of acquiring political information (Converse, 1975). The media are said to possess an agenda-setting ability, defining the importance of various political issues (McCombs and Shaw, 1972). Moreover, different conceptual frameworks have been developed to examine *variations* more precisely in the impact of the media. Thus, "dependency theory" says we should consider the degree to which people are dependent on the media and the nature of that dependency (Ball-Rokeach and Defleur, 1976). Likewise, proponents of this approach argue that before rejecting the influence of the media we must identify the uses to which people put the media (Blumler and Katz, 1974). Those uses may differ from the consequences on which analysts traditionally have focused (e.g., changing the voter's choice), but they are nevertheless important in the world of politics.

PATHS TO RECONSIDERATION

The new portraits of the American public have been painted with different brushes. Fundamental differences obtain in explanations for the attributes of the reconsidered electorate. Two of these explanations concern the relation between the public and the political environment. The first suggests that the public has changed, and therefore responds differently to the stimuli of politics. The second argues that there has been little real change in the public. Rather, politics has changed, and the public's enduring characteristics dictate a different kind of response because of the change in context. In this section, we review these two sets of explanations. The following section provides an overview of methodological disputes and challenges involved in the reconsiderations of the electorate.

A CHANGED PUBLIC

Many scholars suggest that there have been some fundamental changes in the electorate and that these changes are reflected in public opinion and political behavior. This view concedes that the traditional picture of the public may have been correct at one time. Now, however, it is outmoded, for the public has shed its old cloak. Where the electorate may have been wanting, it now meets the demands of democratic political systems and is more than able—if not always ready and willing—to participate rationally and effectively in the political process.

One characterization of fundamental change is found in the literature on "postindustrial" politics (Inglehart, 1976). It is said that the Western societies generally, and the United States in particular, have become postindustrial. That is, they have achieved "affluence; advanced technological development; the central importance of knowledge, the growing prominence and independence of culture; new occupational structures; and with them new life styles and expectations" (Ladd and Hadley, 1978: 184). These changes are significant because they have altered what the public wants out of life as well as the preferred means to obtaining these desires. In other words, there has been a transfiguration in the public's values. This change in value structure has the potential to create fundamental changes in public opinion and political behavior.

How does this change produce changes in political opinions and behavior? Politics affects the satisfaction of personal values. Different political systems, different policy alternatives, different political candidates, organizations, and ideologies may promote the achievement of different values. Thus, people may attempt to achieve their values through the formation and articulation of political preferences and behavior. That is, the individual may evaluate political alternatives by their contribution to the achievement of the individual's values or of need satisfaction. As the distribution of values in society responds to changes in society through postindustrialism, then, the distribution of the electorate's political characteristics also will change. In the American electorate (or portions of it), values reflecting the influence of postindustrialism have been linked to a variety of political attitudes (Pierce, 1979; Sullivan et al., 1979a).

The increasing level of formal education in the American public also is thought to have created some fundamental changes. Increasing education may result in the increased levels of those characteristics that were associated with educational levels in the traditional literature. Thus, greater proportions of ideologues were found among those at higher levels of education in the 1950s. The percentage of ideologues increased with the rise in education. This has led some scholars to speculate that the increase in education led to the increase in conceptualization, although some studies cast doubt on that explanation (Nie et al., 1976). Education also has been linked to changes in political efficacy, political tolerance, and party support.

Fundamentally, both of these explanations are nonpolitical in origin and orientation. The public is now different than it was in the 1950s and early 1960s because of changes in the economic and social system. Changes in aggregate levels of wealth have generated a new set of values; changes in aggregate levels of education have generated increasing levels of political sophistication. We turn now to a discussion of explanations which are more explicitly political in origin and orientation.

A CHANGED POLITICS

The explanations which emphasize a changed politics accept evidence of at least superficial changes in the public's beliefs and behavior. Those changes, however, reflect no fundamental difference in the inherent characteristics of the electorate. Indeed, the shifts in the electorate's attributes are the response of a long-lasting and stable set of individual characteristics to a shifting political scene. The nature of the times, to a large degree, determines how the public's beliefs and behaviors are manifested. The electorate is different because politics has changed, and the public responds to these changes.

The public may, for example, have a certain ability to evaluate presidential candidates on the basis of their ideological positions. Whether or not the electorate actually evaluates candidates in ideological terms depends on the extent to which the candidates use ideological appeals in their campaigns. *The American Voter* found that in 1956 only 12% of the public evaluated presidential candidates and political parties in ideological or near-ideological terms (Campbell et al., 1960). This finding was interpreted by many to suggest that much of the electorate could not articulate ideological evaluations. Yet, studies of the 1964 election, with the presence of an ideological candidate in Barry Goldwater, showed many more people employing ideological terms (Field and Anderson, 1969; Pierce, 1970; Nie et al., 1976).

Actually, this "changed politics" argument is composed of two subgroups that differ rather substantially in their interpretations. First, there are those who interpret the relationship between the public and the nature of politics as fundamentally flattering to the electorate (e.g., Key, 1966; Pomper, 1975). In this view, the electorate is able to independently evaluate politics *when there are real and relevant choices to be made*. It remains able to exhibit rational and consistent behavior even when the political system does not admit to it. When no real choices are present, when political arguments and distinctions are muddied, how is the electorate to make any sense of politics and translate its preferences into coherent and rational political choices? Thus, the public can independently evaluate political alternatives (issues and candidates) when the choices are available to them. The changes in the electorate, therefore, represent changes in the arena of politics and not fundamental changes in the electorate itself.

Second, these same patterns—the shifts in the behavior and beliefs of the public—have been interpreted as confirming original, rather negative, views of the public. Again, there is agreement that the public's superficial characteristics changed because the nature of politics changed. Here it is said, however, that the public has changed because *as always* it depends on political leaders for cues as to the appropriate political responses. What has happened is that the leaders have changed the cues they have distributed to the people dependent on them (Converse, 1975). Again, the fundamental attributes of the public stayed the same—they depend on the cues of political leaders. The cues of the leaders changed, so the responses of the public changed. But, that changing response of the public only confirms the stable character of the public's dependence. The changes in the public are chimerical. The public, following the same old paths, simply received and reflected new signals much the same as always.

METHODOLOGICAL RECONSIDERATIONS

Most possible points of view regarding the current and past level of sophistication among the American electorate are represented in the recent literature. Some scholars believe that the American electorate of the 1950s and early 1960s was terribly unsophisticated, and that the electorate of the late 1960s and 1970s continued to be almost as unsophisticated. Others believe that the earlier electorate was unsophisticated but that the current electorate has improved considerably. Still others believe that the electorate was reasonably sophisticated in the 1950s and continues to be so today. It appears that no one has yet argued that the electorate of the 1950s was more sophisticated than that of today. To a large extent, the three accepted points of view stem from different conceptualizations of the important theoretical concepts involved in analyzing the public's level of sophistication and from different methodologies and methodological perspectives. The following section reviews some of these underlying differences and difficulties.

CONCEPTUALIZATIONS OF IDEOLOGICAL CONSTRAINT

In his seminal analysis, Converse (1964) set the agenda for almost two decades of research on "ideological constraint." He defined a belief system as a system of attitudes in which the idea elements are bound by some form of functional interdependence, which he labeled constraint. Converse then operationalized this notion of constraint as the predictive success that a researcher would have in guessing an individual's attitude on one issue given knowledge of his attitude on another. Converse and others who have accepted this definition of constraint have used various forms of correlation coefficients—calculated between pairs of issues—as an index of the degree of constraint within any population of subjects.

Converse's operationalization has been criticized on several grounds. Luttbeg (1968), for example, argues that simple reliance on correlation coefficients is inadequate because it presumes undimensionality. Luttbeg uses factor analysis and discovers five dimensions that describe the opinions of his mass sample. These factors explain 65% of the variation in responses among his sample of citizens, and he therefore concludes that levels of constraint were higher than Converse's zero order correlation coefficients would indicate. Since Luttbeg's sample of citizens was drawn in 1959, there was no suggestion that things had somehow changed, since Converse's data were collected in 1958.

Marcus et al., (1974) argue that the reliance on any type of correlation coefficient makes the analysis necessarily aggregate rather than individual. They argue further that this type of analysis presumes that there is a single dimension of ideological constraint that must be equally salient for all of the subjects included in the analysis. Most analysts who have used Converse's operational definition of constraint have discussed their results as if they were describing individuals rather than groups. Marcus and his colleagues argue, however, that the correlations describe only groups not individuals. For example, it is possible that in a representative sample of the American electorate, there are diverse sets of ideologies, because the public itself is very heterogeneous.

Assume that a researcher is assessing constraint between two issues, federal aid for medical care and federal aid to education. Assume further that there are four coherent points of view present in the electorate. Conventional liberals support both forms of federal aid; conventional conservatives oppose both forms of aid; a group of moderates feels that education is logically a local function, but that health and medical care are so important that they are basic rights and ought to be a federal responsibility; and a second group of moderates feels that education is the major mechanism for progress and improvement in the society and ought to be a national responsibility, but that medical care ought to be part of the private market system.

In terms of the operational definition of constraint used by Converse and his followers, if this analysis is limited only to the conventional liberals and conservatives, an almost perfect positive item-item correlation will be discovered. If the analysis is limited only to the 2 groups of moderates, an almost perfect negative correlation will be discovered. And, as is the case when analyzing a representative sample of the American electorate, if all 4 groups are included in the analysis, the correlation will be almost zero, if all 4 groups are of approximately equal size. Thus even if each individual in the sample has a reasonably coherent ideology that, in turn, "constrains" his position on various issues, this individual level constraint will not be reflected in the aggregate correlations which characterize the group. The only way to make these 2 levels of analysis congruent, given Converse's definition, is to assume that only the more traditional liberal or conservative positions are truly constrained. The two moderate positions are in some sense "illegitimate," or at least unconstrained.

To examine whether Converse's results reflect the heterogeneity of ideological viewpoints in the electorate, Jackson and Marcus (1975) used a method of individual differences scaling analysis to assess constraint at the individual level. They found high individual levels of constraint in a mass sample using this alternative conceptualization and methodology.

RANDOM MEASUREMENT ERROR

Converse (1964) found that levels of constraint appeared to be low during the 1950s, and that attitude stability was virtually nonexistent. Using a panel survey spanning 4 years, Converse (1970) found that the electorate of the 1950s could best be described as providing random responses to many issue questions. He found low correlations between respondents' answers to questions at time 1 and their answers to the same questions at times 2 and 3.

A number of authors have raised questions about both of these analyses. Since both his analysis of constraint and of attitude stability rely on correlations between measured attitudes, his correlations will be attenuated by imperfect measurement. (See Pierce and Rose, 1974; Achen, 1975; and Erickson, 1978.) To provide a simple illustration, suppose that the model in Figure 1 represents the relation between true attitudes on 2 issues (X_t and Y_t), and the responses to questions designed to measure these true attitudes (x' and y'). If we allow the correlation between the true attitudes on the 2 issues to be represented by r_{XY}, then (under certain assumptions) $r_{XY} = b$. The researcher, however, has only the correlation between 2 measured variables with which to work. If we allow that correlation to be represented by $r_{x'y'}$ then $r_{x'y'} = abc$ (again, under certain assumptions), where a and c are the (unmeasured) correlations between the true attitudes and the measured responses. The latter quantities are thus related to the conventional reliability coefficient used in classical measurement theory. Since a, b, and c are correlations, their range is $+1$ to -1, and unless there is perfect measurement, $r_{x'y'}$ will be less than r_{XY}. The greater the "measurement error" between X and x', and between Y and y', the greater the discrepancy between r_{XY} and $r_{x'y'}$. Since Converse relied on $r_{x'y'}$ all of his correlations were smaller than the correlations between true scores.

In a reanalysis of Converse's data, using a measurement model related to, but more complicated than, that in Figure 1, Achen (1975) found that the correlations between true attitudes were much higher than Converse had estimated both across different issues at the same point in time (constraint), and for the same issue across different points (stability). Erikson (1978) takes issue with aspects of Achen's analysis, but, using different measurement models, confirms Achen's basic conclusion that constraint and stability, once corrected for measurement error, were considerable even in Converse's own data. The issues which revolve around estimating the correlations between true attitudes by correcting for measurement error lie far beyond the scope of the analysis presented here. The point is that much of the disagreement among scholars about the original pessimistic conclusions drawn by Converse and his colleagues revolves around the question of measurement error. Whether "unstable" measured responses reflect respondent instability (nonattitudes) or instrument instability (measurement error) continues to be a matter of considerable debate. In a very real sense, this debate determines many researchers' conclusions about the level of sophistication in the electorate of the 1950s.

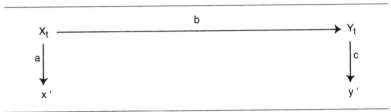

FIGURE 1.1   Simple Measurement Model Connecting True Attitudes (X_t and Y_t) With Their Measures (x' and y')

CHANGED MEASURING INSTRUMENTS

Accepting Converse's (1964) methodology for assessing ideological constraint, Nie and Andersen (1974) traced the item-item correlations across a set of issues from the 1950s through the early 1970s. Their results, also reported in Nie et al., (1976) appeared to document a rather incredible shift in constraint beginning in 1964 and persisting into the 1970s. They linked such changes to the ideological candidacy of Barry Goldwater and the ideological turmoil of the late 1960s. The ideological candidacy of George McGovern kept levels of constraint from returning to the lower levels of the 1950s.

At the same time, Pomper (1972) noted an increase in the relation between partisanship and issue position, resulting in a greater role for issues in voting behavior (Pomper, 1975; Miller et al., 1976; and Nie et al., 1976) and in political behavior generally. The explanations offered were similar to those offered for the apparent increase in issue constraint.

These analyses all relied on the issue questions asked representative samples of the electorate every few years by the Survey Research Center of the University of Michigan. Unfortunately, in retrospect, the SRC changed both its interview format and the content of the issue questions in 1964. The earlier issue questions had been administered by reading a statement to respondents and then asking them to agree or disagree on a 5-point scale; beginning in 1964, the issue questions were asked by reading 2 statements, presenting both sides of that issue, to respondents who were then asked which of the statements best reflected their own point of view. In addition to this changed format, the exact wording of the questions changed. Many of these changes appear to be sufficient to alter the context of the issues under examination. For example, the pre-1964 statement used to measure attitudes toward federal aid to education was: "If cities and towns around the country need help to build more schools, the government in Washington ought to give them the money they need." The post-1964 question designed to measure the same attitude was: "Some people think the government in Washington should help towns and cities provide education for grade and high school children; others think that this should be handled by the states and local communities."[1]

In 1956, 74% of all respondents gave the liberal answer, whereas in 1964 only 38% did. Since 1964 was a watershed in liberal legislation and in federal programs—and the public appeared to support these programs—one might wonder why the electorate of the 1950s appeared to be more liberal on this issue. The change in question wording is a possible explanation. The 1956 question presumes that the state and local levels of government have failed (need help), and thus many respondents who preferred the conservative solution were forced to give a liberal answer. The 1964 wording makes the conservative response more palatable by providing a more meaningful state and local option.

The above reasoning has been used by some authors to suggest that much of the apparent change in ideological constraint in issue voting and in the relation between partisanship and issue attitudes is due not to real changes in these phenomena but to the changes in question format and content. For example, Bishop et al., (1978) used a national sample conducted in the early 1970s, which was asked both the pre-1964 and the post-1964 sets of questions to demonstrate that even at the same time, levels of constraint were lower using the earlier questions. (See also Brunk, 1978; and Sullivan et al., 1978.)

Others remain unconvinced, arguing that the "changed politics" explanation is intuitively plausible, and that there have been changes in mass survey responses to other questions whose wording did not change (Nie and Rabjohn, 1979; Petrocik, 1978). The debate cannot be resolved definitively since, unfortunately, the "changed politics" and the "changed format" occurred simultaneously. It is true, however, that subtle changes in the way a question is worded can have a significant impact on the findings of any research project (Schuman and Presser, 1977; Mueller, 1973).

UNCHANGED MEASURING INSTRUMENTS

The previous two sections have considered the impact, on recent conclusions about the electorate, of the reliability of the measures used (random measurement error) and of changes in questionnaire format and content. These two factors are related. One of the arguments presented earlier implies that the older set of questions was less reliable than the more recent set. This would lead to a greater attenuation of the correlations produced using the older set of questions. Referring to Figure 1, the correlations between true attitudes and measured attitudes would be lower in the pre-1964 questions, producing smaller $r_{x'y'}$'s in that set even if the r_{XY}'s, the correlations among true attitudes, were identical in the 1950s, 1960s, and 1970s.

The question of validity, however, is more difficult to assess than is reliability. Validity refers to whether a particular measure "really measures" what the researcher thinks it does. For example, in the aid to education questions, the researchers who used both questions assumed that each wording was a valid measure of the respondents' true attitudes toward the federal government's role in providing education for the nation's children. Both questions may be valid measures of this true attitude, although the latter may merely be more reliable. Another possibility is that either, or both, are measuring something entirely different from the true attitude under investigation.

Considerations of validity may lead to the ironical conclusion that, when studying changes in mass attitudes and behavior, even the same set of questions repeated over time may produce misleading conclusions. For example, using 5 trust in government items, which were repeated at an eight-year interval in a 2-wave panel study of political socialization, Chubb examined the concept of temporal validity. As he noted: "Indicators are said to have temporal validity if they are related in the same way to the true scores at each wave in a panel study. Temporal validity ensures that the same concept is being measured throughout the study" (1978: 437). Using a statistical technique called maximum likelihood factor analysis, Chubb demonstrated that for a sample of adults, the 5 trust items did not relate in the same way to the true scores in 1965 as they did in 1973. He argued that the political context changed sufficiently between 1965 and 1973 so that even though respondents were technically asked the same questions at the two points in time, the *meaning* of the questions to the respondents had changed significantly. To the extent that, in general, survey items are subject to temporal invalidity, the study of change in the general characteristics of the electorate is problematic. Particular attention must be paid to question wording and format as well as to the political context within which the question is asked.

Another example which illustrates the potential temporal invalidity of questions repeated over time involves the study of political tolerance. In the 1950s, Stouffer (1955) asked two national samples of the electorate a series of questions designed to measure the extent of public support for the civil liberties of communists, atheists, and socialists. He found low tolerance and concluded that the electorate was generally intolerant. In recent years, Stouffer's questions have been repeated, verbatim, and the results have indicated a considerable increase in tolerance (Davis, 1975; Nunn et al., 1978). The conclusion most often reached is that the electorate has become more politically tolerant in the last twenty years.

An alternate explanation is that Stouffer's questions about communists, socialists and atheists had an entirely different meaning to the electorate of the 1950s than it did to the electorate of the 1970s. Political tolerance, understood in a more generic sense than merely tolerance of one particular group, may have been measured reasonably well by Stouffer's questions in the context of cold war fervor and domestic concern with internal subversion of the 1950s. Since that time, detente, increased trade, and culture exchange programs have been established between the United States and the major communist countries, thus completely altering the context within which Americans perceive communism and socialism. The issue of communism is no longer as prominent as it once was. All of these factors no doubt have increased tolerance toward communists and communism within the American electorate.

Both Stouffer and those who have updated his work, however, generalized beyond attitudes toward communism and drew conclusions about tolerance more generally understood. In the current context, this might be especially risky since there is better reason to believe that tolerance of communists has increased than there is to believe that tolerance of all groups and ideas has increased. Sullivan et al. (1979b) have demonstrated that there are a large number of different groups and ideologies that are now salient targets for mass intolerance, and that the norm among the electorate remains one of intolerance. They conclude that while Stouffer's questions may have been valid measures of general tolerance in the 1950s, by the 1970s these questions were temporally invalid for that purpose due to the changed context of politics in the United States.

SUMMARY

In recent years, then, there has been considerable debate over the nature of the electorate. The traditional view emphasizes that the American public has been politically unsophisticated. It sees the average citizen as: viewing politics only in concrete, operational terms, rather than in ideological terms; arriving at stated opinions almost randomly rather than through thought and reflection, thus precluding predictability (constraint) across issues as well as stability of attitudes over time; engaging in sporadic political behavior based almost exclusively on partisan attachments, which, in turn, are learned at a very early age within the family; and uncritically supporting the status quo, both of the political regime and the incumbents who inhabit various political roles.

The revisionist view emphasizes that the American public has recently become reasonably sophisticated. It sees the current electorate as: reasonably capable of viewing politics ideologically; having true opinions on the issues of the day, which are both constrained and reasonably stable over time; engaging in political behavior based increasingly on opinions on important issues and less on partisan attachments; and reasonably critical both of the regime and of unworthy incumbents once they prove their unworthiness.

Some revisionists believe the current electorate is different from the earlier electorate and that both caricatures have been true only at different times. Others believe that the traditional view of the electorate was based on faulty research. Some of the methodological objections of the latter scholars include misguided conceptualizations of research concepts such as ideological constraint; the failure to deal with problems of measurement error; and problems of indicator invalidity, particularly temporal invalidity. These problems have been reviewed here in an attempt to put the following chapters into perspective.

THE CONTENTS OF THIS BOOK

The chapters that follow examine the American electorate from the variety of perspectives described above. New findings, new concepts, and new methods all appear in the following pages. Part Two contains three chapters that examine some basic questions in the recent work on the *structure of public opinion*. In Chapter Two, Hagner and McIver reconsider the question of the degree to which the public's expressions of political opinions reflect true attitudes or are random responses. They employ data from a panel study conducted during the 1976 presidential election campaign, and they explicitly incorporate attitude change into their model, arguing that much opinion instability reflects neither random response nor measurement error, but is a consequence of true attitude change.

Conover and Feldman (Chapter Three) construct a new framework to examine the public's political belief systems. Drawing on the notion of a belief system schema, they suggest that constraint (consistency) in political belief systems can be examined in two dimensions—horizontal and vertical. Vertically, belief system constraint exists when there is a consistency between people's general orientations to politics and their more specific political beliefs, while horizontal constraint obtains when there is consistency among political orientations at the same level of generality or specificity. They demonstrate that substantial vertical constraint is present in the public.

In Chapter Four, Pierce and Hagner look at concurrent increases in belief system consistency and ideological conceptualization from 1956 to 1968, examining two major explanations. One explanation suggests that the increases reflect the public's dependence on political leaders for cues to the nature of politics, while the second contends that responses of the public to recent changes reflect favorably on the electorate's independent ability to comprehend politics.

Part Three contains three examinations of the *sources of public opinion*. Conover (Chapter Five) looks at the processes by which individuals develop and modify images of political figures, particularly candidates for public office, suggesting that both the "image" and the "perceptual balance" theses are inadequate. She develops and applies attribution theory, integrating the two previous approaches. Her discussion makes inferences about candidates' attributes based on information about other behavior or on prior beliefs about the candidate, and applies attribution theory to the development of attitudes about Richard Nixon during the Watergate affair.

Chris Williams (Chapter Six) addresses the problem of explaining patterns of change in public opinion through cohort analysis. In recent years, younger people have exhibited political orientations substantially different from those of their elders. Three alternate explanations have been offered— aging, generational, and period effects, but problems develop in trying to choose among those possible explanations. Williams carefully delineates the relation between observed patterns of change and causal inferences about alternate explanations, proposing a method for identifying "pure effects" models.

In Chapter Seven, Hurwitz and Peffley look at the impact of personality variables on people's perceptions of "anti-deal" (least-preferred) political candidates, finding that personality characteristics are significantly related to variations in perceptions of candidates. They note that social and political variables are usually employed to explain public evaluations of political figures, but that in their study, personality "had the most powerful direct impact on last-choice candidate evaluation, being more important than a variety of social and political variables that have traditionally concerned researchers in the area of political perception."

Part Four presents three studies reconsidering the *content of public opinion*. Chapter Eight, by Pierson, Sullivan, and Marcus, takes a new look at political tolerance in the United States. Traditionally, tolerance has been assessed by asking respondents to indicate their willingness to extend certain rights to a specified set of groups, regardless of respondents' feelings about those groups. Pierson et al. argue that tolerance obtains when respondents are willing to extend civil liberties to their least-liked groups, and that differences in levels of tolerance may be attributed, in part, to differences in the extent to which a group is liked or disliked. Employing their new measure, revisions result in the level and correlates of tolerance in the American public.

Hershey (Chapter Nine) examines the relative impact of race, sex, and sexual role attitudes on support for women's involvement in politics, focusing on sexual role stereotyping and the role of attitudes "toward sexual egalitarianism." Androgynous sex-role attitudes, which combine highly-valued masculine *and* highly-valued feminine characteristics, are examined. Women are more likely to support female political candidates than are either black or white men, but the best predictor of attitudes toward women in politics is the individual's sex-stereotyping of various activities. Support for women in politics, however, is high among people with a "stronger identification with femininity *and* with masculinity."

Chapter Ten, by Carmines and Stimson, argues that political conflict among political parties in the last decade revolved around racial desegregation policy, and that a realignment has occurred (and continues) based on the racial issue. Democrats are incrementally becoming more liberal and Republicans increasingly unified as racial conservatives, over the past decade and a half, resulting in cumulatively large changes over the entire period.

The last section of the book (Part Five) contains three chapters dealing with *party and candidate choice*. In Chapter Eleven, Shively provides a comprehensive overview of recent criticisms of party identification, evaluating the claims that the measure of party identification is multidimensional and that groups of respondents often called "leaning independents" are actually disguised partisans. Shively also examines the stability of party identification and considers several new conceptualizations of party identification.

Weisberg and Fiorina (Chapter Twelve) provide an expanded view of an important approach to explaining voting behavior—rational choice. Rational voting occurs when people estimate the benefits from alternative parties and choose the party with the highest expected benefit. The authors examine the consequences of making this choice under various conditions of incomplete knowledge about the alternatives—uncertainty—which derives from several sources, including the "behavior of competing candidates" (candidates may be vague or they may equivocate), and other uncertainties inherent in the political process. They examine the presence of various voting strategies under uncertainty, concluding that "rational voting encompasses a wider variety of behavior than usually believed."

John Petrocik (Chapter Thirteen) looks at the question of increases in belief system consistency, which, some studies suggest, are the result of changes in question wording and not changes in the public. He concludes that the changes are not totally an artifact of the questions, arguing that issue consistency responds to changes in the political environment. Petrocik similarly considers questions of the rise of political independence and changes in issue voting, demonstrating that the latter is responsive to the ideological character of the candidates. Indeed, he suggests that one can profitably understand the electorate's behavior by the *interaction* between individual characteristics and the changing nature of the political environment.

CONCLUSION

A revolution is occurring in the study of the American electorate, a revolution that rivals in significance the onset of the behavioral approach to the study of public opinion and voting behavior. New methods, new concepts, and new findings have all come together to issue a broad challenge to the traditional picture of the electorate. To be sure, the current challenges and controversies take as their starting point much of the traditional concepts and generalizations, and cannot be divorced from that which it confronts. On the other hand, conclusions about the character of the electorate remain open, both to new discovery about the public's relation to the political environment, and to new concepts and new methods of analysis.

NOTE

1. See the "Editor's Note" in the May, 1978 issue of the *American Journal of Political Science,* pp. 227-232, where all of the questions are listed.

PART II: THE STRUCTURE OF PUBLIC OPINION

2

ATTITUDE STABILITY AND CHANGE IN THE 1976 ELECTION: A PANEL STUDY

Paul R. Hagner
John P. McIver

One of the most serious debates among both past and contemporary political philosophers concerns the political sophistication of the citizens of a democratic regime. This centuries-old debate between proponents of elite democracy and advocates of the populist democratic form centers on a difference of opinion concerning the need for, and the capacities of, citizens to deal with the demands of self-rule. Much of the current empirical work on mass belief systems seeks to prove, or disprove, the proposition that the public is capable of handling the role of "citizen" in a democratic system. Yet the empirical information has not provided definitive answers. Indeed, support for each position is often drawn from the *same* evidence. In this Chapter, we hope to present both new evidence and a slightly modified perspective on one aspect of the current research on belief systems.

Previous work on public opinions as they relate to the polity has concentrated on two dimensions of belief systems: constraint and stability. In this

AUTHORS' NOTE: We would like to thank the following organizations for their assistance in the preparation, collection, and analysis of these data: The Knight-Ridder Newspaper Group; Office of Research and Graduate Development, Indiana University; Department of Political Science, Indiana University; Workshop in Political Theory and Policy Analysis, Indiana University; Department of Political Science, Washington State University. We would also like to thank Edward Carmines, Richard Joslyn, Daniel Minns, and Leroy Rieselbach for their comments and suggestions on an earlier draft of this article presented at the Midwest Association for Public Opinion Research, November 18–20, 1976, Chicago, Illinois. Although we were sorely tempted, none of these organizations and individuals will be held responsible for the contents of this chapter.

chapter we will treat the latter dimension.

If an individual's attitude toward a political stimulus remains constant over time, then the individual holds a "stable" attitude toward that object. This definition has a number of implications for democratic theory. One might confidently say that if the individual has stable attitudes, then the individual has:

> (1) expressed an orientation toward the political world rather than a nonopinion which is formed in responding to a survey, i.e., a response which on succeeding examinations appears to be random, and
> (2) developed a conceptual framework that is sufficiently stable to allow him or her consistently to evaluate the political environment over time.

Pomper (1975) describes other implications of the "responsive voter," that is, the voter who evaluates political phenomena in a consistent fashion over time. A representative who attains office by advocating a set of issue positions should expect constituency approval when he or she attempts to act on these political beliefs. If, however, these attempts are met with indifference or random fluctuations of support, the lawmaker will have little reason to view the election as a guide to his or her activities in government. It is essential to the concept of democratic linkage, therefore, that the content of mass demands remains fairly constant before and after the election. If mass opinion is random, then elections would provide no information for elected officials on the preferences of citizens.

Alternately, attitude stability may not be a "good" for democracy. Bennett (1976) argues that uninformed individuals may hold stable opinions precisely because of their lack of knowledge. One conclusion that may be drawn from Bennett's argument is that attitude *change* is frequently overlooked in discussions of attitude stability. Dennis Thompson (1970) explicitly considered the theoretical effects of attitude change. In *The Democratic Citizen,* Thompson discussed the notion of the *educability potential* inherent in any democratic society. The citizen is assumed to have the ability to adapt to new stimuli and to incorporate these experiences into his or her cognitive framework. This adaptation is essential to the continued life of the polity. The inability of a polity to adapt to changing conditions, particularly to correct for social deterioration, must surely lead to its demise. We would contend that empirical research on political attitudes has systematically ignored adaptation to new information through attitude change. We hope to provide an alternate viewpoint to the traditional literature.

The present state of empirical research on attitude stability is discussed in the next section, along with our evaluation of its continuing inadequacy both in estimating attitude stability and identifying attitude change. We then describe a unique 4-wave nationwide survey of the attitudes of the American electorate during the 1976 Presidential campaign. Data from this survey are used to test the methodologies and conclusions of earlier work. Attitude "change" (as opposed to random variation or measurement error) on 5 issues is identified, and its relation to changes in candidate preference and vote choice is examined in the 1976 election. In a final section, we reflect on the conclusions as they relate to democratic theory and survey research on political attitudes.

THE QUALITY OF PUBLIC OPINION: EMPIRICAL RESEARCH

A series of studies by The Survey Research Center at the University of Michigan during the 1950s produced a picture of the American voter as one whose behavior at the polls is not influenced to any significant degree by the candidates' stands on the issues raised during the campaign. Party identification and candidate appeal rather than campaign issues were better predictors of voting decisions; attitudes on public issues were poorly formed.

Citizen attitudes toward campaign issues were not stable, were often inconsistent, and were not predictable given expressed liberal or conservative predispositions. These conclusions were troublesome to many democratic theorists for they seem to pose problems for this representative democracy. If vote choice is not based on campaign issues, elected officials may not have any guide to citizen preferences.

Why was it that attitudes toward campaign issues were seemingly unrelated to citizens' political choices? Converse (1964, 1970) provided a widely accepted answer. He demonstrated that voter opinions in 1956, 1958, and 1960 did not appear to have any underlying structure (constraint) and that these opinions were not consistent over time (stability). Interview responses (believed to be eliciting attitudes), according to Converse, resembled random variables. The conclusion many have drawn from these findings is that "nonattitudes" on current issues cannot motivate informed political behavior. There are numerous systemic consequences of such findings, the most serious of which is that as elected officials come to believe that mass opinion is unstable, the gulf between citizen preference and public policy will widen. Is this an accurate picture of the American voter? A number of recent studies disagree.

Most of the studies criticizing the SRC research have dealt with more recent elections—i.e., the 1964, 1968, and 1972 Presidential campaigns—in providing counter-evidence.[1] A rise in issue voting is attributed to the existence of a "choice" in each of these elections. Furthermore, much discussion has centered on the increasing sophistication and cynicism of the American people during the 1960s for several reasons including: the end of Camelot, the war in Vietnam, the race riots, and the failure of the Great Society. But, were the 1960s that unique? Did historical events change the electorate? Or can the original SRC conclusions based on the elections of the 1950s be challenged?

A number of researchers (Asher, 1974; Pierce and Rose, 1974; Jackson, 1975; Achen, 1975) have concluded that many of the earlier findings regarding the status of political attitudes as "nonattitudes" may be due to lack of *methodological* sophistication among researchers rather than to a lack of sophistication among American citizens. They have argued that attitudinal stability is much greater than originally estimated. In the next section, these methodological advances are contrasted with Converse's analysis.

SOURCES OF INSTABILITY

The stability of an attitude obtained through survey methods can be defined by the correlation (r_{ij}) between any two administrations of the same question.[2] The amount of variance in a recent response at time j that may be explained by the respondent's position at previous time i is r_{ij}^2. If each responded in the same way at time i and time j, we would conclude that attitudes were perfectly stable over the period separating i and j ($r_{ij} = 1.0$, $r_{ij}^2 = 1.0$). If, however, all responses at times i and j were not identical, the difference between 1.0 and r_{ij}^2 is defined as "instability variance" (σ_I^2). Most of the controversy surrounding the issue of attitude stability has centered on the identification of the source of this instability variation. What are the reasons that a person would give different responses to the same issue prompt at different points in time?

The literature has produced three sources which are possible components of response instability: variation due to respondent response error, variation due to the inadequacies of the measuring instrument, and variation due to the presence of respondent attitude change. More formally, this can be presented as

$$\sigma_I^2 = \sigma_R^2 + \sigma_M^2 + \sigma_{AC}^2$$

where

σ_I^2 is the total response instability variance.

σ_R^2 is the instability variance due to respondent error.

σ_M^2 is the instability variance due to measurement error.

σ_{AC}^2 is the instability variance due to attitude change.

The debate has concentrated on the problem of differentiating respondent-based instability and instability due to the measuring instrument. The difficulty in separating the two lies in the fact that both deal with the relations between true opinions across time and the measurement of those opinions across time. Since true opinion is not directly measurable it must be estimated and the estimation will accentuate the source of instability deemed most important by the theorist.

This is most apparent in the work of Philip Converse (1964, 1970, 1979). In his analysis of the 1956–1960 SRC panel study, Converse found that, even after respondents with "self-confessed" confusion were carefully removed from the analysis, stability correlations for the repeated questions were unusually low and that the observed position shifts closely matched the predictions produced by a model (which Converse termed the "Black-White model") that only allowed for two response patterns: stable and random. Using the first two panel waves as a classification phase in which the respondents were placed in either the stable or the random response pattern group and the third wave as a test of the classifications, Converse found that the majority of those who claimed to have an opinion on an issue were responding randomly or had "nonattitudes" (Converse, 1970; 1979).

In presenting his conclusions, Converse makes two important assumptions: First, there is no appreciable instability due to the weakness or unreliability of the measuring instrument. Second, he assumes that no true attitude change occurs. This is necessary because the Black-White model is underspecified in the presence of stable, random, and change response patterns. Given the fact that he had only three points of measurement, insufficient information existed to distinguish stable, randomly varying, and truly changing attitudes. This second assumption permits identification of the model. Converse argues that this assumption is plausible by noting that (1) respondents should maintain stable positions on the principal political issues of the times; and (2) switching sides on political issues rather than changing intensities of preference are not anticipated.

Converse's assumptions have been questioned by researchers who hold other conceptions of instability variance. Most would argue that nothing can be measured without error. Panel studies, furthermore, present a workable design for reliability assessment through test-retest techniques. While there have been many interesting and sophisticated attempts to use panel designs in the estimation of item reliability, the work which has probably received most attention is Achen (1975), for it deals directly with the same data set used by Converse.[3]

Achen's theoretical formulations are superior to those of Converse's for they consider all three different sources of response instability: respondent error, error due to the measuring instrument, and attitude change. In the first part of his study, Achen attempted to separate instability variation due to respondent error and questionnaire unreliability (which he combined under the heading of "measurement error") and that variation due to "real" attitude change (Achen, 1976: 1231). Achen argued that Converse's original stability correlations were seriously attenuated. When these correlations were corrected by estimates of the reliability of the cross-time issue items, they would yield more realistic and distinct estimates of cross-time response stability. The second part of Achen's work dealt with the problem of which type of error—that due to the respondent or that due to the measuring instrument—was the largest component of measurement error. He reasoned that if Converse was correct and the largest error component was due to respondent instability, there should be a significant difference in the magnitude of estimated measurement error within populations stratified by elite/mass characteristics (education, income, participation, and the like). Such a difference was not discovered by Achen, a finding which he believed strengthened his assumption that "by far the largest part of the error is expected to be due to the vagueness of the questions" (1975: 1222).

Achen believes that the measuring instrument can contribute to response instability in the following way. He states that the largest part of measurement error is the result of question *vagueness*. Item vagueness is due to either the question wording, or to the response categories offered with the question, or both. We believe that Achen has raised an important point. A respondent's attitude toward an object may remain constant from T_1 to T_2 while his or her differentiation of response categories such as "often" and "sometimes" may vary during the same period. We conclude from Achen's work that the more specific and unambiguous the question *and* its response categories, the less response instability is due to measuring instrument unreliability. (See, for example, the SRC party identification question which is both highly stable and reliable).

Achen's work is quite insightful, but three areas of difficulty are of more than passing interest. The first concerns his correction technique. We do not argue that measurement error does not contribute to the measured instability of voter opinions, but rather that the statistical models designed to estimate them *over-estimate* them, because most reliability coefficients are estimates of the *lower bound* of the true reliability of a measure (Guttman, 1953; Novick and Lewis, 1967; Heise and Bohrnstedt, 1971; Armor, 1974; Greene, 1978; Greene and Carmines, 1978). If the reliability estimates of the measurement models are underestimates of the true reliability, the stability of opinions will necessarily be overestimated. Achen's estimate of item reliability may either overestimate or underestimate true reliability. Erikson (1978) argues that if responses to the questionnaire item behave according to a simple causal chain, the Achen procedure overestimates the stability coefficients.

The second reason for concern involves Achen's assumption that change between contiguous time periods is uncorrelated (i.e., change in $T_1—T_2$ cannot be used to predict change in $T_2—T_3$). The assumption of uncorrelated change across time periods does not take into account a very important feature inherent in test-retest designs: regression towards the mean. Bohrnstedt describes the effect thusly: "Any time a variable is imperfectly correlated with itself across time, regression towards the mean can be expected to occur. That is, individuals who obtain a high score on initial measurement can be expected to score lower on remeasurement (1969: 116). Regression toward the mean will result in a negative correlation between changes in contiguous time periods. Erikson (1978) suggests that regression effects will present problems for Achen's parameter estimates: Error variance will be *overestimated* when the correlation between contiguous time periods is negative. This overestimate of the error variance will yield inflated stability coefficients because reliability is underestimated.

The final area of concern, and of prime importance for the present chapter, involves Achen's interpretation of attitude change. While Achen does allow for the existence of attitude change, the assumptions incorporated in his model—that change between contiguous time periods is uncorrelated with change in other contiguous time periods—is unrealistic. Since attitude change involves some cognitive process of attitude modification, a model which treats all real change as a series of random shocks (i.e., change in T_1–T_2 cannot be used to predict change in T_2–T_3) rather than a patterned or developmental process, seems inadequate. It is our belief that the relation between attitude stability over time and attitude change has been explored only marginally. The purpose of this Chapter is to investigate this relation using a different and, we believe, more realistic, model of attitude change.

A MODEL OF ATTITUDE CHANGE

Having discussed the conflicting findings of the two major schools of thought on the instability of political attitudes of Americans, can we offer any insights or resolve the different viewpoints on the same data? Examination of a simplified hypothetical distribution of voter attitudes over a campaign (Figure 2.1) will be used to facilitate discussion.

Each of the two groups of scholars would have very different opinions on what is happening during this campaign. One viewpoint would be that 10–35% of all citizens are inconsistent from one administration of the survey to the next. In addition, half of the electorate has exhibited unstable opinions over the course of the campaign. The conclusion: The electorate holds unstable or random attitudes that should be reason for concern.

The measurement theory group would concentrate on the "corrected" overtime correlations. Attitudes are highly stable over period I–II, low to moderately stable over period II–III, and perfectly stable over the final period of the campaign. Questionnaire reliability, they would argue, is not

FIGURE 2.1 Hypothetical Distribution of Voter Attitudes on One Issue at Four Points in Time

a. Time Periods

Voter Pattern ID	I	II	III	IV	N
A	Y	Y	Y	Y	50
B	N	N	N	N	50
C	N	N	Y	Y	30
D	Y	Y	N	N	30
E	N	Y	Y	Y	10
F	Y	N	N	N	10
G	N	N	N	Y	10
H	Y	N	Y	N	10
					200

b. ϕ (upper diagonal) and % inconsistent (lower diagonal)

	I	II	III	IV
I	—	.70*	.28*	.00
II	15	—	.30*	.30*
III	40	35	—	.80*
IV	50	35	10	—

c. Approximate corrected over-time correlations with a questionnaire item reliable at .75–.80

	.93	.37	.36
		.39	.39
			1.00

perfect. This is why stability coefficients (the uncorrected correlations) appear lower than they really are. Whether or not there is a problem for the polity depends on to whom or what the lower reliability is attributed—respondents or questionnaire design.

Each model has something to tell us about attitude stability. But another look at the data will show us what we do not know. Neither model can adequately distinguish true attitude change from random fluctuation.[4] In part, this may be due to an emphasis on inconsistency between adjacent waves of a survey. Alternately, examining the response patterns for the entire campaign may aid identification of different types of response changes. Such an examination is important because it provides us with more information about the stability of attitudes than is gained by comparing responses to only two waves of the survey at a time. The logic is similar to that underlying "interrupted time-series analysis" (Campbell, 1969). In one group pretest-posttest designs, differences in the measured variable before and after some treatment are evidence of the treatment's effect. Similarly, the continuity of a response over time is evidence of its stability, while the continuity of response before and after a single change is evidence of an opinion change. Multiple response changes, however, would suggest the lack of stable attitudes.

The study of individual response patterns requires some *ad hoc* structure imposed by the researcher. A set of rules such as the one offered below must be adopted to identify attitude change:

(1) *No* response changes across all time periods suggest stable attitudes, e.g., patterns A and B of Figure 2.1a.
(2) *One* change over the course of the campaign is indicative of a "true" attitude change, e.g., patterns C through G.
(3) *Two or more* response changes indicate "unstable" change, e.g., pattern H.

There are, of course, alternates to these rules. "Unstable," as it is used above, has a pejorative meaning attached to it (as has been attached to *any* attitude instability in the past). It is not necessarily an irrational response pattern, however. Increased information or "significant" events may cause a citizen to change his or her opinion more than once. It is important to emphasize that arguing over a set of rules for identifying attitude change is not the purpose here. Rather, this set of guidelines will be used to re-examine the opinion response patterns to see if additional insights into the stability and change of opinions can be gained.

On the basis of the rules outlined above, we differ considerably with an interpretation which classifies up to 50% of the electorate as unstable and assigns this instability to random response. While half of the respondents do not express the same issue position at time I and time IV, 80% of these citizens respond in a manner consistent with our hypothesized pattern of true attitude change; another 10% respond consistently with a pattern of possible attitude change. Only 10% of the nonstable response pattern individuals are readily classified by our scheme as expressing "unstable" attitudes.

Is it reasonable to classify all respondents as perfectly stable during the first and last periods? This conclusion would likely be drawn by measurement theorists based on our corrected stability coefficients. We would find this conclusion hard to accept based on a study of the complete response patterns. Looking closely at period 3–4 (Figure 2.1a), the cross tabulation of responses indicates that 10 percent are inconsistent (patterns G and H). Must all of these off-diagonal responses be attributed to measurement error? Certainly, it is possible that these response patterns are due to measurement error. But pattern G is consistent with our attitude change rule 2. Change at the end of the campaign period seems most likely given the salience of the election and the culmination of candidate media and personal appeals. We believe a finding of perfect stability would be hard to justify in data such as these.

In proposing a new model of attitude change we do not ignore measurement error, for it surely accounts for some response variation. Question ambiguity might account for the response changes in pattern H. Or, random response by citizens may account for this pattern. Or, H could be real change. The point is that each set of assumptions will help us grasp the question—Do citizens express "attitudes" in answering surveys? But none will answer this question completely.

THE 1976 KNIGHT-RIDDER ELECTION STUDY

This chapter is based on data drawn from the 1976 Knight-Ridder Election Study. This study focused predominantly on citizen perceptions and evaluations of the issue orientations and personality characteristics of the presidential candidates. Respondents were also asked for their opinions on a wide range of issues believed to encompass the most salient issue concerns of the 1976 election.

The Knight-Ridder Election Study involved surveying three overlapping national cross-sectional samples. The first wave was completed in January 1976. One thousand one hundred and eighty-eight individuals responded. In wave II (May 1976), attempts were made to contact all wave I respondents. Sixty-one percent (N = 731) of the original respondents were interviewed. In addition, a new cross-sectional sample was surveyed to compensate for attrition bringing the total sample size for wave II to 1,015. Attempts were made to contact all respondents to the second wave in September. Sixty-four percent of these respondents agreed to be reinterviewed. Again, the cross-sectional sample was supplemented with new interviews to bring the N for wave III to 980. The size of the panel (i.e., all respondents contacted in January, May, and September) was 490.

A fourth wave was added by the Department of Political Science at Indiana University on the Wednesday and Thursday following the election. Attempts were made to contact only those respondents who had been interviewed *both* in May and September. Four hundred eighty-eight respondents were interviewed to produce a second three-wave panel for May, September, and November. Overlap of the two three-wave panels yields a unique four-wave survey of the American electorate from warmups for the New Hampshire primary to election day 1976 (N = 365). This four-wave panel is the specific data reported below.[5]

Responses to a series of five issue questions (concerning detente, the economy, regulation of business, defense spending and trust in government) repeated at each wave of the survey, compose the specific data used to examine alternate hypotheses regarding the stability and change of voter attitudes. In the next section we present the stability correlations for the 5 issues over time and contrast them with a set of stability correlations adjusted by Achen's reliability correction method. The final section is a first empirical look at the previously discussed concept of attitude change and relates change to voter choice behavior in 1976.

ATTITUDINAL STABILITY VS. "ADJUSTED" ATTITUDINAL STABILITY

Operationalization of attitude stability entails comparing the similarity of responses to the same question over time. The upper right-hand triangles in Tables 2.1a–e contain the simple correlations between the measures of a single attitude for all of the possible combinations of interview points. Two general observations can be made here.

The first and most obvious observation is that the magnitude of the correlations is relatively low, especially considering the shortness of the period covered by the 4 waves of the survey. The correlations for the 1976 election are not drastically different from those reported for the 1956–1960 SRC panel. Nor does it differ greatly from the magnitude Converse found in the stability correlations for political questions asked in the 1972–1976 panel study (Converse and Markus, 1979).

The second observation has to do with the pattern of the observed correlations. Converse (1964, 1970) argued (on the basis of Markov model requirements) that one should expect contiguous time periods to produce higher correlations than time periods separated by specified intervals (e.g., $r_{12} > r_{13} > r_{14}$) if true attitude change occurs. An analysis of Tables 2.1a–e does not yield any consistent pattern to support this supposition. Again, a first look at the data for 1976 recalls patterns found in the 1956–1960 panel study.

In the lower left-hand triangles of Tables 2.1a–e we show the stability correlations adjusted by Achen's method of measurement error correction. While the relative ranking of the issues in voter stability remained unchanged, the magnitude of the correlations increased dramatically, from a low of 0.55 to a high of 1.22. If we were to draw the same implications from these data that Achen reached with the SRC panel data, we would conclude that the unreliability of the measuring instrument obscured the fact that attitude stability is much more the rule than the exception. For reasons outlined in our earlier discussion, we are not inclined to accept the conclusion that voter attitudes toward these issues were completely stable. Indeed, the frequency with which the Achen estimates of the stability coefficients exceed 1.0 with these data suggests that his model is not appropriate here.

In summary, then, we are hesitant to accept the adjusted stability correlations as accurate indicators of attitude stability for two important reasons. First, the measurement model may overestimate the degree of stability between responses to the same issue due to underestimating question reliability. Second, this model, as well as Converse's, limits any consideration of what we have defined as real attitude change. The real extent of attitude stability likely lies between the unadjusted stability coefficients and those coefficients adjusted for random measurement error.

TABLE 2.1a–e: Simple and Adjusted Overtime Stability Correlations For Five Issue
Concerns, January to November 1976

Upper Right Triangle—Pearson r[a] or Phi[b]

Lower Left Triangle—Adjusted correlations (Achen measurement error correction)

r_{tt} = item reliability

a. Detente[a]

	JAN	MAY	SEPT	NOV
JAN	—	.35	.47	.42
MAY	.55	—	.39	.36
SEPT	.78	.66	—	.50
NOV	.77	.69	.99	—

$.45 < \hat{r}_{tt} < .66$

b. Unemployment/Inflation[b]

	JAN	MAY	SEPT	NOV
JAN	—	.36	.38	.29
MAY	.70	—	.46	.43
SEPT	.74	.88	—	.50
NOV	.55	.83	.96	—

$.52 < \hat{r}_{tt} < .52$

c. Government Anti-Free Enterprise[b]

	JAN	MAY	SEPT	NOV
JAN	—	.53	.55	.38
MAY	1.15	—	.50	.52
SEPT	1.22	1.00	—	.47
NOV	.85	1.01	.95	—

$.41 < \hat{r}_{tt} < .52$

d. Defense Spending[b]

	JAN	MAY	SEPT	NOV
JAN	—	.50	.54	.46
MAY	1.06	—	.51	.59
SEPT	1.14	1.09	—	.55
NOV	.96	1.27	1.18	—

$.46 < \hat{r}_{tt} < .49$

e. Trust Government[a]

	JAN	MAY	SEPT	NOV
JAN	—	.45	.48	.40
MAY ·	.77	—	.43	.39
SEPT	.85	.78	—	.49
NOV	.72	.73	.96	—

$.51 < \hat{r}_{tt} < .61$

ATTITUDE CHANGE AND THE 1976 PRESIDENTIAL ELECTION

Earlier we offered a model (i.e., a series of rules) to estimate the stability and change of attitudes during the 1976 campaign. The model, unfortunately, is not as rigorous or elegant as the "proofs" offered by measurement theorists. We can examine, however, the "construct validity" of this typology of response patterns. There are three steps to construct validation (Cronbach, 1960: 121). First, a construct underlying some set of measurements is hypothesized. Next, substantive hypotheses are derived from the theory involving the construct. Finally, these substantive hypotheses are tested empirically. Support for these substantive hypotheses also provides support for the measurement hypothesis. It is in this sense that a construct is judged to be "validated." Before we examine the relation between attitude change and stability and other relevant variables in the 1976 election, we will use our model to describe the patterns of responses to 5 campaign issues.

In Table 2.2a, we show the amount of response change across time for each of the 5 issues as well as the amount of response change within each period for all of the issues. One point is immediately obvious—response patterns during this period were far from static. (Only 6 respondents exhibited completely stable attitudes on the issues of the campaign.) How much of this is unstable change and how much is attitude change (as we have defined it)? In Table 2.2b, the respondents are classified as stable, attitude changers, or unstable on each issue by their response pattern on all 4 waves. The frequency of attitude changers varies across those issues from 22 to 32%, while the percentage of unstable respondents ranges from 28 to 42%. Stable respondents compose 32 to 50% of the responses to each issue.

One other pattern in Table 2.2a should be identified. The number of response changes decreases on 4 of the 5 issues as the election approaches.

TABLE 2.2a   Percentage of Changed Responses to Issue Questions Between January and November

	JAN–MAY	MAY–SEPT	SEPT–NOV	JAN–NOV
Detente	46.3	43.8	27.4	35.5
Unemployment/ Inflation	35.9	31.5	30.6	34.8
Government Interference with Free Enterprise	33.2	30.1	30.8	27.0
Defense Spending	32.3	30.0	27.0	26.2
Trust in Government	42.2	40.0	32.5	43.5

TABLE 2.2b   A Classification of Respondents by Hypothesized Change Pattern for
             Each Issue Question (N = 365)

	Stable	Attitude Changers	Unstable
Detente	36%	22%	42%
Unemployment/ Inflation	42%	29%	29%
Government Interference with Free Enterprise	46%	26%	28%
Defense Spending	50%	22%	28%
Trust in Government	32%	32%	36%

TABLE 2.3   Percentage responding "Don't Know" within each time period.

	JAN	MAY	SEPT	NOV
Defense Spending	9.9	6.8	6.8	4.2
Government Interference	15.9	6.3	7.9	9.0
Inflation/ Unemployment	5.8	4.9	4.4	4.8
Detente	16.4	13.7	11.2	9.6
Trust in Government	3.8	1.9	1.4	0.8
N =	365	365	365	354

Unfortunately, the surveys were also more frequent; i.e., the period between
waves of the survey was shortest between waves III and IV and longest
between waves I and II. Evidence presented in Table 2.3 suggests, however,
that it is the effect of the campaign rather than length of time between
surveys that causes a reduction in response change. The number of respondents who did not express an opinion on the issues tended to decrease as the
election approached. There is no apparent reason for this decrease in "don't
know" response to be related to the length of time between survey waves.[6]

What evidence can be marshalled to support the classification of respondents as "attitude changers" or as "attitudinally unstable" vis-à-vis the political environment? Two basic hypotheses are proposed and tested.

Page (1978) suggests two possible relations between issue preference and
candidate preference: Opinions on political issues may lead to the choice of
one candidate over all others or, alternately preference for a particular candidate (or the candidate's party) may cause the voter to accept the positions
offered by the candidate. In either case, if one variable changes we would
expect the other variable to change.[7] This relation between change in issue

preference and candidate choice is only expected if the measured response change is an indicator of actual attitude change. If response change is due to random error (caused either by the respondent or the measuring instrument), no relation between response change and candidate choice is expected. This argument forms the basis for our first hypothesis:

1. Attitude change should be associated with a preference change from one candidate to the other. Unstable change is not expected to be associated with a change in candidate preference.

The relation between issue preference and candidate preference is mediated by the election campaign. If we assume that the purpose of campaigning is to provide voters with information about the candidates,[8] then members of the electorate are expected to have greater amounts of information on the candidates as the election approaches. We would expect voters to reduce any incongruency between issue and candidate preference by changing one or the other such that the relation between issue preference and candidate choice increases over time. Measured attitude changes, therefore, should lead to greater congruence between issue and candidate preferences if they are more than simply random fluctuations. If measured change is random, we would not expect change to lead to a stronger relation between the issue positions of the voters and their candidate preferences. This logic underlies our second hypothesis:

2. The relation between issue positions and candidate preference is expected to increase over the election for attitude changers. For respondents with unstable opinions, the relation between issue position and candidate preference should not change during the campaign.

Evidence supporting both of these hypotheses would provide our definitions of attitude change and stability with some degree of construct validity.

Data pertaining to hypothesis 1 are presented in Table 2.4. Respondents identified as attitude changers were most likely to switch preferences asymmetrically; i.e., 80% went to Carter. On the other hand, respondents identified as attitudinally unstable on the political issues of the campaign split their candidate changes evenly. In other words, candidate change among attitudinally unstable respondents apparently occurs randomly—each candidate has a 50-50 chance of new support within this group. These data should only

TABLE 2.4 Shifts in Candidate Support from September to November by Change Categories

	Changer	Low Unstable	Hi Unstable
To Carter	80%	59%	50%
To Ford	20%	41%	50%
	(N = 15)	(N = 41)	(N = 14)

be considered suggestive, however, as the number of candidate switchers for the panel is very low (N = 77).

Table 2.5 contains the data that relate to the second hypothesis. The opinions and candidate choices of attitude changers became more strongly related during the course of the campaign on three issues—unemployment and inflation, government intervention in free enterprise, and defense spending. The same pattern also occurred for individuals classified as unstable on one or two issues. For those respondents who were judged highly unstable (i.e., those who expressed unstable responses to three or more issues), issue positions were less likely to be significantly related to candidate preferences. Surprisingly, trust in government does not appear to be related to candidate preference for any of the groups despite Carter's attempts to make this an issue in the campaign.

Is hypothesis 2 supported? Both the attitude change group and the low unstable group exhibit greater issue voting over time when contrasted with the group of respondents classified hi unstable. It is also likely that many in the low unstable group are true attitude changers. The reason they are not

TABLE 2.5   Correlation Between Opinion on Selected Issues and Candidate Preference in May, September, and November 1976

	MAY	SEPT	NOV
Attitude Changers (1 or more issues + 6 perfectly stable respondents)			
Detente	−.15	−.04	−.03
Unemployment/Inflation	−.05	.19[t]	.32[t]
Government Interference	.03	.36[t]	.26[t]
Defense Spending	.17	.45*	.44*
Trust in Government	−.19	−.12	.01
Low Unstable (Unstable on 1–2 issues)			
Detente	.07	.05	.00
Unemployment/Inflation	.15[t]	.25*	.42*
Government Interference	.12	.26*	.28*
Defense Spending	.20[t]	.25	.31*
Trust in Government	−.09	−.12	.00
Hi Unstable (Unstable on 3–5 issues)			
Detente	.00	−.10	.24[t]
Unemployment/Inflation	−.09	.11	.29[t]
Government Interference	.06	.16	−.12
Defense Spending	−.09	.25[t]	.21
Trust in Government	−.19	−.07	−.07

*Significant at .001 level
t Significant at .05 level

identified as changers is measurement error. (Again, we do not deny that existence of such error, but only wish to reduce the emphasis placed on it.) Fluctuations from true response patterns can lead to the mistaken classification of an individual as stable, changing, or unstable.

CONCLUSION

From our discussion of Converse and Achen, as well as from our own model, the most important problem in researching questions of attitude stability is that of estimating the error variance and specifying it more explicitly. We have shown that how the error variance is specified will greatly influence the nature of the conclusions to be drawn. By allowing for attitude change we also believe that the "condition" of the American citizen is not as pitiful as has been earlier pictured. For the nonrandom respondents, there is a growth of issue and candidate association, even during a campaign that has been described as emphasizing more style than substance. The American voter is not voting randomly, rather there does exist an interaction with opinion and vote choice.

NOTES

1. See Nie et al. (1976) for a recent overview of this literature.

2. It must be pointed out, however, that r_{ij}^2 could equal unity in the complete absence of measured response stability. If, for example, two overtime measures of the same attitude were taken using scale metrics which differed only by a constant, e.g., the value "1" at t_1 is the value "0" at t_2, and the respondents were completely stable in their real attitudes, r_{ij}^2 would equal unity even though every respondent demonstrated a measured response shift. Additionally, if a systemic factor influenced the entire sample so that it changed its response in a manner consistent in magnitude and direction (e.g., if the sample as a whole became more conservative or more liberal), the stability correlation would also achieve unity. These elements are not factors which affect the present analysis given our consistent use of response codings and the fact that the ordinal categories are not sensitive to the minimal total sample shifting which might have occurred over the campaign period.

3. Achen's article (1975) is one of the most recent to appear using measurement theory applied to the study of political attitudes. Asher (1974) and Pierce and Rose (1974a,b) also analyzed Converse's nonattitudes hypothesis using alternative measurement models. Jackson (1975) examined both the constraint hypothesis and the stability hypothesis using a multiple indicators approach to the 56–60 panel. Most of these applications of measurement theory drew on the research of other disciplines—Blalock (1963, 1970a,b), Hannan et al. (1974), Heise (1969, 1970), Lord and Novick (1968), D. Wiley and J. Wiley (1970), and J. Wiley and M. Wiley (1974).

4. This is not to suggest that nonrandom change cannot be studied with Markov models. See Dobson and Meeter (1974) for an analysis of changes in party identification during 1956–1960. Further extensions of the Markov model proposed by Lazarfeld and Henry (1968) seem most appropriate.

5. All of the respondents were interviewed by telephone. The average length of an interview was between 15 and 20 minutes. The initial sample, originally provided by CBS News, was drawn from randomly selected telephone numbers. An attempt was made to obtain full representation of those not often at home by means of four call-backs. No attempt was made to eliminate nonvoters, although some bias may exist if nonvoters tend to live in poorer nontelephone households. Use of randomly selected numbers also provided the means to interview members of households with unlisted numbers.

Does the four-wave panel approximate the initial national sample, or has attrition systematically occurred leaving a potentially biased set of respondents? The only major differences between the original sample and the four-wave panel occur with respect to whether the respondent is registered to vote and whether he or she voted in the 1972 election. Members of the panel were more likely to be registered to vote (86% vs. 79%) and reported voting in 1972 more frequently (81% vs. 72%). On all standard demographic characteristics, as well as party identification, political ideology, and political efficacy, there were minimal or no differences.

6. If individual response patterns were randomly generated, the expected distribution of "stable," "changing," and "unstable" individuals can be computed. For dichotomous variables, 2^4 or 16 possible response patterns exist for a four-wave survey. If each of these patterns occurred with equal frequency, 12.5% of our sample would be judged stable, and 50% would be classified unstable. For trichotomous variables there are 3^4 or 81 possible response patterns. If each were equally likely to occur, 3.7% would be classified stable with 22.2% changers and 74.1% unstable.

7. This argument obviously makes a number of assumptions about the decision processes of voters. These include assumptions that candidates' positions are perceived by the voter, that the issue is salient, and that the candidate does not maintain other prominent issue positions contrary to the voter's preferences. The process may be cumulative with multiple changes on campaign issues necessary prior to switching candidate support or multiple preference changes occurring as a result of a change in preference for president.

8. While many would argue that the campaign should provide information on the candidates' issue stands, others would suggest that the manner in which the candidate campaigns—as an indicator of personality—is more important information (see, for example, Barber, 1972).

3

BELIEF SYSTEM ORGANIZATION IN THE AMERICAN ELECTORATE: AN ALTERNATE APPROACH

Pamela Johnston Conover
Stanley Feldman

The study of mass belief systems is in disarray. Symptomatic of the problem is the recent proliferation of contradictory findings, the growing lack of consensus on the meaning of basic concepts, and the disruptive clash of different theoretical perspectives. This chapter is an effort to solve some of these difficulties. After reviewing past research, the major concepts involved in the study of mass belief systems will be redefined to resolve conceptual conflicts. Then, based on these new definitions we will formulate a framework for studying belief systems, which is a synthesis of old approaches from a new perspective. Specifically, we posit an information processing model in which the pattern of an individual's issue positions is the product of both his existing beliefs and the information provided by the environment. Portions of this model will then be tested empirically.

PAST RESEARCH

A key controversy in the study of mass belief systems concerns the sources of constraint among the elements composing a belief system. The

AUTHORS' NOTE: The authors' names are listed alphabetically. Each author is willing to blame the other for any errors that might be found. This is a revised version of an article presented at the 1979 Annual Meeting of the Midwest Political Science Association, Chicago, April 19–21. The data for the analysis were provided by the Inter-University Consortium for Political and Social Research, which bears no responsibility for the analysis or interpretations.

theoretical basis for this argument is found in Philip Converse's (1964) seminal work: "The Nature of Belief Systems in Mass Publics." Converse argues that constraint can originate either logically, psychologically, or socially. He quickly discounts the likelihood that people rely heavily on logic, leaving two possible explanations: one psychological and one socio-logical. The psychological explanation suggests that a few superordinate or crowning postures toward man and society "serve as a sort of glue to bind together many more specific attitudes and beliefs" (Converse, 1964: 211). Alternately, the sociological explanation posits that constraint originates "socially" when elites organize issues into coherent wholes and then com-municate to the masses information about what issues go together and why. Where constraint originates psychologically, the individual's ability to think and use abstract dimensions is presumed to limit the degree of constraint. Consequently, increases in constraint must be preceded by the expansion of the individual's cognitive abilities. In contrast, the sociological explanation suggests that constraint is learned and depends not only on cognitive abilities but also on the transmission of information from political elites.

Though Converse argued that constraint could either be psychologically or sociologically based, his conceptual and empirical analysis led him to assign primary importance to the sociological sources. In recent years, a number of studies (Bennett, 1973; Jones and Rambo, 1973; Nie and Ander-sen, 1974; Nie et al., 1976; Pierce, 1975) have either elaborated Converse's original argument or attempted to replicate his findings. Though these works criticize the universality of Converse's substantive findings, they do so without attacking the viability of his theoretical framework or the appropri-ateness of his methods of analysis. Their chief theoretical impact has stimu-lated an elaboration and refinement of Converse's original argument pertain-ing to the social sources of constraint (Bennett, 1977; Converse, 1975). Specifically, these studies suggest that Converse's claim that the American public lacks structured belief systems is time-bound as evidenced by the higher levels of constraint characterizing the electorate in the 1960s (Ben-nett, 1973; Nie and Andersen, 1974; Nie et al., 1976). Furthermore, these increases in constraint are attributed primarily to changes in the political environment. As a result of such findings, Converse (1975) recently con-cluded that constraint in a belief system is determined by the saliency and interest of politics to people, factors which are quite responsive to the stimulation provided by the political environment. This theoretical view is congruent with the empirical research suggesting that in the 1950s—a period of limited debate and issue salience—belief constraint was low, while con-straint apparently increased during the 1960s—a time of ideological debate, major political events, and issues (Nie and Andersen, 1974).[1]

Current methodological critiques create serious doubts about the validity of Converse's original conclusions and those of recent studies as well. These

criticisms, which address the reliability of the SRC/CPS questions traditionally employed in the assessment of belief constraint and stability, suggest
that mass belief systems in the 1950s were probably more stable and highly
constrained than Converse indicated (Achen, 1975; Asher, 1974; Erikson,
1979; Iyengar, 1973), and that constraint probably did not increase greatly
between 1956 and 1972 (Bishop et al., 1978; Bishop et al., 1979; Brunk,
1978; Sullivan et al., 1978; and Sullivan et al., 1979).[2] If these critiques are
accepted, they force us to question the substantive findings concerning
belief systems. As a consequence, we must also reconsider the theoretical
framework within which such findings have been interpreted. Specifically,
if constraint is socially determined and *if,* over the past twenty years, the
political environment has become more ideological and thus presumably
more stimulating, *then* why does it appear that there have not been major
increases in the constraint of belief systems? Given such findings, the social
sources of constraint have, perhaps, been overemphasized.

If the structure of mass belief systems is not "socially" determined, then
what is its source and what produces its changes? An alternate explanation,
suggested by Converse (1964), is that constraint is psychologically derived
and thus relatively resistant to rapid change since it depends largely on the
cognitive capacities of individuals and not the political environment. As
developed by Converse, this explanation of constraint treats the role of a
single, broad dimension—the liberal-conservative continuum—in producing a coherent set of more specific issues.

But, though it is theoretically plausible, a substantial body of empirical
findings suggests that constraint could *not* be psychologically derived solely
in terms of a liberal-conservative dimension (Achen, 1975; Hicks and
Wright, 1970; Kerlinger, 1967, 1972; Luttbeg, 1968; Thomis, 1978; Weisberg and Rusk, 1970). The universal reaction, however, is not the rejection
of psychological sources of constraint. A group of researchers—referred to
as "rationalists" by Stimson (1975) and those using the "psychological approach" by Bennett (1977)—have argued that the failure to detect a consistent pattern of liberal-conservative constraint is not an indication that psychological sources of constraint are nonexistent. They question Converse's
implicit assumption that the liberal-conservative continuum is the only basis
for psychological constraint. As an alternative, they posit that constraint
may be psychologically derived either from a multidimensional source or
from a single dimension other than the traditional liberal-conservative continuum (Brown, 1970; Coveyou and Piereson, 1977; Jackson and Marcus,
1975; Lane, 1962, 1973; Marcus et al., 1974; Thomis, 1978).

There are problems with adopting this theoretical perspective as it is
currently formulated. As will be discussed later, the traditional correlational
approach to assessing constraint is no longer justifiable once we abandon the
a priori assumption that a single, known dimension is the primary mode of

organization. Even more problematic is the plethora of unresolved conceptual and theoretical misunderstandings that the psychological approach has
introduced into the study of mass belief systems (Bennett, 1977). Finally,
and perhaps most troubling, the "psychological approach" suffers a serious
theoretical deficiency of its own; it fails to provide an explicit means for the
political environment to contribute to the structuring of beliefs. From this
perspective belief systems appear to develop insulated from environmental
influences. Like the social explanation, the psychological approach is incomplete. Though neither of these theoretical positions seems entirely correct, both contain elements used in our more comprehensive explanation of
the nature and origins of belief system structure. Let us begin our consideration of that framework by redefining certain concepts.

DEFINITIONS

One of the chief difficulties with the mass belief systems literature is the
confusion which abounds over the meaning of certain key concepts. As
Bennett (1977) explains, in the past there was a consensus among researchers about the implicit meaning. But, the theoretical challenge made to the
social constraint argument by advocates of the psychological approach disrupted these existing "shared" definitions without offering any satisfactory
resolution. Consequently, before outlining our framework we must establish
a set of conceptualizations which bridges the gap between the two approaches.

Converse defined a belief system "as a configuration of ideas and attitudes in which the elements are bound together by some form of constraint or
functional interdependence" (1964: 207). Thus, he initially conceived of the
content of a belief system very broadly; the elements composing the system
could be either general or specific, affective or cognitive. Similarly, as
outlined in Converse's definition of constraint, the structure of a belief
system could, in principle, be either uni- or multidimensional; some sense of
linkage about what idea-elements went with one another was the only re-
quirement (Jackson and Marcus, 1975: 95; Lane, 1973: 93; Stimson, 1975:
394).

This broad conceptualization of the content and structure of mass belief
systems has been largely overshadowed by the much narrower operationalizations employed in their study. Specifically, the assumption that constraint
was socially determined dictated the manner in which the content and structure of belief systems were empirically examined. Thus, in content the
emphasis was on specific idea-elements, such as issue positions, since broad
ideological orientations were not expected to be a major component in mass
belief systems. Similarly, the structure of mass belief systems was assumed
to be in terms of the liberal-conservative continuum because that was the

organizing principle which elites—who were thought to structure the masses' attitudes—appeared to use.

In contrast, the psychological approach implies that the content of belief systems should be assessed by general and specific idea-elements, since the latter is assumed to be derived from the former. Consequently, such studies have operationalized belief system content in specific issue positions and general political orientations (Jackson and Marcus, 1975; Marcus et al., 1974; Thomis, 1978). Similarly, the psychological approach suggests that the structure of mass belief systems should be defined not only by the relation among specific elements but also by the links between specific and general elements. This emphasis is reflected in the emphasis on the relations among specific issue positions and more general political orientations (Jackson and Marcus, 1975; Marcus et al., 1974; Thomis, 1978).

It can thus be argued that the sociological and psychological approaches do not differ substantially in their basic theoretical conceptualizations. But, in empirical operationalizations they diverge dramatically, largely as a consequence of their different theoretical emphases. Therefore, the conceptual conflict can be eliminated by developing definitions which provide a theoretical basis for establishing the relations among the various operationalizations of the content and structure of mass belief systems. Towards this end, we provide the following set of definitions.

First, it is necessary to define the nature of the elements composing a belief system. Converse's original definition encompassed virtually all types of elements with little distinction among them. In contrast, the psychological approach discriminates among elements in a general vs. specific orientation. This distinction—which is consistent with Converse's broad conceptualization—is maintained and elaborated. The most general elements of a belief system we label "schemata," while the more specific elements are composed of "attitudes" and "beliefs." Although such a distinction is best seen as a broad *continuum* of belief elements, the explicit differentiation of schemata from beliefs and attitudes is conceptually useful. We would thus expect some variation in specificity within each of these classifications. The important criterion, however, is the relative generality of the objects or class of objects referenced by the belief element. To elaborate, a political schema may be thought of as a *general* cognitive and affective orientation toward politics. In contrast, political attitudes and beliefs represent, respectively, *specific* evaluations and cognitions about politics. A person's political attitudes and beliefs would indicate their position on various issues.

The structure of belief systems—as defined by the concept of constraint—also has been treated differently depending on the theoretical approach. Clearly, Converse's theoretical conception of constraint is general enough to accommodate both empirical treatments. But, to do so, it is necessary to formalize theoretically the distinctions among types of constraint which are implicitly suggested by these two operationalizations. Specifically, based loosely on Bem's (1970) discussion of the structure of belief systems, let us argue that constraint—the functional interdependence among belief elements—may be defined along two distinct dimensions: horizontal and vertical (Bennett, 1977). "Vertical constraint" refers to the relations among the more general elements of a belief system (schemata) and the specific elements (beliefs and attitudes); it is that aspect of belief system structure focused by advocates of the psychological approach. In contrast "horizontal constraint" may be defined as the interrelations among elements of the same type: the relations among schemata *or* the relations between specific elements such as beliefs and attitudes.Horizontal constraint most closely parallels that aspect of belief system structure examined by those taking a social constraint approach.

POLITICAL SCHEMATA AND THE STRUCTURE OF MASS BELIEF SYSTEMS

Our approach to the study of political belief systems differs from previous ones in its emphasis on two points. First, belief systems are not treated as static entities; rather, they are depicted as components in a dynamic process through which an individual relates to the political world. Second, critical to our understanding of the functioning of belief systems is our assumption that they are both the product of, and an input into, the *interaction* between the individual and his environment. With this in mind, let us turn to an examination of the nature of political schemata and subsequently to the development of patterns of constraint within a belief system.

POLITICAL SCHEMATA

Our treatment of political belief systems is built around the "schema" concept which has a strong historical basis in psychology (Bartlett, 1932; Kelly, 1955; and Piaget, 1951) and which has also been the subject of much current research (Axelrod, 1973; Bobrow and Norman, 1975; Neisser, 1976; Stotland and Canon, 1972; and Tesser and Conlee, 1975). Based on the foundation established by such research, our earlier definition may be elaborated: A schema is an internal cognitive structure, derived from past experience, that organizes and guides the processing of information contained in the individual's environment (Markus, 1977).

In order to fully define the concept, however, it is necessary to examine the specific *functions* performed by a schema. First, a schema is a unit of memory in the sense that it is a means of storing information which has been previously collected and evaluated (Markus, 1977). Second, a schema generates expectations about future interactions with the stimulus domain which it encompasses (Tesser and Leone, 1977). Third, and perhaps most important, schemata function as more than simply static memory units or expectations; they also perform a dynamic role in the ongoing processing of information. Specifically, they guide an individual's attention to stimuli, to the extraction of information from such stimuli, and to the subsequent interpretation, categorization, and storage of the information (Neisser, 1976: 55; Markus, 1977: 64).

It is expected that the *structure* of political schemata—the pattern of horizontal constraint among the most general elements of the belief system—may assume a wide variety of forms. An individual may have a single, highly developed schema which guides his perception of political events or he may rely on several schemata which may or may not be related. The *development* of cognitive schemata occurs in response to an individual's extended interactions with the environment: interactions in which the information extracted from the environment is construed in terms of the individual's existing schemata. In effect, schemata not only shape but are shaped by a person's perception of the environment (Minsky, 1975: 256; Neisser, 1976). This suggests that the greater the development of a schema the more resistant it will be to rapid change since, to some extent, perceptions will continue to be guided and structured in accordance with the existing schema. To the degree that the environment dictates both the content and structure of the information received by the individual, schemata are socially determined. At the same time, however, factors internal to the person—such as their existing schemata, their cognitive development, their motives and goals—also determine the nature of the schemata. Thus, social *and* psychological factors contribute to the development of schemata.

Substantively, the schemata applied to political perception are expected to vary in both their development and the degree to which they are explicitly political. Thus, the concept is employed in the same spirit that others have used the terms "ideological principles" (Marcus et al., 1974), "general political orientations" (Thomis, 1978; Searing et al., 1973), "general ideological dimensions" (Jackson and Marcus, 1975), and "core belief system" (Lane, 1962, 1973). The distinguishing feature, and consequently major advantage, of the schema concept with respect to these others is its explicit relation to the dynamic process of perception.

THE EMERGENCE OF CONSTRAINT IN A BELIEF SYSTEM

Our basic assumption is that at any time the overall structure of a political belief system represents the product of the individual's past interactions with the political environment. Thus, in order to understand the evolution of an entire belief system, it is necessary to understand how individual elements develop since, together, their emergence determines the structure of the system as a whole.

In a general sense, the specific elements of a belief system—attitudes and beliefs—resemble schemata in several ways. Like schemata, they may be thought of as cognitive categories within which previously collected information is stored. Also, like schemata, they emerge as a result of the individual's interactions with the environment: interactions which are structured by the person's existing belief system. In essence, new attitudes and beliefs evolve in relation to existing schemata and, as a consequence, with respect to other specific elements of a belief system as well. Thus, the emergence of a pattern of vertical constraint largely determines the nature of horizontal constraint among the specific elements of a belief system. Consequently, a complete understanding of patterns of horizontal constraint may only be attained in conjunction with a consideration of the pattern of vertical constraint.

In general, new elements will be added to a belief system as a consequence of its day-to-day functioning. Given this, the emergence of patterns of constraint are best understood by considering the two general principles which govern the belief system's processing of information:

(1) At some level, the individual must account for all the information provided by the environment.
(2) The ongoing functioning of a belief system can be "driven" either conceptually or by events (Bobrow and Norman, 1975).

Let us explore the implications of these principles.

First, the functioning of a belief system can be "conceptually driven" in the sense that it is motivated by factors (such as personal needs and goals) internal to the individual. Conceptually driven processing tends to be "top-down," in that the individual searches for information which will support the structure of his current belief system—in effect, fitting environmental inputs into existing categories of schemata (Bobrow and Norman, 1975: 141). Such top-down processing becomes more likely the greater the ambiguity in the existing environmental stimuli. Furthermore, where the dominant mode of processing is top-down, new categories (schemata, beliefs, attitudes) will emerge from existing ones largely in response to the personal needs of the individual as opposed to any demands placed on him by the environment. Thus, changes in the patterns of constraint will be instigated largely by internal factors, though they will necessarily occur within the context of environmentally produced information.

This description of a conceptually driven belief system parallels our traditional conceptualization of an ideology. First, the role of an ideology in the development of specific issue positions is usually depicted as one in which general ideological orientations structure the formation of more specific beliefs in the same fashion as the belief system described above (see, for example: Converse, 1964; Thomis, 1978). Furthermore, an ideology is usually described as functioning in a conceptually driven fashion. For example, Abelson (1975) describes the Cold War ideological structure as one in which "an extraordinary number of actual and potential international agents are "understood" as confirming the long range objective of the Communist bloc to control the world, and the need for Free World counteraction" (1975: 274). But, though a belief system may function in a conceptually driven fashion (much like an "ideology" is expected to), it may also operate in a second mode.

The alternative to a conceptually driven belief system is one which is "event-driven" in the sense that activities in the environment create information which motivates the operation of the belief system. Event-driven processing tends to be bottom-up in that the individual searches for a category that will fit the information, rather than looking only for information that will support the belief system (Bobrow and Norman, 1975). Since it is assumed that the individual must process all information to some extent, it can be argued that most event-driven processing is virtually automatic; the information is received, assessed, and routinely stored in the most readily available category. As Bobrow and Norman note, "initially all the data must fit into some schema, but it does not matter if the fit is bad. . . . for most purposes the original interpretation is quite adequate" (1975: 143). Thus, the day-to-day chores of information processing are typically handled by existing categories and, therefore, produce no changes in either schemata or specific attitudes and beliefs. Under certain circumstances, however, changes in a belief system can occur during the course of event-driven processing. Specifically, *unexpected* events, such as the emergence of a new issue or the contextual redefinition of an old one, may trigger in-depth processing for which existing categories are inadequate. In such circumstances, new categories are likely to evolve within the context of the existing belief system (Bobrow and Norman, 1975: 144).

IMPLICATIONS

In summary, let us consider the implications of this approach. First, a political belief system may function in either a conceptually driven or event-driven fashion, and consequently may develop and change in response to *both* psychological and social factors. To elaborate, in a politically unstimulating environment it is expected that political belief systems will function more often in a conceptually driven manner, since there are relatively few environmental occurrences to trigger event-driven processing. Under such circumstances, people's internal needs and goals are the key to understanding the growth and change in political belief systems. The emergence and evolution of both new schemata and specific issue positions will be largely dictated by internal factors. To the degree that internal motives are absent, political belief systems will change little and may be used only sporadically. This description parallels the traditional view of the American electorate in the 1950s.

In a politically stimulating environment, belief systems will continue to function and change in a conceptually driven fashion. But, in addition, belief systems will also have to operate more frequently in an event-driven manner. Thus, there should be greater use of belief systems within the public than there was under less stimulating conditions. Past research has argued that there should also be increases in the constraint of belief systems as a consequence of an increase in political stimulation (Converse, 1975; Nie and Andersen, 1974).

Our perspective suggests that structural changes do not occur quite so easily; with respect to existing issues, constraint is expected to change only if some of those issues become *contextually redefined* in the sense that environmental forces (e.g., political elites or societal events) redefine the general terms or dimensions in which those issues are seen and discussed. Thus, increased political discussion of *existing* issues should stimulate event-driven use of political belief systems; but it is most likely to be routine information processing by already existing categories. From this perspective, though the political environment of the 1960s may have been more stimulating than that of the 1950s, it can be argued that there was no substantial contextual redefinition of most issues which carried over from one decade to the next—issues such as black welfare, social welfare, the Cold War, and school integration. Consequently, a change in constraint among those issues would not be expected—a prediction which is consistent with our earlier interpretation of the data.

Beyond the theoretical implications of our framework, we may also draw certain inferences relevant to the empirical study of mass belief systems. First, some relation is expected between the two general patterns of horizontal constraint—that among the schemata and that characterizing the specific elements of a belief system. But, because of the influence of environmental factors, a particular pattern of schemata cannot be expected to determine entirely the pattern of constraint among specific attitudes and beliefs. Thus, two individuals with the same set of schemata could conceivably have disparate patterns of issue constraint. Second, the structure of a person's underlying schemata cannot be inferred by considering only the pattern of horizontal constraint among specific elements, a point central to the psychological approach (Coveyou and Pierson, 1977; Jackson and Marcus, 1975; Lane, 1973; Marcus et al., 1974). In effect, two individuals could have the same pattern of issue positions and yet have very different patterns of schemata.

EMPIRICAL ANALYSIS

Through the use of survey data, it is difficult to conduct an in-depth exploration of belief systems which are as complex as we have suggested.

Nonetheless, we believe that it is possible to demonstrate how specific schema may be associated with certain patterns of attitudes and beliefs. In this spirit, we offer the following analysis, *not* as a comprehensive test of the posited framework, but rather as an illustration of the viability of certain aspects of our theory.

DATA AND METHOD OF ANALYSIS

Beginnning with Converse's (1964) article, the structure of belief systems has traditionally been assessed solely by correlations among issue positions. Those adopting a psychological approach, however, have heavily criticized this method of analysis because it forces the analyst to decide a priori the structural nature of belief systems. Converse and others, for example, assume unidimensional structuring of the liberal-conservative continuum (Coveyou and Piereson, 1977; Jackson and Marcus, 1975; Lane, 1973; Marcus et al., 1974). To avoid this criticism, the underlying, general elements of a belief system must be considered separately, and preferably their nature should be specified by the respondent. While we were able to meet the first of these requirements, the second was unattainable given the survey data which we employed.

Our analysis begins with the identification of a set of basic political orientations which could be expected to constitute political schemata for many members of the electorate. The sample is then divided into groups of individuals who share the same perspective with respect to a single schema or combinations of schemata. Then, variations between these groups in their patterns of specific issue positions are examined. In effect, our analysis examines the variations in aggregate patterns of vertical constraint that may be associated with different combinations of schemata. Even though this ignores potentially important individual variations in constraint, we feel that this analysis is a useful starting point for demonstrating the relations that may exist between schemata and specific issue positions.

The data employed in the analysis are from the 1976 CPS National Election Study. The schema concept was operationalized in 4 summated rating scales which span the range of societal and political concerns.[3] Specifically, the 4 scales and their reliabilities (coefficient alpha) are:

(1) POWER—the desired power of the federal government (.39);
(2) RESPONSIBILITY—the responsibility of the federal government for solving societal problems (.82);
(3) POOR—the locus of responsibility (society or the individual) for the problems of the poor (.73);
(4) SOCIAL—the locus of responsibility (society or the individual) for the status of social minorities, specifically blacks and women (.69).

Once formed, each scale was collapsed into three categories. The cutting points were selected so that both a sufficient number of cases fell in all categories for each scale, and the absolute position on the scale was not distorted (i.e., subjects were not placed in an extreme category if their response was in the middle). In the case of each scale, those respondents falling in the first category adopted what would traditionally be labeled a "liberal" perspective: They desire a powerful federal government; it is the federal government's responsibility to solve societal problems; the problems of the poor are created by society; and the responsibility for the status of social minorities lies with society. Similarly, subjects in the middle category had a "moderate" perspective, while those in the third category held what would traditionally be labeled a "conservative" perspective. We offer these scales as representative of political schemata since they all reference very broad matters of societal and governmental concern. The RESPONSIBIL-ITY scale, for example, deals with a general perspective on the role of government, but says nothing about the specific societal problems that should be dealt with. Similarly, the POOR scale differentiates general views about the causes of poverty in society without specifying what, if anything, should be done about it.

In contrast to this, the specific elements of a belief system were opera-tionalized in 10 issue questions dealing with a wide range of topics. On each question, the respondents identified their issue positions by placing them-selves on either a 4-, 5-, or 7-point scale. Since ultimately our interest was in examining the pattern of issue positions among a group who shared the same schemata, each of the issue items was converted to a standardized distribu-tion with a mean of zero and a standard deviation of 1. On all the transformed issue items, negative values indicate left-of-center issue positions while positive values represent right-of-center issue positions. Thus, for example, a score of -1.0 would signify that the group mean is a standard deviation to the left of the population mean on that issue.

FINDINGS

Now, let us turn to an examination of our findings concerning the nature of mass belief systems. First, Americans do differ in their general orienta-tions toward politics. Though for each schemata respondents were lost in the scale construction process (a low of 23.8% for the RESPONSIBILITY scale and a high of 37.3% of the sample on the POWER scale), a sufficient number of subjects remained to suggest that these scales capture what are relevant political perspectives to a large portion of the electorate.[4] Further-more, though the distributions for two schemata—government responsibil-ity for social problems and locus of responsibility for social minorities—are somewhat skewed, there is certainly enough variation in all to suggest that these schemata are a viable source of differences in specific issue positions.[5] Even more important is the pattern of horizontal constraint among these schemata. As indicated by the intercorrelations, these schemata are essen-tially independent; only the POOR and SOCIAL scales are substantially related (r = .28). In essence, there is no pervasive mode of liberal-conservative organization linking these schemata to one another; they are each a fairly distinct perspective from which to perceive and evaluate the political world. Furthermore, individuals may have varying combinations of these schemata thus creating more diversity in the perspectives from which politics is viewed.

To simplify the analysis, only those individuals who had extreme positions (category 1 or 3) on a schema scale were considered in our examination of the patterns of vertical constraint between different schemata and specific issue positions. With that in mind, Table 3.1 presents the pattern of issue positions for those groups of individuals with extreme scores on each schema. For those extreme groups on both the locus of responsibility for the poor and social minorities scales, there are distinct, and expected, patterns in their issue positions. Those groups who see society as being responsible for the poor or social minorities tend to adopt issue positions to the left of center, while those who see the individual as responsible develop issue positions to the right of center. In contrast, those groups who differ in their perspectives on the POWER or RESPONSIBILITY scales do not appear to adopt consistent liberal or conservative issue positions. Despite this, as we shall see, the importance of these schemata clearly emerges when their interactive effect with other schemata are examined.

The aggregate patterns of vertical constraint revealed in Table 3.1 are rather unrealistic since individuals are not expected to generate issue positions in the context of a single schemata. Instead, it is much more likely that several schemata interact. Consequently, we consider the patterns of vertical constraint associated with various combinations of schemata. Specifically, the interaction between the POOR and SOCIAL scales is examined since those are the schemata which demonstrate the clearest traditional patterns of constraint with specific issue positions. The interaction of these two schemata produce 4 "extreme" groups, 2 of which are consistent in the traditional sense because they adopt either the "societal" or "individual" perspective on both schemata. Typically, the other 2 groups would be considered inconsistent since the interaction of their schemata combines what would be interpreted as liberal *and* conservative perspectives.

As columns 1 through 4 on Table 3.2 indicate, of these 4 groups, the 2 consistent groups have patterns of vertical constraint that might be expected in the liberal-conservative continuum. With only one exception, individuals with an individual perspective on both the POOR and SOCIAL schemata have beliefs to the right of center. Conversely, those people with a societal perspective on both schemata have issue positions which consistently fall to the extreme left of center. From our point of view, much more interesting are the two middle groups that have what traditional analysts would consider to be inconsistent schemata. Neither of these groups demonstrates a consistent

Table 3.1

TABLE 3.1 Simple Patterns of Vertical Constraint for Extreme Groups on the "Power," "Responsibility," "Poor," and "Social" Scales

Issue (Scale range)	Standard Deviation	Population Mean	High Power	Low Power	High Resp.	Low Resp.	Societal Poor	Individual Poor	Societal Social	Individual Social
Guaranteed Job and Standard of Living (1–7)	2.02	4.41	−.04	.11	−.12	.12	−.49	.49	−.34	.19
Government Health Insurance (1–7)	2.38	3.95	−.02	.09	−.13	.05	−.40	.37	−.36	.14
Aid to Minorities (1–7)	2.00	4.26	−.03	.12	−.05	.10	−.42	.49	−.53	.28
School Integration (1–5)	1.83	3.42	−.15	.16	−.08	.14	−.34	.23	−.57	.26
School Busing (1–7)	1.71	6.07	−.01	.06	.01	.04	−.34	.28	−.69	.29
Urban Unrest (1–7)	1.91	3.20	−.05	−.09	−.09	.08	−.17	−.02	−.55	.35
Rights of Accused (1–7)	2.13	4.26	.03	−.04	−.06	−.01	−.23	.13	−.38	.21
Legalize Marijuana (1–7)	2.19	4.82	.09	−.12	.04	−.02	−.20	.09	−.46	.28
Equal Rights for Women (1–7)	2.07	3.18	−.05	−.09	−.09	.08	−.17	.02	−.55	.35
Allow Abortions (1–4)	1.00	2.41	.05	−.17	−.02	.05	.02	−.02	−.30	.17
			(372)	(512)	(320)	(894)	(542)	(454)	(362)	(1064)

(N = number in group; n's for specific issues vary)

All entries are z-scores

Table 3.2

TABLE 3.2 Complex Patterns of Vertical Constraint: Interactions of the Four Scales

	Individual Poor/ Individual Social	Individual Poor/ Societal Social	Societal Poor/ Individual Social	Societal Poor/ Societal Social	Schema Interaction Societal Social/ Low Power	Societal Social/ High Power	Societal Social/ High Resp.	Societal Social/ Low Resp.	Societal Poor/ Low Power	Societal Poor/ High Power
Guaranteed Job and Standard of Living	.54	.41	-.36	-.67	-.19	-.53	-.43	-.21	-.51	-.54
Government Health Insurance	.41	.19	-.15	-.78	-.06	-.55	-.53	-.12	-.53	-.41
Aid to Minorities	.58	.14	-.12	-.80	-.32	-.52	-.08	-.46	-.55	-.34
School Integration	.35	-.13	.11	-.88	-.27	-.75	-.73	-.46	-.32	-.41
School Busing	.38	-.23	.15	-1.03	-.45	-.72	-.75	-.47	-.34	-.31
Urban Unrest	.47	-.27	-.05	-.58	-.33	-.45	-.56	-.40	-.20	-.26
Rights of Accused	.21	-.47	.04	-.46	-.31	-.25	-.49	-.41	-.24	-.01
Legalize Marijuana	.27	-.27	.24	-.59	-.76	-.18	-.53	-.48	-.21	-.01
Equal Rights for Women	.24	-.55	.24	-.66	-.67	-.49	-.68	-.25	-.37	-.03
Allow Abortions	-.10	-.20	.22	-.26	-.67	-.05	-.35	-.26	-.15	.19
(N = number in group; n's for specific issues vary)	(241)	(43)	(178)	(148)	(63)	(57)	(40)	(163)	(243)	(94)

left- or right-of-center pattern of issue positions; rather each group is to the left on some issues and to the right on others.

Yet, this lack of a consistent liberal-conservative pattern for the middle groups is *not* an indication that these groups have purely random patterns of issue positions. Significantly, the patterns of vertical constraint for the individual POOR/societal SOCIAL group represent an almost perfect mirror image of that characterizing the societal POOR/individual SOCIAL group. Furthermore, and most critical to our argument, the differences between these two groups reflect the differentiation of their fundamental beliefs or schemata. Thus, for example, individuals with an individual POOR/societal SOCIAL configuration of schemata tend to adopt left-of-center or liberal positions on issues relevant to social minorities such as blacks and women—school integration, school busing, rights of the accused, legalization of marijuana, equal rights for women, and abortion. At the same time, however, this group has conservative or right-of-center positions on issues which pertain most directly to the poor: guaranteed job and standard of living and government health insurance. A similar rationale emerges for the issue positions adopted by the societal POOR/individual SOCIAL group.

Based on these findings, several key inferences may be made. First, different combinations of schemata are associated with distinct patterns of issue positions. An individual level examination would be expected to reveal some variation in such patterns of vertical constraint largely because of individual idiosyncracies as well as exposure to different environmental input. Second, this analysis demonstrates the potential error involved in relying on correlation coefficients to infer the underlying nature of an individual's basic political orientation. People differ in the extent to which their schemata may be classified as uniformly liberal or conservative, and this variation is reflected in the pattern of issue positions which emerges. Thus, the absence of a consistently conservative or liberal set of issue positions does not necessarily mean that there is no underlying organization in people's basic political orientations. On the contrary, upon careful examination, their issue positions are likely to reflect a rational outgrowth of their fundamental beliefs concerning the nature and functions of the political system.

We have demonstrated that different combinations of schemata are related to distinct patterns of issue positions. Yet, from both a substantive and methodological perspective, one of the key points of our earlier argument was that the same pattern of issue positions could be associated with a different set of schemata. To test this prediction and to provide another example of the interaction among schemata, we consider the patterns of issue positions associated with variations in the POWER and RESPONSI-BILITY scales among the group with a societal perspective on the SO-CIAL scale.[6] Variations in the minor schemata—POWER and RESPONSI-

BILITY—do make differences in the pattern of issue positions ultimately associated with societal perspectives on the two major schemata.

As columns 5 through 8 of Table 3.2 show, the 4 groups of individuals produced by the combination of the societal category of the social scale with the 2 minor schemata—POWER and RESPONSIBILITY—tend to adopt issue positions to the left of the population mean.nonetheless, despite the overall similarity among the groups, there are distinct variations between them that follow logically from the interaction of the 2 minor schemata with the major one. Specifically, for all but certain social issues—abortion, equal rights for women, legalizing marijuana—the high POWER group has issue positions farther to the left of center than does the low POWER group. Similarly, for all the issues, the high RESPONSIBILITY group has issue positions farther to the left of center than does the low RESPONSIBILITY group. Thus, variations in minor schemata are associated with distinct patterns of issue positions.

Of even greater interest, however, is the marked similarity between the societal SOCIAL/high POWER group and the societal SOCIAL/high RE-SPONSIBILITY group. With the exception of only a few items, the patterns of issue positions are virtually the same, thus demonstrating that different patterns of schemata may be associated with essentially the same pattern of issue positions. This finding assumes even greater validity when we note that there is only random overlap in the membership of the 2 groups; the correlation between the POWER and RESPONSIBILITY scales is only .08. Thus, the overall similarity in these 2 groups suggests the potential for error which exists when one attempts to infer an underlying set of political orientations or schemata from only a pattern of issue positions. But the few differences which do exist illustrate the manner in which different combinations of schemata may be related to subtle, but distinct, variations in issue positions.

One final example will help illustrate the complexities in the way in which schemata combine to influence the development of political beliefs. The last two columns of Table 3.2 present the contrasting pattern of issue positions associated with the interaction of the high and low POWER perspectives with the societal category of the POOR scale. When differences on the POWER scale were just examined in conjunction with the SOCIAL scale, the high POWER group produced a generally more liberal pattern of issue positions, especially on economic and racial issues; this effect is not repeated for the societal POOR group. On many issues the *low* POWER/ societal POOR group actually has issue positions farther to the left of center than does the high POWER/societal POOR group. This pattern often appears on issues—abortion, legalization of marijuana, rights of the accused—for which it can be argued that the low POWER group is simply taking a classic civil libertarian stand consistent with their underlying schemata. This finding is critical, because it demonstrates the complex and nonadditive way in which basic political orientations combine to influence the development of issue positions.

CONCLUSIONS

This chapter has presented a cognitive information processing model of the structure, development, and change of belief systems. One goal of the model is to help reconcile some of the theoretical and operational differences characterizing the sociological and psychological approaches to mass belief systems. At the same time, this perspective goes beyond current conceptualizations to suggest new hypotheses and directions for research. Specifically, based on the concept of cognitive schemata, we have argued that belief systems are dynamic entities that develop and change in response to an individual's interactions with the political world, as well as guiding those same interactions. Consequently, at any one time the structure and content of a belief system will be the result of an evolutionary change affected by both environmental and psychological factors. Further changes in belief systems will occur with respect to existing schemata, since, to a large degree, these will guide new perceptions of the environment.

Our empirical analysis offered a preliminary test of some of the predictions of the model. Given the theoretical argument we present, cross-sectional survey data of the type used here prevents a complete test of the model for three reasons: Individual differences in belief system structure cannot be easily assessed apart from group differences, the content of the schemata must be specified in advance and similarly for all, and the dynamic aspects of the process cannot be directly examined. Despite this, several important conclusions emerge from the analysis. First, the content of people's cognitive schemata are strongly related to the issue positions they hold. As the interactive effects we examined indicate, these relations may be quite complex. This complexity is itself important since it directly affects the way belief systems may be studied. Thus, while some belief systems do resemble those expected from the assumption of liberal-conservative structuring, others are organized along very different lines as would be expected from the observed pattern of schemata. Further care is suggested since the schemata do not necessarily combine in a linear, additive fashion. Drastic changes in issue positions may therefore result from subtle changes in the organization of schemata, and similar patterns of issue positions may result from different sets of schemata.

For the future study of belief systems, this analysis suggests several important correctives on past studies and directions for new research. Most generally, belief systems should be conceptualized and studied as dynamic entities rather than in the purely static manner that has been typical. In doing so, the full range of belief elements, general *and* specific, should be examined since the overall structure of a belief system is a product of both. Similarly, efforts should be made to look at the effects of psychological and sociological factors in the development of belief systems instead of the current tendency to see them in opposition. From a methodological perspective, this suggests that researchers should abandon their simplistic assumptions about unidimensional (liberal vs. conservative) structuring of beliefs, and their misleading use of correlations among issue positions as the sole indicator of belief system structure. Such measures cannot cope with the complexity we have discovered here and deal only with the specific belief elements. Under these circumstances, the consideration of the more general belief elements (schemata) becomes critical. Any a priori judgment of the structure of a belief system will likely fail as a basis for assessing belief system structure in the same manner as the liberal-conservative continuum we have criticized.

NOTES

1. Though, in a theoretical sense, it is possible to separate clearly the social from the psychological constraint arguments, it would be somewhat misleading to suggest that the distinction remains as clear when applied to actual prior research. That is, advocates of a social constraint approach are aware of, and take into account *to some extent,* the psychological argument and vice versa.

2. These critiques are not universally accepted. See Nie and Rabjohn (1979) and Petrocik (1978).

3. The items in the POOR and SOCIAL scales all pose the question of whether the condition of the poor, blacks, or women is a function of the individuals themselves or societal discrimination against the groups. The POOR scale is 6 items long, the SOCIAL scale contains 8 items. The POWER scale combines the responses to 6 items which pose the dilemma of the power of the federal government vs.the rights of the individual in various areas of domestic policy. The RESPONSIBILITY scale is made up of 10 items that assess the respondents' position concerning the responsibility of the federal government for handling a variety of societal problems—largely domestic. For those interested in examining the scales in more detail, the variable numbers (from the CPS 1976 codebook) for each of the scales are: POOR, 3751-3756, 3757; SOCIAL, 3802-3809; POWER, 3554-3559; RESPONSIBILITY, 3716-3725.

4. Respondents were eliminated from the scale by a simple list-wise procedure. Missing data (DK, NA) for any item in the scale caused the respondent to be declared missing for the entire scale.

5. There is no reason why variation on a dimension is necessary for a schema to be an important component of a belief system. Consensual beliefs, as may result from a homogeneous political culture, may be central parts of belief systems for many people. In the present analysis, however, variation in these schemata is necessary to evaluate their role in producing distinctive patterns of political beliefs. A more idiographic procedure would be needed to assess the role of largely consensual beliefs.

6. It should be noted that the POWER and RESPONSIBILITY scales did not produce many variations among those with an "individual" perspective on either the POOR or SOCIAL scale; conservatism appears to be determined by the two schemata already examined—the locus of responsibility for the poor and social minorities scales.

4

CHANGES IN THE PUBLIC'S POLITICAL THINKING: THE WATERSHED YEARS, 1956-1968

John C. Pierce
Paul R. Hagner

In many respects, the 1960s were an important turning point in American politics. That decade can be considered a watershed in the public's political thinking. Indeed, the consistency of the public's political beliefs rose dramatically (Bennett, 1973; Nie and Andersen, 1974). Albeit in a less spectacular fashion, there likewise was an increase in the proportion of the public using sophisticated conceptualizations to evaluate parties and candidates (Field and Anderson, 1969; Pierce, 1970; Converse, 1975; Nie et al., 1976).

The interpretations of the changes in political thinking remain mixed, incomplete, and in some dispute. To be sure, most observers agree that, beginning with the mid-1960s, the American public exhibited a heightened interest in politics while political leaders were clarifying political issues and their own positions on those issues. Substantially less consensus, however, obtains in judgements about whether the increases in the public's belief system consistency represent "the reflected social type or are in fact more autonomously ideological" (Converse, 1975: 107). That is, did the public's beliefs become consistent with each other because people merely adopted and articulated the newly coherent and visible issue positions of favored political cue-givers (e.g., party leaders)? Or, on the other hand, did the public now put its beliefs together in more coherent packages because of a long-standing ability to independently and rationally respond to relevant changes in politics?

This chapter reports the results of an inquiry into the increases in belief system consistency in the American public in the 1960s; it tries partially to disentangle the contributions of ideological thinking and social/political cue-giving. Data are employed from the 1956, 1964, and 1968 election studies of the CPS of the ISR at the University of Michigan.[1] The 1956 study contains the data on which the traditional picture of the public's belief system was developed (Campbell et al., 1960; Converse, 1964). The first major increases in belief system consistency appeared in the 1964 study. The use of the 1968 study provides the opportunity to monitor the continuation of patterns first appearing in 1964.

BELIEF SYSTEM CONSTRAINT: COGNITIVE AND POLITICAL SOURCES

Belief system *constraint* is the extent to which the public's opinions about different issues are related to each other. Constraint is reflected in the consistency of beliefs across a series of issues that share a common dimension (Converse, 1964). Constraint is manifest in the degree to which the public's beliefs on one issue can be predicted knowing their beliefs on other issues. Constraint usually is measured in two ways: aggregate and individual. Aggregate measures look at the strength of the relation (the correlation) between the public's beliefs on issue A and issue B. The result is an aggregated measure of constraint for the public but not necessarily for any individual in the public. On the other hand, individual measures provide constraint levels for each person, looking at the extent to which their responses point in the same (consistent) direction across a series of issues (Barton and Parsons, 1977).

This study employs an aggregate measure of belief system constraint. Five issues relating to domestic policy are chosen in each of the election studies. The relation between the public's beliefs on each issue pair (10 pair in each study) is obtained. Overall constraint is estimated by the average relation among the 10 pairs. There is some variance in the issue content between elections. We chose issues, however, that we felt as closely as possible approximated the same substantive content.[2] The issues were asked in a different format in 1956 than in 1964 and 1968. This has occasioned considerable dispute about the reliability of responses and the appropriate interpretations of changes in belief system constraint.[3] We will not confront that question in detail here, except to suggest along the way that the patterns of changes we observed in the following data argue for forces at work *in addition* to changes in question format.

To force some comparability on the data, and to minimize the risk of cells with insufficient cases in the more disaggregated analyses of the chapter, all responses were grouped into dichotomous categories, corresponding roughly to liberal and conservative beliefs. "Depends," "don't know" and "no answer" responses were eliminated. The relation (constraint) among the dichotomous response categories for each issue pair was obtained through the ordinal statistic phi.[4] Constraint levels, then, are estimated through the average of 10 phis. Most studies of belief system constraint employ the ordinal measure gamma, which has an inappropriate underlying statistical model. On comparable or identical response patterns, phi provides a lower estimate of constraint. The *patterns* of constraint across groups and across years, however, are remarkably similar. Thus, this study's approach produces average constraint levels of .19, .34, and .33 for the 3 years compared to .23, .54, and .51 in Bennett (1973: 556) and to .24, .49, and .51 in Nie et al., (1976: 129). As the analysis proceeds and controls are introduced that disaggregate the samples into smaller groups, the relations are recalculated for each of those groups.

What accounts for the level of constraint or consistency found among the public's beliefs and also for changes in that level? Recent studies have forwarded two sets of substantive explanations. One set concerns the public's sophistication—its inherent cognitive abilities (or limitations, depending on the particular perspective). The other explanation emphasizes the importance of the cues and messages provided to the public by political leaders and the degree to which the public exhibits interest in, attends to, and reflects, the positions of those leaders.

COGNITIVE SOPHISTICATION

It is clear why one would expect cognitively sophisticated people to have more highly constrained political belief systems. The articulation of consistent beliefs may imply the ability to ascertain the content and meaning of political issues, to assess the implications of different issues for each other, and to determine the positions on those issues that are consistent with each other and with some underlying general orientation to politics. That is no series of easy tasks even for the person with considerable intellect and information. But, the growth of objective indicators of cognitive skills, such as the average number of years of formal education, coincided with the dramatic rise in belief system constraint.

Although Stimson (1975) found that the relation of issues to "the liberal-conservative dimension" was stronger among his respondents "high in cognitive ability," surprisingly little other evidence supports speculation about the relation between various measures of sophistication and belief system constraint. Converse concludes, for example, that "the evidence seems fairly clear that consistency of political attitudes . . . is far more dependent on the salience of politics than on educational background" (1975: 104). This is echoed in the recent work by Bennett et al., who found that "education is neither a strong nor a linear predictor of issue constraint among the mass public's opinions on political issues" (1979: 59).

One possible reason for the weak relation between constraint and sophistication may be the measure of sophistication employed. Education, the measure most often used (but, see Stimson, 1975), may imperfectly differentiate among people in politics. In assessing the role of sophistication in constraint, it may be more appropriate to employ a measure of *political* sophistication. That is the approach taken here. As an index of political sophistication this study employs what has become known as the "level of conceptualization." The level of conceptualization, developed first in *The American Voter* (Campbell et al., 1960), is based solely in the character of the political content of the public's evaluations of political parties and their presidential candidates. Distinctions among the *levels* of conceptualization are based in two dimensions: one refers to the content of the evaluations, and the second refers to the sophistication of the remarks (1960: 255). Thus, the levels of conceptualization discriminate among people according to their political sophistication and their criteria for political judgements.

The most sophisticated level of conceptualization is *ideological*, where people (called "ideologues") employ broad, encapsulating or dimensional frames of reference—usually focusing on the liberal-conservative dimension. The second level is labeled *group benefits*, where parties and candidates are evaluated by the benefits or costs they are believed to distribute to social groups (e.g., working people, common men, business people, blacks). In the third level, the prominent reference is the *nature of the times*, the respondents' perceptions of the parties or candidates' effect on the general state of the economy or their probable contribution to peace or international conflict. Finally, the lowest level of conceptualization is *no issue content*. Reference to personal characteristics or traditional or historical attachments predominate here.[5]

The levels of conceptualization have been measured by the same method for 1956, 1964, and 1968. That method is a content analysis, based in a reading of the interview protocols on which are recorded the respondents' evaluations and descriptions of what they like or dislike about the two major political parties and their candidates.[6] That method was employed originally in *The American Voter* and provided the basis for subsequent work by Pierce (1970, 1975). A surrogate measure has been employed in several other locations (Field and Anderson, 1969; Nie et al., 1976), but it produces substantially more people at the higher levels of conceptualization than that found through the original measure and its replications.

Table 4.1 shows the distribution of the public among the levels of conceptualization for the three election years. As that table shows, the proportion of the public at the highest level (ideological) doubled between 1956 and 1964 and maintained that number through 1968. But a commensurate-sized drop occurred in the proportion at the group benefit level, leading several scholars to conclude that only marginal change obtained in the proportion of the public in the upper half of the levels measure (e.g., Converse, 1975). The 1956 distribution—and the data employed here—come from the set employed in the initial measures of the levels (Campbell et al., 1960; Converse, 1964). These data were distributed by the ICPSR in the 1960s, but no longer are available through that source.[7] The 1956 levels, however, are included in the Flanigan/Repass laboratory analysis deck (1969), but that deck omits respondent identification numbers. Thus, the integration of those data with the entire original data set was arduous; it was accomplished by matching respondents' codes across 8 other variables in the deck with those codes for the same variables in the ICPSR master tapes. This resulted in 97% of the respondents correctly matched. The distribution among the levels and the association of the measure with other variables show the missing data to be distributed randomly among the levels.

TABLE 4.1   Levels of Conceptualization: 1956, 1964, 1968

Level of Conceptualization		1956[a]	1964	1968	1968A[b]
Ideological		12%	27%	26%	23%
Group Benefit		42	27	24	33
Nature of the Times		24	20	29	25
No Issue Content		22	26	21	20
	Total	100%	100%	100%	101%
	N	(1740)	(1431)	(1319)	

[a]This distribution comes from the Flanigan/Repass laboratory analysis deck and differs very slightly from that presented in The American Voter.
[b]This distribution is reported in Converse (1975: 102) and is the result of the work of Hans D. Klingemann and William E. Wright.

The possibility remains that the changes in the distribution on the levels measure result from different coders employing varying methods. But prior to the coding of the 1964 and 1968 data sets, a number of the respondents in the 1956 set were recoded until very high reliability obtained. The consistency in the coding between years and its faithfulness to the meaning of the concept are buttressed by the data in Table 4.2, which shows the relations of the levels to several other variables. The relation of levels of conceptualization to psychological involvement in politics, perceptions of party differences, education, and media usage is consistent across the three elections. And, a second and independent replication of the levels measure for 1968 produced a distribution similar to ours (see Table 1). The proportion of ideologues may have increased, but we are confident that the measure is reliable across years.

If belief system constraint is at least partially the product of political sophistication, what might be some of the observed patterns? In one case, in each year the level of constraint might decline as one moves down the levels of conceptualization with constraint the highest among the ideologues. Or, increases in constraint between years might be accounted for by shifts into

TABLE 4.2   The Relationship of Levels of Conceptualization and Four Criterion
             Variables: 1956, 1964, 1968

	1956	1964	1968
Political Involvement	.35*	.38	.36
Party Differences	.39	.45	.35
Education	.31	.31	.32
Media Usage	.29	.31	.32

*The strength of the association is assessed through gamma.

the more sophisticated ranks—the higher levels of conceptualization. The constraint might remain the same in each level, but the overall constraint would increase from the greater proportion of the public at the higher levels conceptualization. Third, constraint might increase more at the lower levels of conceptualization, creating the suspicion that social/political cue-giving is at work. Finally, there might occur some more intricate patterns of change, revealing an interaction between the nature of the political environment and the particular level of conceptualization. The changes in the campaign emphases (e.g., ideological in 1964; more group oriented in 1968) may have had special meaning for the belief system constraint of people at the relevant levels of conceptualization (ideological and group benefits).

POLITICAL SOURCES

A number of writers suggest that the increase in constraint is a consequence of changes in the nature of politics. More precisely, political leadership is given the major role in the heightened consistency of public beliefs (Pomper, 1975; Miller and Levitin, 1976; Converse, 1975; Nie et al., 1976). It is argued that in the early 1960s political leaders changed their behavior. While they may have previously differed on issues (McClosky, 1960) these differences were not expressed in their public rhetoric. Beginning in 1964, however, they made those differences explicit. Throughout the 1964 presidential election campaign rhetoric, coherent sets of issues were presented to the public and the alternate positions on those issues were explicitly laid down for all to see. This change in leader behavior took place when the public's constraint changed. Thus, the level of constraint has been hypothesized to depend largely on the character of elite politics.

Yet, the nature of the public's response to changes in politics has been given two rather different interpretations. On the one hand, it has been seen as a "responsive" or rational reaction to an increasingly *relevant* differentiation in politics (Pomper, 1975; Nie and Andersen, 1974). The public's beliefs became more coherent because it made sense to do so, given that political alternatives were presented more coherently. On the other hand, it also has been suggested that the public responded because of an ultimate *dependence* of many on the cues provided by political leaders. The most articulate proponent of this position is Philip Converse:

Various reference group cues and other social mechanisms could help to create ideological patterning of political attitudes and behaviors on the part of individuals, even though these patterns might not be accompanied by much explicit understanding of the more overarching and abstract reasons why these patterns go together in the conventional "ideological" sense [1975: 106].

Thus, it may be that the public "fell into positions of heightened ideological clarity without any clear recognition of the fact that they were doing so" (1975: 106). This demands only some "elastic motivational characteristics such as interest and attentiveness," and these were strongly stimulated during the politics of the early 1960s.

The social/political forces explanations agree that three variables are crucial: attentiveness to politics, interest or involvement in the content of politics, and some perceptions of the differences among political leaders. Clues about whether the large constraint increase stems from social or sophisticated cognitive sources should be provided by the manner in which belief system constraint fluctuates over time (1956-1968) within levels of attention, interest-involvement, and perceived differentiation *controlling for the level of political sophistication*.

Thus, in the subsequent analysis we employ measures of attention, interest-involvement, and perceived political differentiation. Attention is measured by respondents' reports of their media use. Involvement is assessed through an index combining responses to questions about interest in the election and care about who wins the election. Perceived differentiation is calculated by summing the number of issues on which the respondent perceives a difference between the Republicans and the Democrats. On each measure for each year, the distributions are divided into "high" and "low," as near to the mid-point (median) as possible. This provides continuity in the relative positioning of people across years when the precise construction of the measure differs (e.g., perceived differentiation). It also maintains adequate cell sizes when examining constraint levels.[8]

FINDINGS AND ANALYSIS

CONSTRAINT AND CONCEPTUALIZATION LEVELS

Past research into belief system constraint has produced conflicting evidence regarding the public's ability to connect political issues. Constraint levels did undergo a significant upward movement during the period 1956 to 1964 and seemed to stabilize in 1968. But raw aggregations such as these do not resolve the debates about whether the upward shift was a function of political sophistication or of political and social forces. Looking at belief constraint across levels of conceptualization should allow us to better evaluate the sources of the increased belief constraint. If all levels of conceptualization show the same increase in constraint, either the connecting of issues together coherently is unrelated to political sophistication in a *direct* fashion, or the change in question wording has had a consistent impact at each conceptualization level. If, however, those who conceptualize politics in a more ideological manner show greater increases in constraint, it would indicate a differentiation of constraint across a cognitive sophistication dimension. Conversely, if the lower conceptualization group demonstrates greater increases, it would give credence to the argument that constraint results from an unsophisticated "dependent" response to the temper of the political environment.

The data provide an unexpected fourth pattern. Figure 4.1A presents the relation between belief constraint and levels of conceptualization for 1956, 1964, and 1968. In 1956 and 1964, the relation between levels of conceptualization and constraint was irregular. In both years, the lower two levels showed higher constraint than group benefits respondents. Thus, if we accept the levels of conceptualization measure as one indicator of sophistication, even in apparently low salience eras (e.g., the 1950s), something in addition to cognitive skills is at work in constraint levels.

The increase in constraint between 1956 and 1964 observed at the aggregate level is clearly observable at each conceptualization level. While ideologues have somewhat higher levels of constraint in both years (supporting the sophistication argument) the increase for all levels is roughly proportionate. This can be seen more clearly in Figure 4.1B which plots the change in average constraint for each conceptualization level. While ideologues evidence the greatest magnitude of change between 1956 and 1964 it was not substantially greater than that at the other levels. This may indicate that either *changes* in constraint levels are unrelated to sophistication, or the effect of question change was undifferentiated across respondents.

The period from 1964 to 1968, however, casts some shadows on the last conclusion. While ideologues, nature-of-times, and no-issue respondents showed little or no change from the 1964 constraint levels, the group benefit respondents showed a very large *increase* in constraint. Tables 4.1A and 4.1B show that there was a differential change in the constraint of this group which cannot be accounted for either by an appeal to a general increase in sophistication or by change in question wording. This upsurge in constraint levels by those who evaluate political objects on the basis of their group connections seems very plausible in light of the stratification and conflict which attended the 1968 election. Converse has noted that "by 1968 group antagonisms within the electorate itself had reached a sufficiently politicized peak that high levels of consistency across issue domains could be maintained" (1975: 106). Thus, the recognition of the group-polarized nature of 1968 politics might have been a convenient way for group-benefits respondents to evaluate the important political issues of the day. The evidence suggests that the nature of the political environment did have differential impact on the level of constraint during this period. The largest change, however, occurred not at the very upper or the very lower extremes of political conceptualization, but within that group that tended to evaluate political phenomena in a manner congruent with the temper of the political environment. What is important is that this group-oriented, referent-based coherence took place in the upper half of the levels of conceptualization measure, rather than in the lower reaches with apparently fewer cognitive skills.

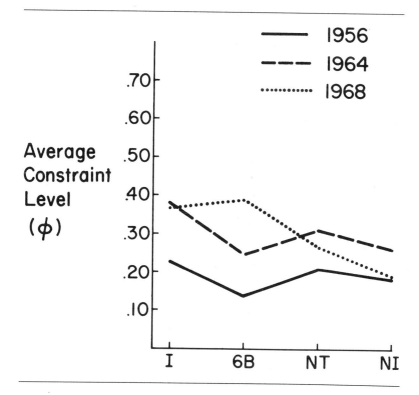

FIGURE 4.1A   Belief System Constraint Within Levels of Conceptualization: 1956, 1964, and 1968

CONSTRAINT AND LEVEL OF INFORMATION EXPOSURE

If the general increase in belief system constraint, which is relatively constant across all conceptualization levels from 1956 to 1964, was due to the impact of the increased volume of political rhetoric and coherent cue-giving found in the 1960s, differences in constraint levels should obtain between those groups which sought out campaign-related information and those who did not. Figure 4.2 does show that those who used the media for political information had higher levels of constraint in each year than those

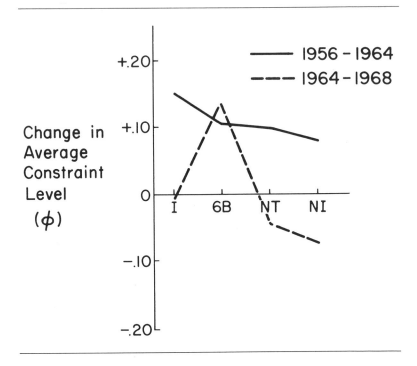

FIGURE 4.1B   Change in Levels of Belief System Constraint Within Levels of
Conceptualization: 1956–1964 and 1964–1968

who did not seek out political information. A close look at the graphs,
however, will show that the relative separation between the 2 exposure
groups *decreased* in 1964 and 1968. Thus, at this level, it would seem that
difference in exposure levels became less important during the 1960s.

The data in Figure 4.2, however, might obscure the disproportionate
effect that information exposure could have on those groups which conceptualize politics in nonideological terms. If cue-giving is occurring at the
lower ends of the political conceptualization spectrum, we should see a
widening gulf between those who were exposed to the increased temper of
the times and those who were not. Figure 4.3 presents constraint levels
stratified across exposure levels and conceptualization levels. For the first
three conceptualization levels there is very little difference between the
exposure groups in constraint levels. Only in the no-issue group do we see a
marked difference in constraint levels between the two exposure groups.
Differences in information exposure do show their greatest impact among
people with the least sophisticated conceptualization of politics.

Figure 4.4, however, shows that the exposure level difference in constraint is not a reflection of the increased cue-giving environment of the

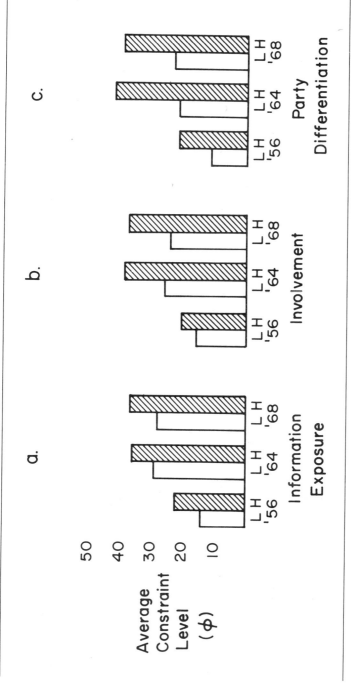

FIGURE 4.2 Constraint Across Levels of Attention, Political Differentiation, and Involvement

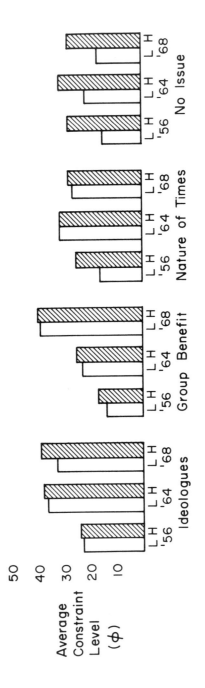

FIGURE 4.3   Information Exposure, Levels of Conceptualization, and Belief System
Constraint: 1956, 1964, and 1968

1960s. The change in constraint levels for the nonissue group remains very low for both periods. If the 1964 campaign rhetoric had had a substantial impact on those low conceptualization groups who sought out campaign information, we should have seen a noticeable increase in constraint levels between 1956 and 1964. This is simply not the case. At the lowest levels of conceptualization, differences in information exposure have a constant effect which is relatively immune to changes in the temper of political environment.

The other conceptualization groups differ very little with respect to information exposure. The 1964–1968 group benefit increase was experienced equally by both exposure groups. The equalization of constraint levels for the nature of the times group in 1964 (Figure 4.3) also seems unrelated to differences in information exposure in that the greatest 1956-1964 change was evidenced in the low-exposure group. Thus, while there are some differences across exposure levels, changes in constraint levels generally are unrelated to exposure to political information within any of the conceptualization levels.

CONSTRAINT AND CAMPAIGN INVOLVEMENT

While information exposure does not have an observable effect on changes in constraint levels the degree to which a respondent felt personally involved in the campaign does provide some interesting results. Figure 4.2 shows that, in contrast to exposure, the proportional constraint difference between low and high involvement groups increases between 1956 and 1964. While the low involvement group in 1964 had higher levels of constraint than the high involvement group in 1956, the high involvement group showed a greater proportionate rise in constraint levels. The initial implication is that as people felt they had more at stake in 1964, as opposed to 1956, they were better able to or more highly motivated to sort through political issues.

Was the greater increase among the highly involved in 1964 due to the effect of the heightened political rhetoric on lower conceptualization groups? The evidence indicates this. Figure 4.5 presents the constraint level for each conceptualization level stratified by involvement level. In the ideologue and group-benefit classifications between 1956 and 1964, there was an apparent covariation in constraint levels for both involvement levels. The nature-of-the-times respondents showed a smaller degree of covariation and the no-issue respondents showed very little. While the low involvement, no-issue respondents in 1956 and 1964 show approximately the same level of political constraint, the high involvement, no-issue respondents in 1964 show substantial increases over the corresponding 1956 group. Figure 4.6 presents a graphic demonstration of this. While the higher conceptualization level groups show little change across involvement levels for the period 1956–1964 as one moves down the conceptualization ladder, the difference

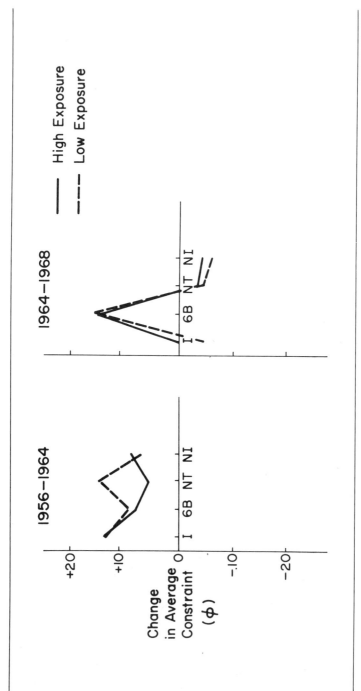

FIGURE 4.4   Change in Levels of Belief System Constraint Across Levels of Information Exposure and Levels of
Conceptualization: 1956–1964 and 1964–1968

between high and low campaign involvement becomes much more pronounced. Such pronounced differences are not to be found in the period 1964–1968.

Exposure to political rhetoric is not enough to cause serious differences in belief system constraint. It appears that the less sophisticated respondent must feel personally involved with the outcome of the campaign before he or she can be influenced by the more dramatic campaign environment. There is a connection between the nature of the political environment, political sophistication, and constraint. But, there remains one other aspect of the social/political environment which may help illuminate the sources of the increase in belief system constraint and, at the same time, shed further light on the substantial increase in constraint found in the group benefit respondents in 1968.

CONSTRAINT AND POLITICAL DIFFERENTIATION

In addition to the influence of information exposure and involvement, the degree to which individuals see the political environment as being polarized may have an impact on their ability to connect political issues. Using a measure which separates respondents into high and low levels of perceived political differentiation, a significant gap between the average level of belief system constraint obtains for each group (Figure 4.2c). For each election year, the constraint level for the low differentiation group is about half that of the high differentiation group. The public's perception of the issue differences in the political parties does relate to their ability to consistently respond to related political issues. Yet, the relationship between levels of differentiation and constraint is fairly constant across the different campaigns.

Is the effect of perceived differentiation maintained within each conceptualization level? Figure 4.7 shows that for the ideologue and group benefit respondents in 1956, there are only minimal differences between the differentiation groups, but the difference becomes more pronounced for the nature-of-the-times and no-issue respondents. In 1964, all conceptualization levels reflect the same comparison between the two differentiation levels. In 1968 the two lower conceptualization groups show a drop-off in overall constraint and a lessening of the difference between the differentiation groups. The 1968 ideologues maintain approximately the same level of constraint and proportional difference in the differentiation groups. The group benefit respondents in 1968, however, show an *increased* level of constraint at both differentiation levels with the high differentiation group showing the greatest proportional gain. The respondent's perception of the polarization of the political environment did influence their constraint levels and this effect depends in some way on the conceptualization of political phenomena.

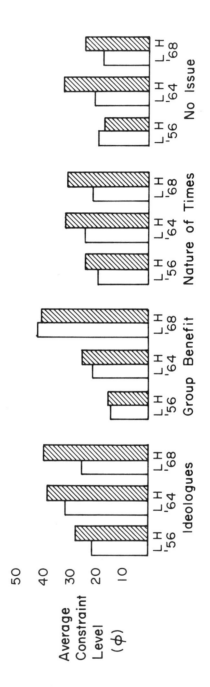

FIGURE 4.5   Political Involvement, Levels of Conceptualization, and Belief System
Constraint: 1956, 1964, 1968

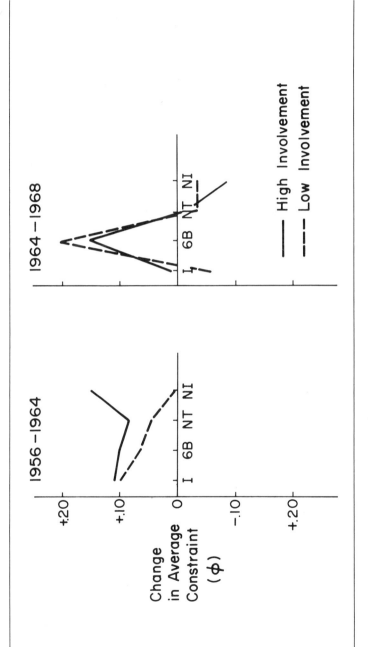

FIGURE 4.6   Change in Levels of Belief System Constraint Across Involvement and
Levels of Conceptualization: 1956–1964 and 1964–1968

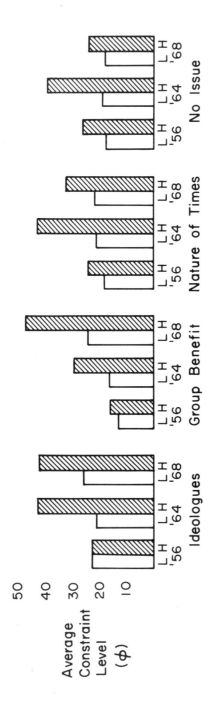

FIGURE 4.7   Political Differentiation, Levels of Conceptualization, and Belief System
Constraint: 1956, 1964, 1968

Again, looking at change across elections (Figure 4.8), a remarkable difference obtains between the change patterns of each differentiation group. Between 1956 and 1964, the low differentiation group changed very little across all levels of political conceptualization. This contrasts dramatically with the change evidenced for those respondents who did differentiate the political parties. During this period there is a general improvement of belief system constraint only among those who felt that the political parties differed in their positions on the political issues of the day.

The change curves from 1964 to 1968 strengthen the above conclusions, especially via the rather dramatic rise in constraint evidenced by the group benefit respondents. While those group-benefit respondents who saw few party differences exhibited an increase in constraint levels, this increase was not substantially higher than that of the corresponding group of ideologues. But group benefit respondents with a high level of political differentiation produced a great change in constraint levels. It seems, then, that the group conflict nature of the 1968 campaign, coupled with a high perception of party differences across a wide range of issues, had a strong impact on the way group benefit respondents associated issues. Again, the political environment had a differential impact on the constraint levels of the conceptualization groups. This is buttressed by the significant drop off in the constraint levels of the high-differentiation, nature-of-the-times and no-issue respondents. Without the more dramatic cues of the 1964 campaign and lacking a group-oriented conceptualization of politics, these two conceptualization groups had less of an impetus to form consistent positions on related issues.

CONCLUSION

Recent studies have raised the question of whether the increase in belief system constraint stemmed from a sophisticated, ideological response to politics or from a more dependent, cue-taking response. Moreover, some scholars recently challenged the constraint increases by contending that they reflect only question wording alterations. In the latter case, if change in constraint level were simply and only an artifact of changes in questionnaire wording, we would not expect to see the variations in change patterns demonstrated in each conceptualization level stratified by involvement and political differentiation.[9] The overall rise in constraint between 1956 and 1964 lends credence to some uniform effects of questionnaire modification. The disaggregated analysis presented here, however, suggests the presence of other factors as well. The conclusion forwarded here is that respondents with differing levels of conceptualizing politics (reflecting differences in sophistication and content) show different levels of constraint as a result of

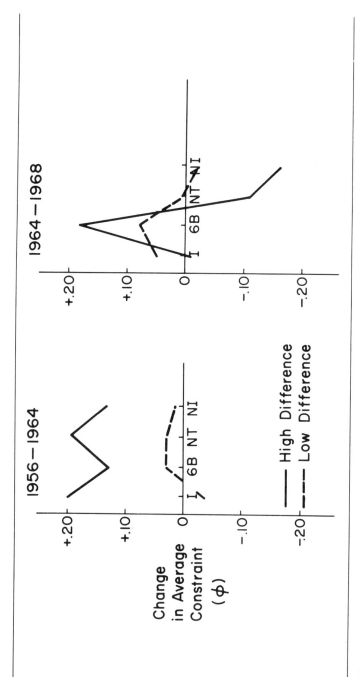

FIGURE 4.8   Change in Levels of Belief System Constraint Across Political Differentiation and Levels of
Conceptualization: 1956–1964 and 1964–1968

differing involvement and political differentiation levels within different elections. That is quite a few "differents." But it does lead to the more general conclusion that cue-giving within elections affects the level of mass belief system constraint for certain kinds of people. This effect becomes more apparent when the citizen feels a personal stake in the outcome of the election and sees the political system containing significant amounts of issue differentiation. The more citizen duty oriented factor of information exposure does little to disturb the trends established in larger aggregation levels. Rather, it is when the citizen personally feels involved with the electoral contest or sees politics as an arena of choice that his or her ability to synthesize political issues improves.

Yet, the importance of involvement and differentiation have been noted in earlier studies (e.g., Nie and Andersen, 1974; Pomper, 1975). This study's contribution is concerned with how the impact of involvement and differentiation are tempered by the interaction of political sophistication (i.e., levels of conceptualization) and the nature of political cues. Thus, for example, high perceived political differentiation is very important in the increase in constraint from 1964–1968 for group benefit respondents. The 1968 election was replete with group related issue cues from the political parties and their leaders. By the nature of their level of conceptualization, group benefit respondents are sensitive to group related cues and relatively able to deal with them in a sophisticated manner. Indeed, when group benefit respondents perceived high levels of differentiation their constraint level skyrocketed during the same period that the ideologues' constraint remained relatively stable.

We see further tasks necessary to pin down the suggestions generated by these results. First, there obviously must be a longer period of analysis. Not only must the 1960 data be filled in, but 1972, 1976, and 1980 data must be generated. The problem is that comparable measures of the level of conceptualization do not exist for those election years. Relative to the original measure, presently available surrogate measures mostly overidentify the number of ideologues in the electorate. Thus, an alternate measure is needed that is both valid and reliable as an index of conceptualization in those years where the original, protocol content analysis is absent. Second, the same relations need to be examined while using an *individual* measure of belief system constraint. The aggregate measure used here impedes analysis in several ways. For example, it does not allow the identification of individual variations in constraint, inhibiting the use of multivariate techniques that would allow the more precise allocation of influence to the variables used in this study.[10]

The elements of the public's political thinking have been central to estimates of the American citizen's capability for intelligent participation in politics. Too often, the public has been painted in broad, sweeping strokes.

The results presented here add to the growing view of the complex relation between American citizens and their political environment. Indeed, the structure of the public's array of political opinions is affected by no less than the interaction among the level of conceptualization, the nature of political campaigns, and the individual's exposure to, involvement in, and perceived differentiation of, politics.

NOTES

1. The data were collected by The Center for Political Studies and distributed through the InterUniversity Consortium for Political and Social Research. Neither the CPS nor the ICPSR bear any responsibility for the analysis and interpretation presented here.

2. The following items were employed to measure constraint in each of the three election years:

1956		1964		1968	
Guar. Jobs	(VAR 33)	Guar. Jobs	(VAR 78)	Std. Living	(VAR 66)
Medical Care	(VAR 38)	Medical Care	(VAR 74)	Medical Care	(VAR 64)
Big Corps	(VAR 47)	Gov. Power	(VAR 71)	Gov. Power	(VAR 62)
School Aid	(VAR 53)	School Aid	(VAR 66)	School Aid	(VAR 60)
Electric Power	(VAR 59)	Electric Power	(VAR 344)	Job Equality	(VAR 73)

3. The literature examining the effect of changes in question wording is growing. See the Petrocik chapter in this volume for an examination and review of that question and literature.

4. The model that underlies the constraint correlation assumes that a liberal response on one issue will be conjoined with a liberal response on another issue. Thus, perfect constraint would be indicated by complete homogeneity within the position cells (off-diagonal cells would equal zero). Perfect null constraint relations are then defined as the proportional independence of one issue response from the other. These underlying model states correspond to those described by Weisberg (1974) as "strong monotonicity" and "independence." The appropriate statistic to use given these model constraints is phi, in the 2 × 2 case. Yules Q, the 2 × 2 nominal form of gamma, is based on a different underlying statistical model and tends to overestimate relations based on the model assumed by the constraint theorem (see Reynolds, 1977 and Hildebrand, 1977 for a straightforward discussion of the distinction between the two measures).

5. For much more detailed discussions of these distinctions the reader is referred to Campbell et al. (1960) and Converse (1964).

6. The authors wish to acknowledge their appreciation for the granting of access to the microfilm copies of the 1964 and 1968 interview protocols. The coding of the 1964 data occurred in February of 1968. The coding of the 1968 data took place in June of 1969. Both tasks were accomplished in the Center for Political Studies at the University of Michigan.

7. Personal communication from Philip Converse.

8. To preserve space, the precise construction of the measures is not presented. Interested readers may contact the authors for details.

9. Achen (1975) argues that the effects of question unreliability are relatively constant across important socioeconomic indicators. And, Sullivan et al., note that "If changes in question formats indeed explain the patterns of correlations, then such changes in format should affect all sub-groups within the samples" (1978: 243).

10. We are currently engaged in exploring some of these same questions through the use of an individual measure of belief system constraint.

5

THE PERCEPTION OF POLITICAL FIGURES: AN APPLICATION OF ATTRIBUTION THEORY

Pamela Johnston Conover

In recent years, a number of studies have stressed the critical role that candidate images play in the vote choice process (see, for example, Declerq et al., 1975; Kelley and Mirer, 1974; Kirkpatrick et al., 1975; RePass, 1976). Despite this increased interest, however, the subject of candidate images remains shrouded in ambiguity. To some extent, there is disagreement over the nature and content of candidate images, a term which will be defined here as "the beliefs (information) which an individual holds about a candidate as a person"—his personality, experience, and ability.[1] To an even larger degree, there is uncertainty concerning the processes through which candidate images develop and change. The goal of this chapter is to resolve some of this ambiguity beginning with a review of previous approaches to the perception of political candidates. It should be noted that, though the focus is on political candidates, the theoretical perspective is applicable to the perception of all types of political figures.

PAST RESEARCH

There has been considerable disagreement about the sources of candidate images. On the one hand, there are the advocates of an "image thesis" that is derived largely from early studies of mass advertising and mass communica-

AUTHOR'S NOTE: The data used in this chapter were originally collected by John D. Holm and were made available through the Inter-University Consortium for Political and Social Research. Neither bears any responsibility for my analyses or interpretations.

tions. The image thesis posits that candidate images are stimulus determined in the sense that the image is a direct representation of the stimuli or information presented by the candidate, e.g., his speeches, actions, and press coverage (Blumler and McQuail, 1969). This suggests that candidates have a large measure of control over the images which people hold of them; by adopting certain forms of behavior and presenting themselves in a particular fashion, candidates determine the images. Thus, the image thesis effectively minimizes the effect of the perceiver on perception.

In opposition to the image thesis is the "perceptual balance" approach, which is based on cognitive consistency theories (Insko and Schopler, 1972). Underlying this approach is the assumption that, as perceivers, people are motivated by their need for consistency. Where an individual's beliefs are in conflict or incongruent with each other, he or she experiences a tension or uncomfortable feeling that can be alleviated by altering the source of the tension—the inconsistent beliefs. Thus, if on the basis of a prior belief (such as party identification) a voter develops a favorable evaluation of a candidate, subsequent perceptions that conflict with this are likely to be altered to avoid any evaluative inconsistency. As Sigel explains, "in order not to experience any imbalance or stress, partisans, especially, will see in a preferred candidate what they wish to see—even if it is unrelated to objective reality" (1964: 484). This implies that voters or perceivers are likely to engage in selective perception and distortion to maintain evaluative consistency among beliefs. Thus, candidate images should differ from voter to voter depending on the voter's particular beliefs.

The evidence pertaining to this controversy has been inconclusive; neither position has been uniformly confirmed.[2] In one of the most often cited studies, McGrath and McGrath (1962) provided evidence for both theories, though they interpreted their study as supporting the image thesis. Specifically, on a number of activity traits (such as aggressive, active, and dynamic) they discovered that partisans agreed in their evaluations of the 1960 presidential candidates, thus providing support for the image thesis. Yet, their study also revealed a number of partisan differences in candidate evaluations.

The McGraths' study was heavily criticized by Sigel (1964) who argued for a perceptual balance explanation of image formation. In her own study of the 1960 election, she demonstrated that partisans' evaluations of their own candidate tended to be more highly correlated with their images of the ideal president than were their images of the opposing party's candidate (i.e., Democrats saw Kennedy as being closer to their ideal than Nixon and vice versa). This evidence was interpreted as supporting the perceptual balance theory. But Sigel also found that there was substantial agreement among partisans in their perceptions of the two candidates as indicated by their responses to the question of why they might or might not vote for each candidate. In short, neither Sigel nor the McGraths have been successful in resolving the conflict. In more recent years, subsequent works have also failed to end the debate (Hughes and Western, 1966; Blumler and McQuail, 1969; Brownstein, 1971). Thus, to date, the evidence does not warrant rejecting one theory in favor of the other.

Furthermore, there are problems with both approaches that suggest that perhaps *neither* one is an accurate depiction of the development of candidate images. Empirically, the image thesis is damaged significantly by findings that indicate that perceptions of political candidates do vary, often systematically, from person to person. Theoretically, the image thesis is seriously marred by its failure to outline in greater detail the specific role which perceivers play in formulating a candidate image.

Similarly, there are major problems with the perceptual balance approach. Empirically, tests of balance theory against other explanations of belief formation have shown that balance theory predictions are often unsupported (Fishbein and Ajzen, 1975). More specific findings also present difficulties for the perceptual balance approach. For example, voters rarely form negative images of political candidates (Nimmo and Savage, 1976), a finding that conflicts with the balance theory prediction that voters will attribute negatively evaluated traits to candidates of the opposing party. Furthermore, balance theory does not provide systematic predictions concerning which traits will and will not be involved in a voter's maintenance of cognitive consistency. Thus, it fails to account for the finding that candidate characteristics, like party identification, appear to prompt selective perception only with respect to certain traits (Blumler and McQuail, 1969). Finally, balance theory suffers theoretically because it does not specify fully how people deal with ambiguous information, nor does it adequately take into account individual differences in the ability to tolerate stress.

In reaction to such inadequacies, some researchers have attempted to develop a framework which combines these two approaches. Notably, Nimmo and Savage (1976) have posited that candidate images are the product of "stimulus-perceiver transactions" involving symbolic exchanges between voters and candidates. But Nimmo and Savage do not move much beyond a general distinction of the broad outlines of their theoretical resolution. In contrast, this chapter suggests a theoretical framework which clearly specifies the relative roles of the voter and the candidate in the formation of images.

THE DEVELOPMENT OF CANDIDATE IMAGES

Candidate images—the beliefs a person holds about a candidate—are the product of two inferential processes. First, the beliefs composing a candidate's image may represent "causal attributions": beliefs inferred from the candidate's behavior. Or, second, the image may be the result of "trait inferences": beliefs inferred from the voter's prior beliefs. The discussion of both these processes and their relative contributions to the development of candidate images is based on an assumption that is central to a number of psychological theories: Namely, as perceivers, people have a need to predict and control their environments (Decharms, 1969; Harvey, 1963; Kelly, G. A., 1963; Kelley, H. H., 1972; Piaget, 1929; White, 1959). Where the environment itself does not provide the information necessary for such predictions, individuals are expected to create the essential information from their beliefs (Bruner, 1964).

Specifically, where the voter lacks information or has ambiguous information—ambiguous in the sense that the information does not enable the voter to make causal attributions—then he is forced to rely on his prior beliefs in determining the candidate's image.[3] To elaborate briefly, based on candidate characteristics or political cues, such as party identification, voters are able to divide candidates into groups that they associate with various patterns of attributes or stereotypes. Consequently, once a candidate is perceived as belonging to a particular group (i.e. Democrats, incumbents, liberals) the voter may make trait inferences according to his stereotype or expectations about group characteristics. Since the voter's prior beliefs are critical to the formation of new beliefs, this trait inference, like perceptual balance, results in images which are largely perceiver-determined. But, despite their shared emphasis on the voter's role in determining candidate images, there is a fundamental difference between the two: trait inference *does not* require that the voter's inferences necessarily preserve the evaluative consistency among attributes, i.e., negatively evaluated characteristics need not always produce negative inferences (Peabody, 1970; Fishbein and Ajzen, 1975).

Whether voters are forced to rely on trait inference depends largely on the amount and nature of the available information. If voters have access to unambiguous information—unambiguous in the sense that they are able to make causal attributions—then the image should be heavily influenced by the candidate's behavior, and, consequently, the need to make trait inferences should be reduced. Thus, it becomes essential to determine under what conditions voters will be able to make attributions. With this in mind, let us consider in greater detail the nature of that process.

CAUSAL ATTRIBUTIONS

In addition to trait inferences, the development of candidate images involves making "causal attributions"—the forming or changing of beliefs—based on the candidate's behavior. The present treatment of this process stems from attribution theory which focuses on the manner in which people attempt to discern the causes of their own and other's behavior. It is based on the assumption that, when confronted with a person's behavior, the perceiver must determine if it was caused by some aspect of the situation, by chance, or by some underlying personal disposition of the actor. Thus, the voter will gain information about a candidate to the degree that the cause of the behavior may be assigned to an internal disposition or trait. In recent years, the literature concerning the different versions of attribution theory has grown enormously (Harvey et al., 1976; Heider, 1958; Jones and Davis, 1965; Kelley, H.H., 1967, 1972, 1973; Shaver, 1975). Consequently, rather than exploring any of these treatments in great depth, the following simply outlines the points common to most variants of attribution theory and then discusses their relevance to the development of candidate images.[4]

Causal attribution is the amount of information gained about an individual from the observation of his behavior (Jones and McGillis, 1976: 391). It refers to a change in the voter's belief that associates a candidate with a particular trait (Fishbein and Ajzen, 1975). Most versions of attribution theory concur in the basic steps characterizing the attribution process. Three major steps may be delineated: (1) the observation of behavior; (2) the evaluation of the behavior; and (3) the making of a causal attribution (Shaver, 1975). Let us consider each of these steps separately as they apply to the perception of political figures.

The Observation of behavior. The first step in the attribution process is the voter's observation of the candidate's behavior. In making such an observation, the voter not only records the candidate's behavior but he also attempts to determine what aspects of the environment the candidate may be reacting to (Jones and McGillis, 1976). In many elections, third parties—television, radio, and newspapers—will mediate the voter's observation of the candidate (Graber, 1976), thus playing a critical role in structuring the voter's causal analysis. For example, by focusing on the audience at a campaign appearance, the media may suggest to the voter that the candidate was possibly reacting to the audience rather than revealing his true attitudes.

The media not only influence the *nature* of the voter's observation, but they also help to determine the *likelihood* of it. Specifically, the more media focus on a candidate's actions, the more likely the voter is to receive information that will allow him to make a causal attribution. Furthermore, the media coverage allocated to a particular candidate is likely to vary depending on both the type of office (national vs. local) and the type of race (a primary vs. a general election). This suggests that the more prominent the office and race, the greater the available information about the candidates and, consequently, the more likely the voter is to make an attribution based on the candidate's behavior.

Finally, to some degree, voters themselves influence how much they observe a candidate's behavior and, consequently, how much information they possess. Interested voters pay attention to the media and even attend campaign functions that provide information unavailable to the average voter who depends on third parties for information. Uninterested voters neither make a special effort to gather information nor do they take full advantage of the information provided by the media. Consequently, the greater the voters' interest in a campaign, the more information they will obtain about a candidate, and thus the more likely they are to make an attribution based on the candidate's behavior.

The Evaluation of behavior. The second phase encompasses three more specific steps: the identification of behavioral effects, the estimation of the likelihood of those behavioral effects, and an evaluation of the intentionality of the behavior (Jones and McGillis, 1976). After observing the candidate's behavior, the voter attempts to gain an initial picture of the candidate's objectives by identifying the *effects* or consequences of his behavior (Jones and Davis, 1965; Jones and McGillis, 1976). Guiding such an analysis is the voter's assumption that the candidate acted purposively either to cause or avoid specific behavioral effects. Thus, behavioral effects are "possible causes" of the candidate's behavior. Once such effects have been identified, the voter attempts to link the effects with some stable attribute of the candidate.

The first step toward the formation of such a link is estimating the likelihood (i.e., expectancy) of each behavioral effect. Prior beliefs are the critical basis from which such expectancies are generated; thus, it is at this point where the two processes of image development—trait inferences from prior beliefs and causal attributions from behavior—interact. Two types of prior beliefs may contribute to the development of an expectancy (Jones and McGillis, 1976). First, in accordance with the inferential process described earlier, experiences may be *category-based* in the sense that they are derived from the voter's belief about *other* persons who are similar to the candidate with respect to some attribute. Thus, for example, the candidate's partisanship, ideological orientation, incumbency status, and general status as a candidate may all act as categoric cues in the derivation of expectancies. Second, once the voter has observed the candidate on several occasions, expectancies may be *target-based* in the sense that they are derived from information about that specific candidate. Clearly, the greater the available information about a candidate then the more likely it is that a voter will be able to use target-based expectancies to evaluate the candidate's behavior.

Once these expectancies have been generated they will be used to estimate the likelihood of each behavioral effect. But they will also be used by the voter to determine whether the candidate had the knowledge and ability to act intentionally (Jones and McGillis, 1976). Only if the behavior is judged intentional will it be possible for the voter to make a causal attribution. In extreme cases of expectancy disconfirmation, it is likely that the voter will decide that the candidate's behavior was unintentional. For example, in 1976, strong supporters of Jimmy Carter might have found his "ethnic purity" statement to be very unexpected. They might have concluded that Carter did not intend to make a racist remark, and thus no causal attribution would have been made. In most cases, however, the candidate's behavior is likely to be judged intentional. Subsequently, the voter will proceed to the final steps of the analysis: the inference of intentions and dispositions.

The making of a causal attribution. As Jones and McGillis explain, making an attribution is a two-step inference:

> The first step concerns the relationship between perceived effects and inferred intent; he dominated the group and really intended to. The second step concerns the relationship between intention and disposition: he was intentionally dominant in this situation and is really a dominant character in general [1976: 416].

The inference of intentions from behaviorial effects follows almost automatically if the behavior is deemed intentional. In contrast, the movement from transitory intentions to more stable dispositions is less easily made. In this respect, the decision rule governing the voter's analysis may be described as follows: the *fewer* and the *more unexpected* the inferred intentions, then the more likely it is that a causal attribution will be made from a behavioral observation (Jones and Davis, 1965; Jones and McGillis, 1976). In essence, voters are expected to gain the *most* information about a candidate from unexpected or "out-of-role" behavior; expected behavior, in contrast, reveals nothing new about the candidate. This information gain will then be reflected in changes in the voter's beliefs or expectancies—changes in the subjective probability associating a candidate with an attribute (Jones and McGillis, 1976).

By definition, "out-of-role" behavior should occur less frequently than "in-role" behavior. Thus, it can be argued that most of a candidate's behavior is expected in terms of either category or target-based expectancies, and therefore is relatively uninformative to voters in the sense that they are unable to make causal attributions about the candidate. For several reasons, however, a candidate's behavior may still have a substantial effect on image formation. First, the media are expected to publicize more heavily sensational or unexpected events (Chaffee and Patrick, 1975), in effect, sampling proportionately more from "out-of-role" than "in-role" behavior in selecting what to present to voters. Second, there is a general bias in the news toward the presentation of negative items which often pertain to unexpected behavior (Galtung and Ruge, 1965).

IMPLICATIONS

In summary, researchers have generally argued that candidate images are either stimulus- or perceiver-determined. This chapter also posits that two processes—one which emphasizes the perceiver's role and the other the stimulus' role—underlie the development of candidate images. But there the similarity ends. In contrast to perceptual balance approaches, the cognitive model presented here emphasizes the role of the voter's prior beliefs in enabling him to infer candidate traits in those electoral situations where information is missing or ambiguous. From this perspective, voters are not expected to distort relatively unambiguous information, nor are all inferences predicted to be evaluatively consistent. Consequently, the cognitive model is considerably more complex than the "perceiver-determined" process presented by past researchers.

Others have argued that candidate images are largely stimulus-determined. Similarly, this chapter has also argued for a process of image development in which the stimulus plays a significant role. Again, however, the two differ considerably. In the image thesis employed by political scientists, the voter's role was largely unspecified; candidates were depicted as determining or projecting whatever image they chose and the voters were assumed to adopt that image in its entirety. In contrast, in the attribution process, the voter plays a very significant and well-defined role in interpreting the candidate's behavior. Consequently, the candidate's behavior is seen as influencing the voter's images, but it by no means determines them.

Finally, in contrast to past research, this perspective stresses that these two processes interact with one another and that both may contribute to the development of candidate images, though not necessarily equally. Beliefs generated from prior beliefs may be an important basis for judging a candidate's behavior and subsequently making causal attributions. The reverse may also occur; information gained from a candidate's behavior may be instrumental in activating trait inferences in accordance with a voter's stereotypes, the voter's reliance on one or the other of the two processes will be determined by the amount and the ambiguity of the information that he has about the candidate; the less information and the greater the ambiguity then the fewer the causal attributions from the candidate's behavior and the greater the impact of the voter's prior beliefs on his candidate image. In concrete terms, then, potentially the candidate's behavior will have the greatest impact in prominent elections characterized by unexpected events in which voter interest is high.

HYPOTHESES, DATA, AND METHODS

Given that the relative impact on an image of a voter's prior beliefs and a candidate's behavior depends primarily on the "informativeness" of the behavior, it becomes critical to assess the empirical validity of the attribution process just described. To test the basic propositions derivable from attribution theory, it is necessary to employ panel data so that revisions in expectancies or beliefs may be measured. In addition, the data must focus on some out-of-role behavior in order to maximize the likelihood that respondents have some opportunity to make attributions. Unfortunately, there were no readily available data sets concerning political candidates that met these requirements. Consequently, this study treats a campaign incident which, though it occurred during the 1972 presidential election, did not become really important until after the election: the Watergate incident. Though Nixon was no longer a political candidate when discussions of Watergate reached their peak, the incident, nonetheless, allows for a fair assessment of attribution as it applies to the perception of candidates and office-holders alike.

Given this choice of a "candidate" and a campaign incident, the propositions to be examined empirically may be outlined. The out-of-role behavior is Nixon's participation in Watergate, which is defined as including both the original Watergate break-in as well as the subsequent cover-up. Thus, the dependent variable is the degree of attribution: the amount of change or the revisions made in beliefs about Nixon as a result of his perceived participation in Watergate. Based on the earlier description of attribution, three independent variables which may influence the degree of attribution are identifiable: (1) the observation of behavior; (2) the prior expectancies of the behavior; and (3) the judgment of intention. Each of these variables contributes directly to the outcome of attribution and also influences the steps following it.

As with many campaign incidents, direct observation of Nixon's behavior as it occurred was virtually impossible for all but a few members of the public. Consequently, the focus is on the amount of information which individuals collected about Nixon and Watergate. Specifically, it is posited that:

Hypothesis 1.0: The greater the amount of information an individual has about Watergate the more likely he is to make causal attributions about Nixon as a result of Watergate.

An individual's expectancies about Nixon specifically and politicians in general should also influence whether or not attributions are made based on Watergate. Such expectancies are inferred from prior beliefs. In this instance, based on the assumption that most people would evaluate Watergate in a negative or neutral fashion, it is inferred that negative beliefs lead to high expectancies of a Watergate type of behavior, while positive beliefs result in low expectancies. In the analysis, two types of prior beliefs will be examined: (1) categoric beliefs about politicians in general and partisan groups of politicians, and (2) target-based beliefs about Nixon in particular. The following propositions will be examined:

> Hypothesis 2.1: The lower the expectancy that politicians in general will participate in activities such as Watergate the more likely an individual is to make causal attributions about Nixon as a result of Watergate.
>
> Hypothesis 2.2: The lower the expectancy that Republicans will participate in activities such as Watergate the more likely an individual is to make causal attributions about Nixon as a result of Watergate.
>
> Hypothesis 2.3: The lower the expectancy that Nixon would participate in activities such as Watergate the more likely an individual is to make causal attributions about Nixon as a result of Watergate.

Finally, Watergate should have an effect on a person's beliefs only if Nixon is thought to have acted intentionally—that he had both the ability to carry out his intentions and knowledge of the consequences of his actions. Yet, before Nixon's behavior may be judged intentional, he must first have been perceived as being involved in the Watergate incident. Given that within the limits of the data set there is no way to determine if an individual believes Nixon's participation to have been intentional, Nixon's perceived involvement in Watergate will be used as a surrogate test.[4] Specifically, the following hypothesis will be examined:

> Hypothesis 3.0: The greater Nixon's perceived involvement in Watergate the more likely an individual is to make causal attributions about Nixon as a result of Watergate.[5]

DATA

The data to be used in the analysis were originally collected by John D. Holm and were made available, in part, by the Inter-University Consortium for Political and Social Research.[6] The panel survey was conducted by phone and the respondents were randomly selected from the Cleveland Metropolitan Directory. The first wave of interviews (360 respondents) was conducted the two nights preceding the beginning of the Ervin Committee Senate Hearings in the Spring of 1973, while the third and final wave of interviews (135 of the original respondents) was conducted the weekend immediately following John Dean's testimony.

MEASUREMENT INSTRUMENTS

Observation of behavior. Because information about Watergate could have been obtained through a variety of third-party sources—the news media, family, and friends—several different questions formed an index of the "observation of Watergate." Specifically, during the third period, respondents were asked how much attention they had paid to Watergate in "keeping up with news" as well as how much they had discussed Watergate with their friends and with their family. The responses to the questions were then summed to form an index ranging from 3 (low attention) to 9 (high attention), with a reliability (coefficient alpha) of .75 (Nunnally, 1967).

Prior expectancies. Both category and target-based expectancies were assessed though questions asked at the first period. Specifically, category-based expectancies about politicians were measured by three questions pertaining to whether politicians are perceived as being: (1) devoted to the service of the country; (2) honest in that they tell us what they think; and (3) able to maintain their integrity and still succeed in politics. Agreement with these ideas was scored "0" since they represent positive beliefs about politicians and thus a low prior expectancy of a Watergate type of behavior. Similarly, "don't know" responses were scored 1 and disagreement or negative beliefs were coded 2. The responses were then summed to form an index of "General Expectancies" ranging from 0 to 6 with a low score indicating a low prior expectancy of a Watergate type of behavior (coefficient alpha = .54).

Categoric expectancies about Republicans were measured indirectly. Based on the assumption that partisans will have a lower expectancy of negative behavior from members of their own party, it was inferred that Republicans would have a lower expectancy of Nixon's participating in Watergate than would Democrats. Thus, a measure of "partisan expectancies" ranging from 1 to 5 with a low score indicating an inferred low prior expectancy of Watergate behavior was created from the respondents' partisan self-identifications; Republicans received a 1, Independents a 3, and Democrats a 5.

Finally, target-based expectancies were estimated by considering the respondent's prior beliefs about whether certain attributes characterized Nixon. In particular, at the first period, subjects were asked to choose between five pairs of traits—honest/dishonest, sincere/insincere, competent/incompetent, reliable/unreliable, and ethical/unethical—one of which they felt best described Nixon. Negatively evaluated traits were scored 2, "don't know" responses 1, and positively evaluated traits 0. The responses were summed to form an index of "Target-Based Expectancies" ranging from 0 to 10 with a high score indicating a highly negative evaluation of Nixon and thus a high prior expectancy of Watergate type of behavior (coefficient alpha = .87).

Perceived involvement. Potentially, Nixon's involvement in Watergate could have occurred at several different stages in the incident, each of which was considered. Specifically, during the third time period, respondents were asked whether they thought that Nixon knew in advance about the Watergate bugging and whether or not he participated in a cover-up of the incident. Negative responses were scored 0, "don't know" responses 1, and positive responses 2. The responses were then summed to form an index of "Perceived Involvement" which ranges from 0 to 4 with a "4" indicating a very high perceived involvement (coefficient alpha = .50).

Degree of attribution. The dependent variable in the analysis is the amount of information gained about Nixon—the degree of attribution made—as a result of Watergate. Operationally, the degree of attribution is defined by the changes in the target-based expectancies occurring between the first and third periods. For each of the five trait pairs the response at the first period was subtracted from that at the third, and then the five individual item differences were summed to form a measure of net belief change.[8] The resulting measure ranges from -10 to $+10$ with a high positive score indicating a large amount of attribution or belief change in the predicted direction—greater negative evaluations of Nixon. Finally, it is important to note that there are potentially very serious problems associated with the use of a change score as a dependent variable (Harris, 1963).[9] An awareness of such problems, however, allows for proper caution to be taken in the interpretation of results.

FINDINGS

THE STEPS OF THE ATTRIBUTION PROCESS

A separate examination of each independent variable indicates that there is sufficient variation to suggest that some individuals would have made attributions about Nixon based on Watergate. In particular, over three-quarters of the sample report medium-to-high observation of Watergate. Furthermore, in terms of both categoric and target-based expectancies, Nixon's participation in Watergate appears to have been very unexpected by at least a third of the sample. Finally, most respondents perceived Nixon as being at least partially involved in Watergate. Thus, for a number of individuals the Watergate incident provided ample opportunity for making dispositional inferences about Nixon. Given this, let us turn to an examination of the relations among the various classes of independent variable.[10]

During political campaigns (or, in this instance, Watergate), the public has considerable control over the amount of information which they gather about the behavior of political figures. Is the variability in behavior observation at all related to prior beliefs? As illustrated in Table 5.1, there is virtually no relation between either general or partisan expectancies and the observation of Watergate; Pearson's r equals .003 and .09. In contrast, target-based expectancies are clearly related to the observation of Watergate ($r = .37$); the more negative Nixon's image (i.e., the higher the expectancy of negative behavior) then the greater the observation. Such a finding is congruent with experimental studies that have shown that perceivers tend to engage in "cognitive bolstering" in which their current expectancies influence the nature of their future perceptions (Zadney and Gerard, 1974).

Similarly, there are several reasons for expecting some positive relation

TABLE 5.1   Intercorrelations Among Independent Variables[*]

	Observation Scale	General Expectancies	Partisan Expectancies	Target Expectancies	Involvement Scale
Observation Scale[a]	1.00				
General Expectancies[b]	.003[c]	1.00			
Partisan Expectancies[b]	.09	.26	1.00		
Target Expectancies[b]	.37	.24	.42	1.00	
Involvement Scale[a]	.25	.33	.28	.55	1.00

[a]Measured at time 3.
[b]Measured at time 1.
[c]Not significant at .01 level.
[*]Entries are Pearson product-moment correlations.

between prior expectancies and perceived involvement. Recall, prior expectancies enter into the determination of the intentionality of a behavior; if expectancy disconfirmation is very extreme, the behavior is likely to be deemed unintentional. As applied to Watergate, this suggests that if Nixon's image is extremely positive, then it is likely that he will be perceived as being involved in Watergate. Cognitive bolstering represents a second reason for expecting a positive relation. A perceiver's expectancies may lead him to attribute certain intentions to actors *prior* to observing their behavior. This may result in the perceiver selecting those aspects of the actor's behavior which are relevant to confirming such previously attributed intentions (Zadney and Gerard, 1974). With respect to Watergate, people expecting negative behavior from Nixon should be more likely to focus on that information which would confirm their negative expectations; consequently, they should be more likely to perceive Nixon as being involved in Watergate.

Both of these arguments receive indirect support from the data. First, there is a moderate, positive relation between general expectancies and perceived involvement ($r = .33$); the higher the expectancy that politicians will engage in dishonest behavior then the higher the perception of Nixon's involvement in Watergate. Second, party identification is also positively correlated with perceived involvement; the less Republican the respondent, the more likely he is to perceive Nixon as being involved in Watergate ($r = .28$). Finally, there is a very strong, positive relation between an individual's target-based expectancies and perceived involvement; the higher the expectancy that Nixon would engage in dishonest sorts of behavior the greater an individual's perception of his involvement in Watergate ($r = .55$).

Since if an individual has little information about Watergate it may be difficult to assess Nixon's involvement in the incident, some positive relation is expected between the observation of Watergate and Nixon's perceived involvement. And, in fact, that is what is found ($r = .25$). Yet, because target-based expectancies have a moderate, positive relation to both behavior observation and perceived involvement, the relation may be spurious.[11] To determine if this is the case, the effects of target-based expectancies are controlled. As predicted, the relation between behavior observation and perceived involvement virtually disappears (partial $r = .05$, sig. $= .1$). Thus, behavior observation has very little direct effect on perceived involvement.

In summary, this analysis suggests that prior expectancies or beliefs play a critical role throughout the entire attribution process. They influence how much behavior observation (i.e., information gathering) occurs as well as the nature of that observation—what aspects of the behavior are focused upon. There also appear to be certain differences between categoric and target-based expectancies. Specifically, target-based expectancies are more influential throughout, a finding which concurs with experimental investigations (see, for example, Ajzen, 1977; Nisbett et al., 1976).

THE CORRELATES OF ATTRIBUTION

Before examining the correlates of attribution, let us consider the dependent variable itself. As indicated in Table 5.2, a number of respondents behaved as predicted; they either made no attributions at all (40%) or they developed higher expectancies of a Watergate type of behavior (positive change—42.8%). But, a number of respondents (16.9%) experienced negative change; their expectancies that Nixon would engage in negative sorts of behavior *declined* as a result of Watergate. In effect, Nixon's image grew more positive over the period studied. Though such negative changes tended to be relatively small in number and magnitude, they, nonetheless, require some explanation.

TABLE 5.2   Frequency Distribution of the Degree of Attribution Variable

Amount and Direction of Change	Percentage
High Negative Change (−10 thru −6)	1.4%
Low Negative Change (−5 thru −1)	15.5%
No Net Change (0)	40.0%
Low Positive Change (+1 thru +5)	33.3%
High Positive Change (+6 thru +10)	9.5%
	99.7%*
	(n = 135)

*Does not total to 100.0 due to rounding

Perhaps the most plausible explanation is that the negative changers were those respondents who had extremely low expectancies that Nixon would perform any negative behavior; they rejected the idea that Nixon was involved in Watergate. This would explain the lack of any belief change; but to account for negative change, the argument must be taken a step further. Specifically, it is posited that negative changers are those respondents who saw Nixon's perceived *noninvolvement* in Watergate as being informative. In effect, it is argued that they took Nixon's claims of honesty in the face of such adversity as an indication that he was truly honest, and thus their images become more positive. Empirical support for this explanation is provided by the positive relation between perceived involvement and attribution ($r = .24$).

Now, let us turn to an examination of the attribution process as a whole. Given that the steps are related, a multivariate analysis was undertaken; the degree of attribution variable was regressed on the behavior observation, general expectancies, partisan expectancies, target-based expectancies, and perceived involvement variables (Table 5.3).[12]

TABLE 5.3   Multiple Regression Analysis of Attribution on Behavior Observation,
Prior Expectancies and Perceived Involvement

	b^*	B^{**}	Standard Error	Significance Level
Behavior Observation	.33	.18	.14	.023
Prior Expectancies				
General	.16	.12	.11	.143
Partisan	.35	.19	.16	.026
Target	−.52	−.68	.074	.001
Perceived Involvement	3.36	.48	.20	.001

*Unstandardized regresson coefficients.
**Standardized regression coefficients.

Looking at the standardized regression coefficients, it is apparent that behavior observation has a positive, though somewhat weak, impact on attribution, providing mild support for hypothesis 1.0. The weakness of the impact is in all likelihood a result of the fact that the observation of behavior is but the first step which an individual takes towards making an attribution.

Next, we see that both hypotheses 2.1 and 2.2 are unsupported though not strongly disconfirmed. Both general and partisan expectancies have a positive, albeit weak (and in the first case insignificant), impact on attribution. In effect, if a behavior is expected in terms of categoric beliefs, then a subsequent attribution becomes, if anything, more, rather than less, likely. The most plausible explanation for these findings seems to be that categoric expectancies are most important in determining the nature of behavior observation (i.e., what is focused on) and, consequently, the determination of the intentionality of behavior. Ultimately, the effect of the categoric expectancies on these intervening steps of the process is reflected in a slight positive effect on the final attribution. In this respect, perceivers appear to use categoric and target-based expectancies in a different fashion, with the latter being relied on more heavily, if they exist.

In contrast, the prediction (hypothesis 2.3) concerning target-based expectancies was confirmed; they have a strong, negative impact on attribution. In essence, the lower an individual's expectancy that Nixon would engage in negative behavior, the greater the attribution as a result of Watergate. But this same finding is also predicted on purely statistical grounds; regression effects should result in those with lower scores experiencing greater change (Bereiter, 1963; Lord, 1963). Because the statistical bias introduced through the use of change scores coincides with the theoretical prediction, it is impossible to determine how much of the impact is attributable to the substantive processes posited herein and how much is really a statistical artifact. Given this, the confirmation of hypothesis 2.3, though encouraging, is tentative.

Perceived involvement also has a large impact on attribution that is only slightly smaller than that of the target-based expectancies (beta weight = .48

as compared to $-.68$). But unlike the case of the target-based expectancies, this finding may be interpreted as providing substantial support for an earlier hypothesis (3.0). The greater the perceived involvement, then, the greater the attribution in the predicted direction. Thus, it appears that the most critical factors in determining the degree of attribution are target-based expectancies and perceived involvement.

Finally, the multiple correlation coefficient for the regression is .56. Thus, focusing only on the preceding steps of the process explains approximately 32% of the variance in attribution (multiple $R^2 = .315$). This suggests that either a more complex regression model of the process would be more appropriate, or that certain factors outside the attribution process are exerting an influence on the degree of attribution made as a result of Watergate. The first possibility was tested with a regression model of the attribution process which included a multiplicative term designed to capture the interaction between target-based expectancies and perceived involvement.[13] This model explained no more of the variance than the simple additive model, nor was the interaction term significant. Consequently, it is probable that other factors outside the process (as specified herein) are having an impact on attribution. For example, Nixon's handling of the Watergate hearings or his treatment in the press are factors which could have produced belief change. This explanation is particularly likely given that there was no control for outside factors in the analysis.

CONCLUSIONS

In summary, the empirical analysis of the determinants of attribution provides considerable support for the theoretical view of attribution outlined earlier. As predicted, behavior observation and perception of involvement are positively related to attribution. Also as predicted, target-based expectancies were negatively related to attribution, so that the more unexpected a behavior the greater the attribution (though in some part, this finding may be a statistical artifact associated with the use of change scores). The major exception to this pattern of confirmed hypotheses occurred with respect to categoric expectancies, which, contrary to prediction, had a slight, positive impact on attribution.

This empirical confirmation of attribution has broader implications for our understanding of the perception of political figures. In contrast to the argument made by proponents of the "image thesis," it appears that politicians cannot and do not control the images which the public has of them. This by no means suggests that a politician's behavior has no impact on the public's images. Rather, it implies that any influence of the politician's behavior on his image is necessarily mediated by the perceiver and his existing beliefs. Even potentially informative behaviors are interpreted within the context of the perceiver's existing beliefs or expectancies. Furthermore, where the candidate or politician's behavior is uninformative the impact of prior beliefs on image formation is expected to greatly increase. Thus, candidate images are best described as being neither wholly stimulus- nor perceiver-determined. Instead, they represent the product of a perceptual process involving both the candidate and the voter.

NOTES

1. An in-depth consideration of the controversy surrounding the term "candidate image" is beyond the scope of this chapter. See Nimmo and Savage (1976).

2. Not included are a number of works which focus on the perceptions of a candidate's issue positions (as opposed to the perception of the candidate's image). See, for example: Granberg and Brent (1974), Kinder (1978), King (1977–1978), Page and Brody (1972), Shaffer (1978), and Sherrod (1971).

3. This discussion is based on literature from the field of social psychology, having to do with both "implicit personality theories" (Bruner and Taiguiri, 1954; Hastorf et al., 1970; Schneider, 1973) and stereotyping (Hamilton, 1976).

4. This overview of the attribution process is a general synthesis of a number of different attribution theories. As such, it no doubt does injustice to some of the complexity embodied in the more specific theories.

5. Since some respondents may perceive Nixon to have been involved in Watergate but not responsible for his actions, this measure probably overestimates the number of respondents who perceive Nixon's behavior to be intentional; consequently, it underestimates the true relation to attribution.

6. Where expectancy disconfirmation is very extreme—the behavior is very unexpected—then the perceiver may decide that the behavior was unintentional.

7. ICPSR Study 7352.

8. To conserve space, changes in each trait were not examined separately. Theoretically, it is possible that Watergate may have affected perceptions of Nixon on some traits but not on others. In fact, changes in each of the individual traits were similar and tended to follow the pattern of changes which occurred in the overall index.

9. First, to some extent, change scores are related to, or depend on, the initial score. This relation is reflected in what is commonly referred to as "regression effects"—the tendency of subjects with initially lower scores to make greater gains than those with initially higher scores. The second major problem with change scores is their unreliability which underestimates the relations between change scores and other variables. Using internal consistency reliablity estimates (rather than the preferred replicate test estimates), the reliability of the change scores was calculated and found to be .60. Thus, the correlation between the observed change scores and the true change scores would be about .77 (Lord, 1963).

10. Given the varying reliabilities of the measures, the correlations corrected for attenuation were also examined. The largest increases in the correlations occurred among those relations involving either the general expectancies or perceived involvement scales. Of special interest is the corrected correlation for the relation between perceived involvement and target-based expectancies: .84.

11. The relation is described as spurious rather than intervening since both behavior observation and perceived involvement were measured at time 3, while target-based expectancies were assessed at time 1.

12. The regression model assumed the following form:

$$Y = B_0 + B_1X_1 + B_2X_2 + B_3X_3 + B_4X_4 + B_5X_5$$

where
Y   = attribution
X_1 = behavior observation
X_2 = general expectancies
X_3 = partisan expectancies
X_4 = target-based expectancies
X_5 = perceived involvement

13. The regression model was of the following form:

$$Y = B_{0'} + B_1X_1 + B_2X_2 + B_3X_3 + B_4X_4 + B_5X_5 + B_6X_4X_5$$

where X_1, X_2, X_3, X_5 are defined in note 12. The target-based expectancies scale was first reversed so that it ran from high to low expectancy of Watergate behavior.

6

A SOCIALIZATION EXPLANATION OF POLITICAL CHANGE

Christine B. Williams

INTRODUCTION

Political socialization is the *process* by which individuals acquire behavior, attitudes, and information about politics from other members of their political system. Individuals, however, do not merely passively absorb political content, they are active participants in learning, restructuring content to conform to their own cognitive ordering of experiences: The transmission of political content is *interactive*. Changes in political content—over the life cycle or across generations—reflect changes in the underlying patterns of socialization. Socialization is a *dynamic* process that continues throughout the life cycle.

That the study of socialization helps to understand political continuity, i.e., system maintenance or stability over time, long has been recognized (Easton and Dennis, 1969). But what may be more important for our day is its ability to explain political change. We see changes in all segments of society, changes that are profoundly affecting the American political system. We need to understand the processes at work: why adults already socialized to one set of behaviors, attitudes, and information about politics currently are changing them; and the reasons young people today are acquiring different political information, attitudes, and behavior than the generation that preceded them.

Recent studies of children, adolescents, young adults, and adults reveal distinct changes in political content for each age group (Arterton, 1974; Greenstein, 1974, 1975; Dennis and Webster, 1975; Gilmour and Lamb, 1975; Pomper, 1975; Miller and Levitin, 1976; Sigel and Hoskin, 1977; *inter alia*). Contrasting the post-Watergate period with the 1950s and 1960s, four trends stand out:

(1) Individuals are more apathetic about politics. For example, the activism of college students during the Vietnam period has given way to a pragmatic orientation toward college as a means to secure technical job training or to prepare for a specific career (Newsweek, May 14, 1979: 110–112). Looking at a more conventional form of political activity, voter turnout has declined steadily over the past two decades, from 62% in 1952 to 54% in 1976. Among 18 to 20 and 21 to 24-year olds, the percentage voting remains considerably lower than the national average. Only 38% of the former, and 45% latter, age group voted in 1976. Finally, surveys of the upcoming generation of voters show declines in high school students' levels of political information and interest (National Center for Education Statistics, 1976).

(2) Individuals are more cynical about politics. Children and adolescents do not hold the idealized images of their government and its political authorities so prevalent among those studied in the 1960s (Dennis and Webster, 1975; Greenstein, 1975; Sigel and Hoskin, 1977). Since 1972, young people, and especially college students, compose one of the most alienated groups in contemporary society (Flanigan and Zingale, 1975). In 1964, 62% trusted the government most of the time, but by 1974, only 33% did so; looking just at young people, in 1965, 42% trusted government just about always, compared with 11% in 1973 (Campbell, 1979: 89–95). The percentage of Americans expressing feelings of political distrust, powerlessness, and meaninglessness doubled between 1956–1960 and 1972 (Gilmour and Lamb, 1975: 16–21).

(3) The current generation is more liberal than either their parents or the population as a whole, especially on social issues or matters of life style.[1] While 44% of 18–24 year olds and 29% of 25–35 year olds classify themselves as politically liberal, only 20% of those 35 and older do so (Pomper, 1975: 93). According to Miller and Levitin (1976), these "New Liberals" are more disposed to support the counterculture and political protest, and less inclined to espouse law and order and other "Establishment" values. Liberal and anti-Establishment candidates, e.g., Wallace in 1968, McGovern in 1972, have received their strongest support from young voters (Flanigan and Zingale, 1975; Pomper, 1975).[2]

(4) Young people are far less partisan than their elders: 18 to 24-year olds represent the highest proportion of independent identifiers of any age group. In 1974, 56% of this group identified themselves as independent or leaning independent. The partisan ties and voting decisions young people do make tend to reflect issues or candidates rather than emotional or inherited loyalty to a party label. National trends confirm an overall decline in partisan identification over the past two decades: from 47 to 39% Democratic and 27 to 22% Republican, while Independents increased from 22 to 37% (Malbin, 1975). Conversely, issue voting, as measured by the average correlation between political attitudes and vote choice, has increased from $+.18$ to $+.42$ over the same period (Nie et al., 1976).[3]

LIFE CYCLE, GENERATION, AND PERIOD EFFECTS

To disentangle the causes of these political changes presents both theoretical and methodological problems. The reported trends were inferred from cross-sectional data that contrast the survey findings of the 1950s and 1960s with those of the 1970s, i.e., post-Watergate period. Thus we have only the observed changes from which to make inferences about causality. If our comparisons span at least two age groups and at least two points in time, four patterns of change are theoretically possible. On the one hand, both age groups could show the same pattern—direction and amount—of change: in this case, either (1) both change equally, or (2) neither changes at all. On the other hand, the two age groups could show different patterns: then, either (3) one changes and the other remains the same, or (4) both change, but in different directions or by different amounts.

Although each of the previously described trends conforms to only one of these patterns (the fourth), the problem of causality is not solved. It remains complicated because any observed pattern of change can have more than one cause, and the several causes are not readily disentangled. The changes we observe have three alternate causal explanations: *maturation, generation,* and *period*. As Abramson noted:

> Age differences may result from generational effects, for "age may mark an historical epoch in which the person has matured or undergone some special variety of experience that has left an imprint on his attitudes or behaviors." On the other hand, age differences may result from the differing position of people in the life cycle, for "age may serve as an index of the length of time that the individual has lived in a specified state or engaged in a specified behavior" [1976: 471–472].

Miller and Levitin's description of the "New Politics" attitudes of youth contrasts the generational and maturational explanations:

> "Youth" may stand as an indicator of the unique experiences held in common by the youngest voters, experiences separating them from the older cohorts in the electorate. "Youth" may also indicate a lack of accumulated political experience, the absence of tested loyalties, or a limited amount of intellectual and emotional commitment, all of which contribute to shaping assessments of the New Politics [1976: 113].

Finally, the observed changes may be the result of period effects, or "dynamic mutations in response to historic events during the full life span of the persons under study" (Converse, 1976: 19).

The methodological problem in selecting among causal explanations is that the present generation cannot simply be compared with its elders, the preceding generations: Time period and age are confounded. The preceding generations differ from the present one both in age (older), *and* in the time period (political era) of their socialization. The effects can be separated only if one variable can be held constant, i.e., controlled, while changes in the other, across generations (cross-sectional analysis) or over the years (longitudinal analysis), are examined. Unfortunately, it is not possible to examine the three effects simultaneously.[4] The necessary control is lacking using either cross-sectional or longitudinal analysis alone. To illustrate, the generational hypothesis would compare young people with older people at the same point in time (t_1), apparently controlling time. Similarly, the maturational hypothesis would compare one generation, or birth cohort, with itself over succeeding points in time, apparently controlling generation.[5] In both cases, the third variable remains confounded with one of the other two: in the first, age and generation are confounded; in the second, period and age are confounded.

Past efforts to assess the effects of life cycle, generation, and period on political content have focused on the methodological aspects of the problem. As a result, important theoretical issues have been overlooked. Aging often is associated with an increasing resistance to change. The relation can be explained by social learning theory: Each repetition of a learned response reinforces the response and thus strengthens its recurrence; hence, habits formed at an early age are maintained and strengthened over the years. Habitual behavior, however, can be extinguished, essentially by reversing the process—discontinuation of positive reinforcement, negative reinforcement, or punishment. On closer examination, then, reinforcement does not lead to an unambiguous prediction with respect to aging and changing.

Cognitive development suggests an alternative theoretical explanation of the socialization processes involved, postulating a sequence of hierarchical developmental stages in which individuals are able to comprehend progressively more abstract levels of content. Some cognitive theorists (Rokeach, 1968) argue that, at advanced stages of development, beliefs, attitudes, and opinions become closely interrelated, forming a complex system whose most central components are most resistant to change. Belief systems, however, may be individual specific, and incorrect assumptions about belief centrality will impair prediction. To return to the earlier example, neither cognitive development nor social learning theory dictates that partisanship must *increase* with age, although its conceptual (i.e., ideological) sophistication should.[6]

In contrast to the life cycle explanation, the generational explanation assumes that within birth cohorts, political content remains stable across time. It adopts a static, if not deterministic, view of socialization where the political era in which individuals come of voting age is seen as their most important and lasting political experience. Thus, partisan identification is largely a function of the historical epoch in which a generation reaches political maturity; once acquired, it is retained throughout adult political life. The view directly conflicts with prevailing definitions of socialization as a dynamic process that continues throughout the life cycle. According to the latter perspective, new experiences modify, or are modified by, preceding and succeeding ones: Individuals' partisan identifications *may* change.

For the electorate as a whole, this implies that political change need not await generational replacement. (See also Shively, forthcoming).

The changing patterns of partisan identification most commonly associated with period effects are political realignments. During a critical realignment period, traditional patterns of voting behavior are intensely disrupted as large blocks of the active electorate shift their partisan allegiance (Burnham, 1970).[7] While the appearance of realignments has been marked by uniform periodicity, existing time series data generally can do no better than compare generations on either side of a single specified cutpoint, e.g., those who came of voting age before and after 1928–1932. Other cutpoints, e.g., World War II, 1964, have been suggested (Abramson, 1976, 1979; Converse, 1976), but are not accorded the same theoretical status. Lacking a greater number and longer time series of clearly identifiable and bounded political eras on which researchers can agree, period effects either are neglected entirely, assigned whatever variance remains unexplained after other effects are taken out, or are inductively inferred from visual, ad hoc inspection of the data. Cohort analyses have made no attempt to define and measure period effects as short-term forces. We return to these theoretical issues later.

CAUSAL INFERENCES ABOUT CHANGE

The problems in disentangling generation, maturation, and period effects come more clearly into view when we attempt to infer causality for each of the four patterns of change. As demonstrated below, a single pattern of change allows more than one inference about causality. The choice among competing explanations, then, will depend on the assumptions made. Since these assumptions more often are implicit than explicit, it is important they be examined for each pattern of change.

In the first two cases, all groups show the *same* pattern of change, direction and amount, from one time period to the next (t_1 to t_2, or by extension, t_1 to t_n). Pattern one (all groups change equally) supports the conclusion that aging affects all groups in the same way. In other words, aging is an incremental process: A one year increment in age results in a unit increment of change, regardless of present age. Change is a linear function of age. The pattern *also* supports the conclusion that some environmental change from t_1 to t_2 has affected everyone in the same way. Whether maturation or period effects account for the observed pattern of change, there is no *new*, independent effect for generation.[8] All birth cohorts replicate the same change pattern (see Table 6.1).

The second pattern (*no* change for any group) leads to the inference that either there are no aging effects, *or* that the years between t_1 and t_2 are insufficient to observe them. The latter interpretation is all the more plausible considering that the maturational model is premised on developmental stages, each of which spans several years. Similarly, we can conclude that there are no period effects, *or,* that the years between t_1 and t_2 are insufficient to observe them. Recall that periods refer to political eras, and the best documented of these are realignments, which occur in 25–35-year cycles. Finally, the stability of all birth cohorts means that while past generational effects may be maintained, there is no new, independent generational effect (see Table 6.1). This is consistent with the fixed effects deterministic model of generation described above. This otherwise trivial case illustrates the important point that even an absence of change from t_1 to t_2 *need not rule out any of the three causal explanations, given appropriate assumptions.* It also underscores the need for longer time series data.

TABLE 6.1   Casual Infrences from Four Patterns of Change[9]

Observed Change Pattern	Alternative Causal Inferences: Maturation, Generation, Period
(1) All groups change equally from t_1 to t_2.	*maturation:* aging affects all groups equally, regardless of present age—effects are incremental.
Example 1: *Example 2:*	
t_1 t_2 t_1 t_2	*period:* environmental change affects all groups equally (1st example, pure period effects).
G_1, G_2, G_3 ⁔ G_3 ⁔ G_2 ⁔ G_1 ⁔	*generation:* no new, independent generational effects but past generational effects may be maintained (2nd example).
(2) No groups change (at all) t_1 to t_2.	*maturation:* no aging effects *or* t_1 to t_2 insufficient time frame to observe them
Example 1: *Example 2:*	*period:* no period effects *or* t_1 to t_2 insufficient time frame to observe them
t_1 t_2 t_1 t_2	
G_1, G_2, G_3 ⁔ G_3 ⁔ G_2 ⁔ G_1 ⁔	*generation:* no new, independent generational effects, but past generational effects may be maintained (2nd example, pure deterministic model of generation).
(3) Different groups show different patterns of change from t_1 to t_2: at least one group *changes,* and at least one group stays the same.	*maturation:* aging threshholds or other deterministic maturational model, e.g., young are more susceptible to change
Example 1: *Example 2:*	*generation:* generational model *not* wholly deterministic: Change affects some generations but not others as a function of their different past histories, e.g., stable vs. unstable period conditions during formative years.
t_1 t_2 t_1 t_2	
G_3 ⁔ G_2 ⁔ G_1 ⁔ G_3, G_2 ⁔ G_1 ⁔	*period:* mixed effects model only—interaction of period with generation or aging

(4) Different groups show different patterns of change from t_1 to t_2: all groups change but differ in direction or amount.

maturation: each age group at its respective points along a prescribed maturational curve

generation: pure effects, *non*deterministic model of generation: each generation responds differently to environmental, e.g., period, effects as a function of its unique political history

period: mixed effects model only—interaction of period with generation or aging

Example 1:

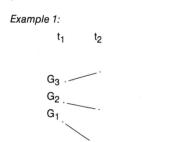

where G_1 = youngest birth cohort $\quad\quad$ t_1 = first time point
$\quad\quad$ G_2 = middle birth cohort $\quad\quad\quad\quad$ t_2 = second time point
$\quad\quad$ G_3 = oldest birth cohort
and $\quad$ t_1 to t_2 is confounded with age, A_1 to A_2;
$\quad\quad$ G_1, G_2, G_3 is confounded with age, A_1, A_2, A_3.

In the third and fourth cases, different age groups show *different* patterns of change. Pattern three, where at least one group changes (direction or amount) and at least one group stays the same, is consistent with a maturational model. It only need stipulate that stages represent threshholds, which do not precisely correspond to birth cohorts or years, $t_2 - t_1$, or that aging proceeds according to a deterministic rather than linear model. For example, young people may be more susceptible to change, or change more rapidly, than adults. The pattern is also consistent with a generational model if we assume that birth cohorts differ in stability as a function of their unique political histories. For example, cohorts entering the electorate following a realignment period may be less volatile than their parents (Beck, 1974), or some (older) generations may be insulated from any changes in the environment, i.e., period effects. Because some groups experienced no change from t_1 to t_2, period effects can be inferred only in interaction with age or generation.

Finally, any or all of the three models of change can explain the fourth pattern where all groups change but differ in direction or amount). The maturational explanation requires that the trends for each age group or stage conform to a prescribed nonlinear maturational curve. Differences in direction or amount of change reflect the groups' different locations along the curve. The generational explanation only need relax the assumption of determinism. Birth cohorts *may* change over time, but the patterns differ as a result of their unique political histories. To account for the fact that all groups do not change in the same way, period effects can have occurred only in conjunction, i.e., interaction, with age or generation (see Table 6.1).

Under the appropriate assumptions, then, none of the three models, maturation, generation, or period, can be definitively ruled out as a causal explanation of any theoretically possible pattern of change. If interactive effects are involved, it becomes difficult to ascertain the relative impact of each component (Mason et al., 1973). Period effects are, perhaps, the most troublesome: Existing data sets are insufficiently long to permit observation of those periods of most theoretical interest, namely realignments. At best, available data include two such political eras. This is less of a problem if we are interested instead in short-term, interelection period forces. But even with sufficient time intervals, other measurement problems remain. Neither a priori definitions nor post hoc assignments based on observed trends in the data provides a wholly satisfactory measure of period effects.[10] Given this dilemma, cohort analysts often assign to period effects whatever variance is unexplained after either life cycle or birth cohort effects have accounted for as much variance as they can (cf. Abramson, 1976: 476–477). The practice may seriously underestimate the impact of period on political change.

THE PURE EFFECTS MODELS

The preceding section began with a set of observed patterns of change and examined the causal inferences that could be made about each. We were unable to select among the competing explanations of change on either theoretical or methodological grounds. We therefore turn to an examination of the pure effects models, maturation, generation, and period, their underlying assumptions, and predicted patterns of change.

Ideally, a time series analysis of maturation, generation, and period effects would use longitudinal panel data in which the same individuals are reinterviewed at later points in time (Abramson, 1976). Because specific individuals' political experiences may differ widely from those of their birth cohort or age group (cf. Jaros et al., 1968), repeated cross-sectional surveys introduce measurement error. However, both the maturational and generational models assume that (st)age (or birth cohort) is the theoretically relevant unit of change. At issue, then, are only those experiences individuals hold in common as members of a collective unit (Dalton, 1977: 461). From this perspective, the measurement error lies in improperly designating individuals' stage or cohort, not in using an aggregate unit of analysis.

The time series comparisons of interest are:

C1: the same birth cohort (G) with itself across time (t), or

G_1 at t_1 vs. t_2 vs. t_n; G_2 at t_1 vs. t_2 vs. t_n; G_n at t_1 vs. t_2 vs. t_n;

C2: across birth cohorts at a single point in time, or

G_1 vs. G_2 vs. G_n at t_1, or t_2, or t_n; and

C3: birth cohorts across life cycle stages, i.e., as they age (A), or

G_1 at A_1 thru A_n vs. G_2 at A_1 thru A_n vs. G_n at A_1 thru A_n.

Table 6.2 contrasts the underlying assumptions and predicted patterns of change for pure maturation, generation, and period effects models under each comparison.

Any outline of the major assumptions and predictions that underlie these pure effects models are, of necessity, an oversimplification. The purpose here is to find a set of comparisons that uniquely identify maturation, generation, and period effects. The oversimplification, of course, is that the real world is rarely so "pure." The descriptions that follow, therefore, should be regarded as prototypes against which observed patterns of change can be compared.

Comparing birth cohorts with themselves over time, a pure effects maturational model predicts changes in political content as the cohort ages. At any single point in time, each cohort is at a different (st)age, and hence a different point along the prescribed maturational curve.[11] Consequently, patterns across generations will differ, depending on their (st)age proximity. The prediction assumes that the time interval includes at least one stage change, and that no cohort includes more than one developmental stage. (The latter might cause life cycle effects within cohorts to cancel out.) The pure deterministic model of generation assumes that early political experiences are the most important and enduring. Hence the model predicts no change within birth cohorts over time. Subsequent experiences have no perceptible impact. Finally, assuming the observed time series is long enough to encompass two or more political eras, the pure period effects model posits an identical pattern of change for all groups.

The second comparison looks at (vertical) differences between generations at single points in time. To the extent (st)age is closely correlated with birth cohort intervals, a pure effects maturational model will produce generational differences. If the intervals are too small, birth cohorts at the same developmental stage will have the same maturational trend; hence there will be no intergenerational differences between them. If the interval contains more than one developmental stage, life cycle effects may cancel out. The pure effects generational model predicts the same pattern of differences. Because each birth cohort's political history is unique, no two generations will be at the same level. (This of course would not be true of a nondeterministic model of generation.) Unlike the two preceding cases, all generations would be affected equally by period effects. Consequently, the pure effects model here predicts no differences between generations: The pattern of change moves across time only.

The third comparison follows a birth cohort as it ages, comparing it with the others when they were the same age, i.e., at earlier points in time. The pure effects maturational model predicts no change: Each generation follows the same prescribed maturational curve. It is, of course, necessary that the time frame include sufficient points along the curve—developmental stages—to trace it. In contrast, the pure effects generational model predicts differences between cohorts: Each reached the specified level of age during a different political generation, i.e., era. A deterministic model, however,

TABLE 6.2 Predictions of Pure Effects Models for Three Comparisons

Pure Effects Model	C1 (G_1 at t_1 to t_n)	C2 (G_1 vs. G_2 at t_1)	C3 (G_1 vs. G_2 at A_1 to A_n)
I: MATURATION (Aging)	*Prediction* CHANGE—changing pattern across t_1 to t_n; differs for each G (horizontal comparisons)	*Prediction* CHANGE—level differs G_1 to G_n for each t (vertical comparisons)	*Prediction* NO CHANGE—the same pattern from A_1 to A_n for each G, despite differing t (no vertical change from G_1 to G_n at A; horizontal change from A_1 to A_n for all Gs)
	Assumptions Time interval t_1 to t_n encompasses at least one developmental stage for each birth cohort; cohort intervals encompass no more than one developmental stage	*Assumptions* same as C1 (specifically, age and generation are closely correlated)	*Assumptions* (A) correctly operationalizes developmental stage, and A_1 to A_n includes more than one stage
II. GENERATION (birth cohort)	*Prediction* NO CHANGE t_1 to t_n	*Prediction* CHANGE—level differs G_1 to G_n for each t	*Prediction* CHANGE—across A_1 to A_n, levels differ for each G.
	Assumptions deterministic model of socialization (after entering the electorate, birth cohorts are relatively stable: *subsequent* period effects t_1 to t_n have imperceptible impact)	*Assumptions* same as C1 (specifically, birth cohorts do not regress or progress to the same levels as other cohorts)	*Assumptions* same as C1 (specifically, each birth cohort is imprinted with its own unique socialization experience that is stronger than, or offsets, both age and period effects)

III: PERIOD (Nature of the times)	*Prediction* CHANGE—changing pattern across t_1 to t_n, identical for all Gs *Assumptions* t_1 to t_n encompasses the relevant period of change, and a sufficient number of periods (more than one); if political eras are defined a priori, period effects will conform to (correctly) specified cutpoints	*Prediction* NO CHANGE—levels the same G_1 to G_n at each t *Assumptions* Period effects are absent by definition, i.e., held constant; *preceding period effects no longer having an impact at present t*; they have discrete beginning and end points, no lag (assumption probably untenable since it is unlikely that individuals begin each period with a clean slate, or that period perfectly overlaps with each G)	*Prediction* CHANGE—across A_1 to A_n, levels differ for each G *Assumptions* because, and to the extent, each G also represents a different time period t_1 to t_n, same as C1 (specifically, A_1 to A_n encompasses the relevant time points and a sufficient number of periods)

where C1 compares the same birth cohort (G) with itself across time (t), or G_1 at t_1 vs. t_2 vs. t_n; G_2 at t_1 vs. t_2 vs. t_n; G_n at t_1 vs. t_2 vs. t_n;

C2 compares across birth cohorts at a single point in time, or G_1 vs. G_2 vs. G_n at t_1, or t_2, or t_n; and

C3 compares birth cohorts across life cycle stages, i.e., as they age (A), or G_1 at A_1 thru A_n vs. G_2 at A_1 thru A_n vs. G_n at A_1 thru A_n.

also stipulates that after a birth cohort comes of political age, its pattern remains stable. The same prediction holds in the case of the pure effects model, but for a different reason. The trend (horizontal comparison) depicts not only aging, but also the passage of time; assuming the interval includes more than one period, these effects will show up as intergenerational differences. Across generations, then, the effects of period occur at different points along the age continuum, specifically, on the diagonals. Hence, the pure effects period model predicts lagged differences between generations at specified levels of age.

The preceding discussion has shown that a single observed pattern of change can lead to different inferences about causality. Given appropriate assumptions, none of the four patterns rules out generation, maturation, or period effects. An examination of the pure effects models contrasted their underlying assumptions and predictions across three time series comparisons. Together the three comparisons uniquely identify the pure maturation, generation, and period effects models, providing a prototype against which to compare observed patterns of change for actual data. Time series data for one of the patterns of political change described at the outset will provide a useful example.

EXPLAINING CHANGING PARTISAN IDENTIFICATION

Abramson's (1976, 1979) cohort analysis of changing patterns of partisan identification, 1952–1976, can illustrate the three comparison test of maturation, generation, and period effects. Visual inspection of Figures 6.1 and 6.2 reveals that the pattern of mean partisan strength for whites across ten birth cohorts does not conform to any of the pure effects models.[12] The observed pattern of change for the three comparisons is: C1—CHANGE, C2—CHANGE, C3—CHANGE. In other words, these data support a mixed effects model in which generation, period, and maturation interact. This conclusion can be verified by examining each comparison in turn.

Figure 6.1 illustrates the first two comparisons; C1 is made horizontally and C2 is made vertically. Figure 6.2 merely slides the horizontal trend line for each succeeding generation shown in Figure 6.1 backward until all birth cohorts are matched vertically by age group instead of by time, i.e., year. This permits us to make the third comparison between groups at the same stage in the life cycle across all stages, i.e., as they age. In Figure 6.1, period remains confounded with age for the horizontal comparisons, and generation with age for the vertical comparisons. Similarly, Figure 6.2 confounds period with age horizontally and generation with period vertically. The horizontal comparisons represent both aging and temporal change; the vertical comparisons represent different birth cohorts as well as different points in time.

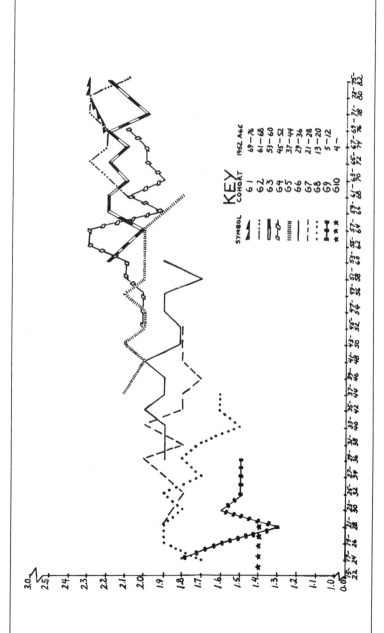

FIGURE 6.2   Mean Partisanship of Whites, 1952–1976, by Age

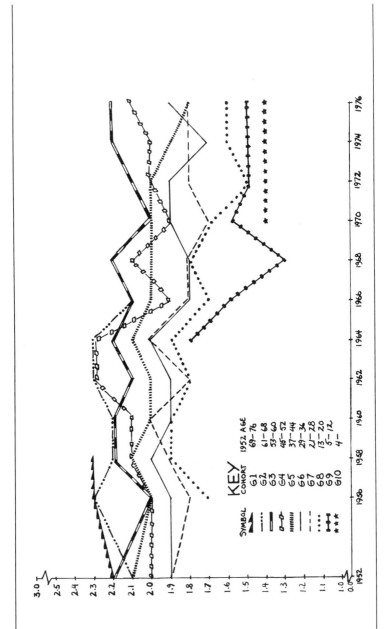

FIGURE 6.1   Mean Partisanship of Whites, 1952–1976, by Cohort

The first comparison follows each birth cohort over time, i.e., period, as it ages, a total of 24 years. The years between 1952 and 1976 may signify movement within (short term effects) or across periods (long term effects). Ignoring individual birth cohorts, the aggregate change in mean partisanship among whites from 1952 to 1976 is $-.3$;[13] the average individual cohort change for the same period is $-.1$. Comparison C2, Figure 6.1, measures intergenerational change at single points in time. The absolute vertical difference between generational pairs at t, averaged over all time points, is /.1/. Since Figure 6.2 merely shifts the vertical intersections of the trend lines in Figure 6.1, the horizontal comparisons for C3 yield the same change statistics as C1, $-.3$ and $-.1$. The comparisons of interest, however, are the intergenerational, i.e., vertical, differences between age groups. The mean difference between cohorts at each A, averaged over all age groups, is $+.1$. Assuming that Figure 6.2, taken as a whole, depicts the complete life cycle maturational curve, the aggregate change from youngest to oldest age group, ignoring individual birth cohorts, is $+.6$.

Following the designation used in Table 6.1, Abramson's data for changing partisan identification, 1952–1976 can be simplified to:

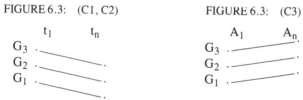

FIGURE 6.3:   (C1, C2)   FIGURE 6.3:   (C3)

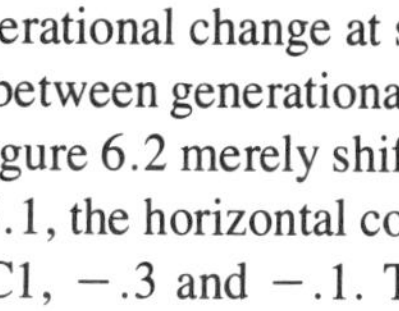

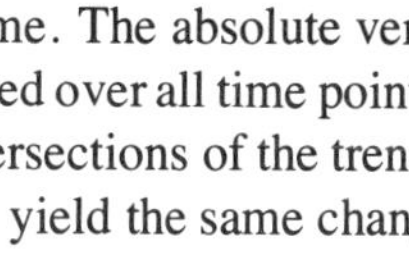

Based on Table 6.2, the figures for pure maturation, generation, and period effects simplify to:

FIGURE 6.4:   (C1, C2)   FIGURE 6.4:   (C3)

I: *Pure Maturation Effects*

Example 1:   Example 2: 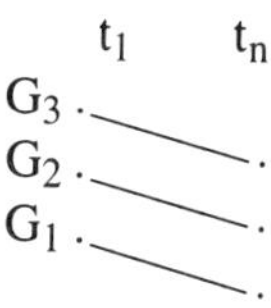   Example 1: 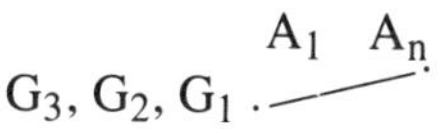   Example 2:

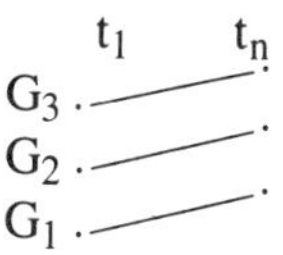

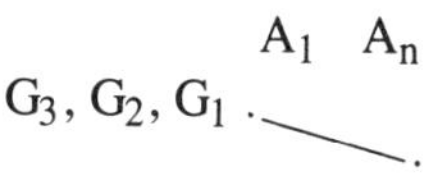

II: *Pure Generation Effects*

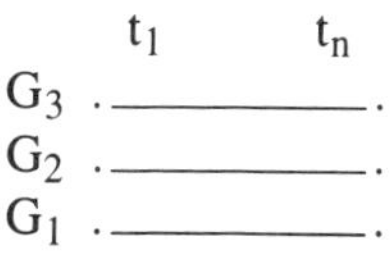

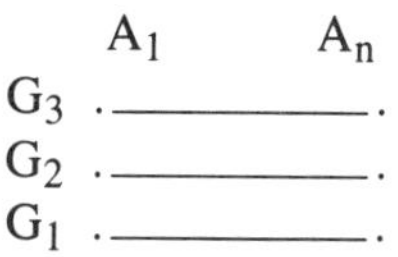

Continued on 126

III: *Pure Period Effects*

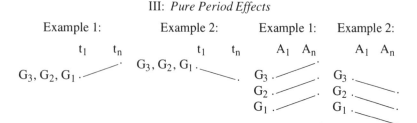

The three comparisons, and hence Figures 6.4: (C1, C2) and Figure 6.4: C3, uniquely identify the three pure effects models. Comparing the figures for Abramson's data on partisan identification with each pair of figures for the pure effects maturation, generation, and period models rules out cases I and III in Figure 6.4 above. Assuming the stipulation of no differences between birth cohorts (I, Figure 6.4: C3 and III, Figure 6:4 C1, C2) to be stringent precludes a pure maturational or period explanation of partisan change.

The more controversial question surrounding cohort analyses of party identification, however, is the fit with the pure effects generational model (Abramson, 1979; Converse, 1979). Specifically, are the horizontal trends for each birth cohort significantly greater than zero, ruling generation out as the single and most appropriate causal explanation of the data?[14] Calculating absolute change from t_1 to t_n for each cohort, a single sample difference of means t-test shows that 8 of the 10 means differ significantly from zero. The two exceptions, oldest and youngest cohorts, are based on a small number of data points, and one, the oldest, only narrowly fails to achieve significance at the .05 level.[15] The significance tests, therefore, confirm the original assessment that changing patterns of partisan identification from the 1950s to the 1970s have been caused by a combination, i.e., interaction, of maturation, generation, and period effects.

That a mixed effects model should be the most accurate causal explanation of changing patterns of partisan identification is neither very surprising nor enlightening. It is consistent with our intuitive sense of the complexities of the real world; it is also the source of its explanatory weakness. The mixed effects model probably generalizes to nearly *all* patterns of political change that interest researchers, and, consequently, is no longer useful. The key question then becomes the *relative* impact of generation, maturation, and period, or more simply, which effect is strongest? We have come full circle: The identification problem is indeterminate; no empirical solution is possible.

To proceed with cohort analysis, researchers have, of necessity, assumed that one of the effects is constant, i.e., at least two groups have an identical effect on the dependent variable (Mason et al., 1973). The assumption may be implicit—one of the three effects simply is ignored—or it may be based on "outside evidence" about which of the three is in a "steady state" (Converse, 1976; Shively, forthcoming). Errors of the former type are readily exposed. In the latter case, the inferential error of determining which effect is constant solely from observation of the data under study is also obvious and generally recognized. It means, however, that we ultimately must return to theory to avoid making the same inappropriate predictions, inferences, and conclusions about patterns of political change that plague this literature. The next section deals with the theoretical implications of the complex and often subtle sets of assumptions surrounding changing partisan identification.

SOCIALIZATION AND PARTISAN CHANGE

Political socialization plays a central role in the acquisition, modification, and extinction of partisan identification. Studies consistently report positive correlations of .5 or .6 between parents' party affiliation and that of their offspring (Sears, 1975: 123–124). Levels of agreement increase when both parents hold the same affiliation or are strong partisans, and reach their highest level, 60% agreement, during adolescence. There is greater parent-child agreement on partisan identification than on most other political issues (Jennings and Niemi, 1974).

Parents, acting as socializing agents, clearly transmit certain attitudinal political content (e.g., partisan identification) to their children.[16] The transmission process is, however, an imperfect one in which other socializing agents and environmental forces share, if not compete for, influence over the content of socialization. Finally, individuals shape, as well as are shaped by, the agents and events with which they come into contact. The strength and nature of parental and other partisan cues seem to ebb and flow, causing or caused by secular political realignments (Beck, 1974; Baker, 1978). Two theories of political socialization, Identification and Cognitive Development, are particularly relevant to understanding the partisan and electoral changes that have occurred from the 1950s to the 1970s.

IDENTIFICATION

The Identification model is premised on the social learning theory concept of reinforcement. It views party loyalty as a learned response, dependent on reinforcement for its persistence: Without positive reinforcement, a response is extinguished. One of two identification mechanisms is at work. Approved behavior (party loyalty in this case) either is linked directly to a reward, or is motivated by a desire to be like the role model, i.e., socializing agent. These mechanisms explain both the acquisition and maintenance of party identification. Initial responses to party labels are reinforced—positively or negatively, directly or indirectly—by parental, and later peer, approval or disapproval (Reynolds, 1974). The first time an individual votes, party label cues the appropriate behavior.[17] The act of voting reinforces partisan attachments, which grow stronger with each repetition of the behavior. The persistence of learned voting habits depends on continued positive reinforcement, whether internalized or from valued role models (i.e., socializing agents), at least intermittently. There is no reason to assume that positive reinforcement always will occur, or that it will continue over the course of the life cycle. Individuals mature, role models change, and political events intervene, each with some effect on people's political outlooks.

Since the 1960s, regard for political parties has diminished in all segments of the electorate. Fewer people seem to attach cue value to party label. The decline in turnout over the past two decades suggests that for many, voting is no longer reinforcing. Since the transmission of partisan identification from parents to offspring is not wholly successful, a weakening of ties in adults (socializing agents) signals even greater partisan losses in upcoming generations. Indeed, today's youth are infrequent voters, often split their tickets, and are the most likely to switch and vote for different parties election to election. In the space of a few generations, American political parties could lose most of their base of support.

The foregoing discussion of reinforcement underscores the dynamics of socialization and suggests a need to rethink the generational explanation of partisanship. To the extent a birth cohort shares a common political history which differs from that of other cohorts, generation is a meaningful descriptive construct. A cohort's history, however, should not be considered static, indelibly determined at the time it enters the electorate. Socialization continues throughout the life cycle, constantly changing the "historical" imprint. Just as experiences mediate learning new content through assimilation, new experiences can modify what has gone before through accommodation. Although recent experiences generally have only incremental effects on what was learned first (primacy), crises or other traumatic events can have more important consequences, both for individual political behavior and for the larger political system. Thus we see that generations differ not only from each other, but also from themselves over time. Generation becomes a summary measure for *past period effects that have been maintained over time; since only one birth cohort enters the electorate at a given point in time, these effects compose a unique set for each generation.*

COGNITIVE DEVELOPMENT

The cognitive development model of political socialization treats a different dimension of partisanship. According to this theory, as individuals mature, they develop progressively more complex ways of processing content and move from a concrete to an abstract level of thinking. Having had neither personal contacts with the larger political environment, nor behavioral political experience, children merely assimilate party label (Easton and Dennis, 1969). As they mature, the label is linked with party platform, candidates, and so forth, as well as with the individual's other political attitudes and behaviors. By adolescence, the stage of formal operations, the cognitive development model postulates that individuals are capable of logical thought and have begun to develop an interconnected belief system (Connell, 1971).[18]

As attitudes become more firmly embedded in the belief system, they are more resistant to change (Rokeach, 1968). To the extent that partisan identification is one such element in an individual's belief system, strength of partisanship should increase with age, i.e., developmental stage.[19] In an era where the number of partisan identifiers is decreasing and parties are losing political viability, the condition of belief centrality probably does not hold for many people. Nor can it be assumed that strong partisan ties necessarily represent a higher or more sophisticated level of ideological thought. To define ideological sophistication in partisan terms presumes a certain bias toward the American two-party system. If, as critics charge, there are no meaningful differences between the two parties and their candidates, voters cannot be faulted for failing to find them.[20] Unlike the European prototype with which they are unfavorably compared, American political parties lack clear ideologies, and shun programmatic platforms.

A cognitive development interpretation of life cycle effects posits a specific maturational trend across cognitive stages for all birth cohorts, irrespective of period. To specify the shape of the maturational curve across the life cycle will require both theoretical and empirical refinements in the concept of stage as it relates to partisanship. From a cognitive developmental perspective, as individuals mature, they develop more complex belief systems: There is no presumption that strength of partisan identification increases with age. Strong partisanship is a function of belief centrality; it is not a prerequisite for ideological sophistication. To equate the two oversimplifies and misspecifies the theoretical basis of the relation, leading to inappropriate age predictions that then fail to confirm the presence of life-cycle effects. In other cases, researchers have concluded that the mass public lacks political sophistication, or does not measure up to requirements for democratic citizenship. What is needed, then, are more appropriate tests of the maturational model than those provided by existing cohort analyses of party identification.

REEXAMINING GENERATION, MATURATION, AND PERIOD: SOME ALTERNATIVE TESTS

Jennings and Niemi's (1975) cohort analysis of partisan affect, political preference, participation, and cognition offers supporting evidence for the

argument that generation and maturation are not mutually exclusive explanations of political change. Their findings show that older individuals are
not resistant to environmental change, and that differences between parents
and their children are not merely a function of the generation gap between
them. Indeed, they conclude that, on balance, the forces of convergence
seem to outweigh those creating divergence, bringing the two generations
closer together in 1973 than they were in 1965 (Jennings and Niemi, 1975:
1335).[21] For 7 of the 10 types of political content they investigated, a hybrid,
i.e., interactive, model most accurately explains the observed patterns of
change. Their analysis is, however, post hoc, and like other cohort analyses,
depends on the questionable assumption that ignore the convergence of trend
lines—younger to older generation—represents aging or life-cycle effects;
flat, parallel trend lines represent generational effects; and overlapping,
congruently moving trend lines represent period effects. Only C1 and C2 are
taken into account. The illustration underscores a final and important point:
To derive appropriate predictions and make correct casual inferences about
political change requires a theoretical understanding of the socialization
processes at work.

The cognitive development interpretation of ideological sophistication
described above suggests a theoretically viable test of the maturational
explanation of political change. In general terms, ideology refers to a consistent way of understanding and relating to politics, which need not follow
conventional liberal—conservative lines. The usual, albeit not undisputed
(Marcus et al., 1974), measure of ideological sophistication is the intercorrelation between attitude positions or sets of positions—foreign and domestic
policy, party identification, vote choice, and the like.[22] Much of the current
debate in the literature concerns whether the electorate is more issue oriented
and ideologically sophisticated today than it was in the 1950s and early
1960s. (See Petrocik's chapter in the volume for a review of the topic.) This
chapter is less concerned with the fact of political change than with its
underlying dynamics. The question, then, turns on whether the intercorrelations between attitudes increase with age, i.e., stage, as a cognitive development model of life cycle would predict.

The cognitive development model's prediction is straightforward: Correlations between salient issues should increase with stage, or, operationally,
with age. The prediction in the case of the generational model, however, is
unclear. The way particular issues are linked together is, in part, a function
of the political era in which a person lives (Nie and Andersen, 1974). The
problem lies in knowing whether past (i.e., generation) or present period
effects are controlling. Assuming the underlying theoretical premises of the
predicted age relationship are now correctly specified, correlations should
increase, though not necessarily linearly, over the life cycle, i.e., across
developmental stages. Depending on the definition of attitudinal consis-

tency imposed, the level, i.e., magnitude, of correlations will differ among birth cohorts. (While the operational measure of consistency is, of necessity, fixed, actual issues may be linked differently across time.)

Failure to find the expected life-cycle effects in this test clearly would refute the maturational explanation, but does not confirm a generational one. The ambiguity surrounding expected period effects precludes that conclusion. Maturation and generation should not be regarded as mutually exclusive explanations of political change nor this illustration a critical test of them.

To summarize the argument, partisan identification is not a developmental concept. Partisanship in itself is not an ideologically more sophisticated (complex or abstract) way of thinking about politics. Social learning theory explains the positive relation between age and partisanship by reinforcement mechanisms. Yet current trends suggest a decline, not an increase, in partisan identification as individuals age and new cohorts enter the electorate, replacing older ones. What individuals learn and transmit to their offspring can be unlearned through the same socialization process: Socialization is dynamic. Thus birth cohorts differ not only from each other as a function of their unique political histories, but also from themselves over time. Generations represent the mirror through which past period effects are seen.

CONCLUSION

This chapter has identified a set of problems that characterize most cohort analyses of party identification and the study of political change more generally. The major arguments can be summarized as methodological, theoretical and analytical issues.

Methodological issues. While the identification problem generally is acknowledged in principle, the confounding of maturation, generation, and period effects often is ignored in its specific contexts. Insufficient attention has been given to measurement problems and specifically to the operational definitions of developmental stage (vis à vis age and birth cohort) and period (i.e., cutpoints). In addition, existing time series may include insufficient data points. Finally, birth cohorts must be compared at the same age, different time as well as at the same time, different age. Three comparisons (and two graphs) are necessary to identify the pure effects models uniquely.

Theoretical issues. The underlying assumptions and predictions, especially with respect to the maturation model, have been misspecified. The age relation is one glaring example. Ideological consistency suggests a more appropriate test of aging effects. The theoretical meaning of concepts in relation to political content needs reexamination and refinement: for example, specifying a maturational curve or distinguishing between past (i.e., generational) and present period effects. Underlying all of these theoretical issues is an understanding of political socialization as a dynamic rather than static or deterministic process.

Analytical issues: findings and conclusions. Largely because of the identification problem, inaccurate causal inferences have been drawn about observed patterns of change. A common problem here is misspecification of the change patterns for the pure effects models. Effects are attributed erroneously to maturation, generation, or period explanations when a mixed effects model more correctly characterizes the data. A related error is to conclude that disproving one model (i.e., maturational) confirms its "opposite" (i.e., the generational model). This both commits a logical fallacy and disregards the identification problems discussed above.

To understand the changes taking place in the American political system, we must first understand the socialization processes through which they are occurring. The study of political change is a complex one; its dynamics raise difficult methodological, theoretical, and analytical issues.

NOTES

1. More recent studies (late 1970s) report a surge of neoconservatism on the nation's college campuses. (See Frankland et al., 1979 for a brief summary.) A poll of American college freshmen indicates that the return to traditional values is widespread. The percentage of those identifying themselves as middle-of-the-road politically is up 11% from 1970, paralleling similar increases in the proportion of self-identified conservatives in the nation as a whole. Consistent with Miller and Levitin's (1976) findings, however, the number endorsing traditional liberal positions on so-called social issues has increased (Newsweek, February 26, 1979; New York Times, January 22, 1978).

2. In 1972, 50.7% of 18–24-year olds voted for McGovern, compared with 39.0% of 25–35-year olds, and 31.8% of those 35 and older (Pomper, 1975: 93).

3. Other researchers (Sullivan et al., 1978; Bishop et al., 1978) contend that the supposed increase in issue voting is actually an artifact of method; specifically, question wording and coding.

4. The problem is one of identification. With 3 unknown effects but only 2 diagnostic variables, the problem is underidentified and technically indeterminate. Each of the 3 variables—period of study, years of age, and date of birth (cohort)—is completely defined by the other 2, i.e., linearly dependent. The selection of a particular age group in a particular year dictates the date of birth: only *one* cohort can be observed (Converse, 1976; Mason et al., 1973).

5. Cohort analysis extends the time series using repeated cross-sectional surveys. Thus one birth cohort is compared with itself across time, controlling for generation, but leaving period and age confounded. Implicitly, birth cohorts are compared with each other at each single point in time, across all time points in the series.

6. An analogous argument can be made with respect to increasing Republican identification or with age.

7. Realignments may consist of *demographic changes* in the voting population as newly enfranchised citizens enter the electorate or of *individual conversions* as voters step across party lines, permanently changing their partisan identification (Sundquist, 1973). Beck's (1974) socialization theory of partisan realignment treats only the latter type of wholesale defection—youth's defection from inherited partisan orientations.

8. It may be, however, that *past* generational effects are being maintained.

9. Jennings and Niemi (1975) use similar diagrams to depict pure and hybrid maturation, generation, and period effects. Whereas they begin with assumptions about what diagram is consistent with each of their causal models, the strategy here is just the reverse: to begin with the theoretically possible observed patterns of change, and show that all three causal models, singly or in interaction, are consistent with each pattern diagrammed. As Tables 6.1 and 6.2 demonstrate, some of their assumptions can be challenged.

10. If periods are defined a priori (deductive approach), cutpoints *must* be specified correctly. There is insufficient agreement on the appropriate periods, as well as insufficient numbers of them, i.e,. long enough time series in existing data sets. Post hoc definitions of period based on observed trends in the data (inductive approach) create verification problems: The same data that were used to identify the periods later are marshalled to confirm the presence of period effects.

11. The maturational model is premised on developmental stage, which is not perfectly correlated with age, its operational definition. (St)age is used to denote the discrepancy between concept and indicator.

12. The ten birth cohorts listed by age in 1952 are: 69–76, 61–68, 53–60, 45–52, 37–44, 29–36, 21–28, 13–20, 5–12, and 4 or younger.

13. Abramson collapses the SRC scale of partisan identification so that strong partisans are scored as 3, weak partisans as 2, independents who lean toward a party as 1, and pure independents and apoliticals as 0 (Abramson, 1976: 471). The aggregate change in mean partisanship from 1952 to 1976 is computed as $\sum_{G_1}^{G_n} \overline{X}_{t_n} - \sum_{G_1}^{G_n} \overline{X}_{t_1}$.

14. A purely deterministic model of generation predicts no (zero) change: After coming of political age, birth cohorts remain stable over time. The appropriate significance test, then, is whether the slope of the horizontal trend line deviates significantly from that prediction of no or zero change. Deviation is measured in positive *or* negative units of change from t_n to t_{n+1}. The resulting mean is the average of these deviations for each cohort across time, for all cohorts, and is reported in *absolute value* terms.

15. Significance tests of the absolute changes across age groups for each cohort yield similar results.

16. Attitude generally is defined as a predisposition to respond favorably to an object (Kiesler et al., 1969); in this case, to a party label, its candidates, platform, and the like.

17. Party identification remains the single most important predictor of vote choice, despite its precipitous decline since 1960 (cf. Nie et al., 1976: 164–173). It should be noted that although the importance of issue preferences and candidate orientation have increased, both also are correlated with partisan identification and to a greater degree than in the past (Pomper, 1975).

18. In general, a belief system is a set of interrelated (by constraint or functional interdependence) beliefs, attitudes, and opinions (Converse, 1964). Beliefs are composed of an individual's values and world view—what constitutes reality—(universal truths, Rokeach, 1968); attitudes are enduring predispositions toward objects or people, whereas opinions refer to specific people, events, and so forth, rather than to broad classes of attitude objects. They are the most subject to change.

19. Theorists differ over the nature and sequence of developmental stages. Many (e.g., Connell and Kohlberg) subscribe to Piaget's basic conception of a hierarchical progression that culminates with formal operations, usually attained by adolescence. Erikson (1950) departs from most psychoanalysts' deterministic view of stage by positing a life-long evolution of eight stages: Oral Sensory, Muscular-anal, Locomotor-genital, Latency, Puberty and adolescence, Young adulthood, Adulthood, and Maturity. The predicted linear relation between age and partisanship (inaccurately attributed to the maturational model) depends on a full life-cycle conceptualization of stage.

20. Empirical studies of the American public's level of ideological sophistication indicate that, prior to 1964, few adults conceptualized politics in ideological terms (Nie and Rabjohn, 1979). By one estimate (Converse, 1964), only 2 to 3% of the public qualifies as pure ideologues; most people are unable to differentiate parties and issue positions along liberal or conservative or other dimensions. Levels of attitudinal constraint, as measured by the intercorrelations among attitude domains, are low, particularly in the mass public.

21. Jennings and Niemi's conclusions are subject to the caveat that parent-child comparisons tap generational, but not actual age, differences, and to the limitation that 2 time points 8 years apart are insufficient data for the kinds of causal inferences they wish to make about political change. (See Tables 6.1 and 6.2.) Their analysis shares with other cohort analyses of partisan identification the problems regarding assumptions and predictions described in the text.

22. The relation between party identification and issue position entails some of the same problems as the assumption that partisanship represents a greater degree of ideological sophistication than independence. Maturation almost certainly will interact with period, and possibly generation, effects. More importantly, the prediction for life-cycle effects remains tenuous. The expected relation depends on the willingness to assume that parties articulate, and are perceived in terms of, clear ideologies and distinct issue positions. It further assumes that the issues selected are relevant, i.e., partisan, ones. The latter is also problematic in the suggested issue consistency test.

7

PERSONALITY AND THE EVALUATION OF ANTI-IDEAL CANDIDATES

Jonathon M. Hurwitz

Mark A. Peffley

Candidate perception and evaluation literature has typically been structured by the stimulus-perceiver controversy. Reviewers of the debate (Nimmo and Savage, 1976; Conover, this volume) have noted that the central argument has concerned whether the perception of the social stimuli is determined primarily by characteristics of the candidate—the image position—or of the perceiver—the perceptual balance position. Not surprisingly, most major studies (Blumer and McQuail, 1969; Nimmo and Savage, 1971, 1974; Sigel, 1964) have found evidence for both effects, although the results have generally been interpreted in support of one position or the other.

Unfortunately, most of the literature has been seriously limited in several respects. For one, studies typically concentrate on either hypothetical "ideal" candidates or actual front runners in high-level governmental elections. The findings, consequently, have led to what Sears (Sears and Whitney, 1973) has labelled as the "positivity bias"—the tendency for electors to perceive political figures in consistently favorable terms. Such uniformly positive ratings, with little variation across candidates or perceivers, have presented methodological problems for some forms of statistical analysis (Watts, 1974: 133–136). A second difficulty with the research is its tendency to investigate only a very limited number of sources of individual differences among perceivers, generally examining only the role of partisanship and ideology.

While not denying the importance of the image thesis, it is our purpose to suggest and examine an additional, and currently ignored, source of perceiver variation—personality—to add greater depth and structure to the political perception literature. More specifically, we hope to determine if personality factors are equally, if not more, important causes of candidate perception as other more traditional explanations such as politcal and social influences. Further, although the use of secondary analysis dictates that this study is exploratory, we hope to specify and test several hypotheses regarding situations under which psychological factors should be most important as determinants of political perception.

This research will use a fundamentally different methodology in an attempt to remedy the difficulties noted above. Most significantly, we have concentrated on least-preferred, or "anti-ideal" political candidates to introduce greater variation in perceptual judgments. We find, consequently, considerable difference between individuals in their evaluations and, contrary to Sears' expectations, a great deal of negativity in perceptions. Further, it will become apparent below that least-favored candidates are likely to elicit differential perception based on the personality of the evaluator. To the extent that negative evaluations are motivated by fears and anxieties, we would expect to find a significant role for the perceiver's personality in guiding his judgments of "anti-ideal" candidates. And, finally, by focusing on least-preferred candidates, we are able to explore the lower, as well as the upper, bounds of the perceptual process.

THE ROLE OF PARTISANSHIP AND IDEOLOGY

As noted, perceiver determination perspectives have been applied in only a limited context to the candidate image literature, with most studies focusing narrowly on political predispositions as a source of perceiver differences in candidate evaluation. In replication of Sigel's (1964) study, which was among the first to document the importance of partisanship in forming evaluations, Nimmo and Savage (1974) found some evidence that partisan groups tend to perceive their party's candidate more favorably than the candidate of the opposition party. In their study of the 1972 presidential election, the researchers noted that subjects with a partisan identification tended to view their own party's candidate as a "great statesman" and, importantly, to rate the opposing contestant negatively, seeing him as a "partisan campaigner" (i.e., ambitious, self-serving, and so forth). Not only did an individual's affect toward the candidates seems to be influenced by his party label, but the cognitive content of his images of the two candidates was similarly affected.

As with partisanship, ideology can be expected to serve as an anchor in a person's conception of a political figure. Individuals may judge candidates who are closer to them on an ideological scale more favorably or attribute more desirable traits to them. Surprisingly, almost all research on ideology has related it to the vote and not to candidate perception, although Rusk and Weisberg (1972) suggested the importance of ideology to candidate evaluations. The authors looked at feeling thermometer ratings of a number of political objects, and scaling analyses yielded both ideological and partisan dimensions that "explained" individual ratings.[1]

PERSONALITY AND SOCIAL PERCEPTION

One neglected variable in the literature on political perception is personality. Most of the evidence leading us to expect personal dispositions to be a determinant of candidate evaluation have come from social psychological research in social (person) perception. Perhaps the earliest examination of dispositions in this context employed the California F (pre-fascism) scale to analyze the effect of authoritarianism (Adorno et al., 1950) on the accuracy of person perception. Newcomb (1961), noting the tendency of authoritarians to project undesirableness onto others, predicted that high-F individuals would suffer from inaccuracy in interpersonal evaluation. In fact, in his study of friendship development, he found this tendency of self-projection among authoritarians who were substantially less accurate in their judgments than low-F subjects.[2]

There are other explanations for Newcomb's findings which have little to do with authoritarian projection. Rokeach (1960), for instance, has argued persuasively that individuals who score high on the F scale are merely a conservative subpopulation of a broader group with a closed minded belief system. These dogmatic perceivers are characteristically unable to assimilate information which is ambiguous or incongruent with their present beliefs. Because dogmatism is statistically associated with both intolerance of ambiguity and authoritarianism (Knutson, 1972: 343), it can be speculatively inferred that Newcomb's findings were less the result of authoritarian projection than of the tendency of dogmatists to simplify and distort perceptual reality; this view is reinforced by Steiner and Johnson's (1963) findings that strongly authoritarian individuals are less likely to see both good and bad attributes in other persons. In sum, although the degree to which authoritarianism and dogmatism are distinct entities is not known, there is an abundant literature that adequately documents the relation between the personality construct and social perception.

Related to dogmatism is Kelly's (1955, 1963) work on cognitive complexity, which Harvey et al., (1961) have defined by the criteria of differentiation (the number of cognitive dimensions employed in perceiving the social world) and integration (the flexibility of interrelatedness among the dimensions). Both conceptions have been applied extensively to social perception with the general consensus as summarized by Bieri et al.'s (1966) review that more complex perceivers are able to observe greater differences between themselves and others than are more cognitively simple perceivers. Further, Bieri (1961) has demonstrated that complex individuals are better able to form a balanced, integrated impression of other people.

Authoritarianism, dogmatism, and cognitive complexity are only three of a number of cognitive-psychological dispositions that influence social perception. Other research has been conducted on traits such as intelligence (Taft, 1955), hostility and aggression (Sarason and Winkel, 1966), prejudice and ethnocentrism (DeFleur and Westie, 1959), personal values (Mueller, 1966), Machiavellianism (Christie and Geis, 1970), locus of control (Rotter, 1966), and "repressors/sensitizers" (Altrocchi, 1961).[3] Much of this literature has been reviewed by Warr and Knapper (1968: 195–206), Tagiuri (1968), and Schrauger and Altrocchi (1963).

ATTRIBUTION AND THE ROLE OF PERSONALITY

Conover's treatment of attribution theory (in this volume) provides additional justification for expecting various personality types to perceive candidates differently. Attribution theory postulates that when information is missing or ambiguous, persons will use their existing dispositions and beliefs to generate the information necessary for prediction. Applied to an electoral campaign, the theory would predict that when a voter receives ambiguous or inconsistent messages about a candidate's image he will rely heavily on his predilections when attributing various traits to the candidate. Thus, substantial variation will exist in the way candidates are perceived. Fiorina and Weisberg (in this volume) point out that even in presidential campaigns, where more information is available to voters, uncertainty about the candidates' issue positions is likely to be considerable. Naturally, a voter's judgments about a candidate's *personal* image traits (as opposed to issue and party positions) tend to be subjective and not amenable to reliable verification and thus will be even more a product of his beliefs and dispositions.

From this theoretical perspective, a voter's personality figures importantly into candidate perception. By one definition, an individual's personality is "an organized and stable set of enduring dispositions" (Lieberg and Spiegler, 1974: 125). A voter's personality may thus be treated as a convenient and economical summary variable, representing a wide array of dispositions on which he may draw to interpret a candidate's behavior.

Just as important, these stable dispositions are assumed to give rise to more transient attitudes, beliefs, and motivational states which, according to attribution theory, should affect perception. For example, a number of studies have found personality to be an important determinant of political attitudes and beliefs which are clearly relevant to the process of political perception. A substantial body of literature has related various personality dimensions to such important political predispositions as isolationism (Sniderman and Citrin, 1971: 401–417), conservatism (McClosky, 1958: 27–45), democratic personality (Sniderman, 1975), political intolerance (Sullivan et al., 1979), and political efficacy (Milbrath, 1962). Importantly, these effects of personality are independent of other social and political attributes of the perceiver.

In light of the important role of personality in social perception and attribution, it is surprising that very few studies in the image literature have investigated its impact on the perception of political figures. The results of two studies are suggestive of the benefits of drawing measures of personality into the analysis. Leventhal et al. (1964) report a significant relation between authoritarianism and candidate preference when liberal versus conservative ideology is salient in a campaign. High authoritarians were likely to prefer more conservative candidates, largely irrespective of partisanship.

A second study draws from Rokeach's insights on dogmatic belief systems. In their San Francisco Bay Study, Kernell et al. (1973) found that respondents who scored higher on their inflexibility scale (essentially similar to the dogmatism scale devised by Rokeach) were more likely to support President Johnson and presidents in general under a variety of conditions. Importantly, inflexibility was the most important predictor of presidential support, more important than social variables (age, sex, race, and socioeconomic status [SES]) and some political factors (evaluation of American government; the authors did not report findings for ideology and partisanship). Though the results of this study may be tied to regime and community support, it is clear that, along with Leventhal et al.'s research, they suggest the various ways in which personality may shape the perception of political figures.

PROCEDURES

To investigate the importance of personality variables on candidate evaluation, data from Sullivan et al.'s (1979) Tolerance study were analyzed. The data were collected in interviews with a random sample of 398 adults (265 of whom completed questions on candidate evaluation) in the Twin Cities (Minnesota) area during the spring of 1976. Candidate rating questions were asked only until the party primaries so that respondents selected candidates from a field of 8 candidates (see below).

INDEPENDENT VARIABLES

The Twin Cities study included two personality variables—a self-esteem inventory and a measure of Maslow's need hierarchy. The first psychological variable, self-esteem, has most frequently been treated as a stable, enduring personality disposition, much along the lines of Allport's (1966) definition. Although there is a lack of consensus about the etiology of the trait, a great deal of research specifies psychological and behavioral correlates of the syndrome of low self-regard. Empirically, it has been associated with feelings of inadequacy, futility, guilt, disaffection, withdrawal, isolation, loneliness, and anxiety (Sniderman, 1975: 73–101). Further, it has been linked with a wide array of behavioral manifestations.[4]

The general prognosis for individuals who hold themselves in low esteem, as characterized in the literature, would have to be described as bleak. Their insecurity and doubts about their own worth can quite often lead to feelings of helplessness and vulnerability. Because they see themselves as prey to a difficult environment, they are likely to feel a chronic and persistent mood of anxiety and, possibly, persecution. Further, it has been shown that individuals may project their dislike for themselves on their social and professional acquaintances. They may become cynical, distrustful, and suspicious of those in their environment (Sniderman, 1975: Ch. 2, 3).

For our purposes, self-esteem has been measured by questions first used by McClosky (derived from the Minnesota Multi-Phasic Inventory) in 1955 and subsequently by Sniderman in 1975. Although these researchers disaggregated self-esteem into measures of personal unworthiness, status inferiority, and interpersonal competence, Sniderman found the first to be by far the best predictor of behavior and, consequently, Sullivan et al. used only the eight-item unworthiness scale in their Twin Cities survey, with each item measured on a five-point Likert type of format. Following Michel's (1968: 6) additivity principle that postulates that the trait measurement is simply the relative frequency of its occurrence, an individual's responses were summed across the eight questions to determine his self-esteem score on a scale ranging from 8 (extremely high) to 40 (extremely low). In most respects the scale seems to be a reliable indicator of the trait (alpha = .756) with all scale items measuring the same underlying construct.

Abraham Maslow's (1970) theory of personality assumes that each individual is predominantly motivated by one or more of five psychic needs which influence the individual's attitudes and behaviors: (1) physiological, (2) security or safety, (3) affection or belongingness, (4) esteem, and (5) self-actualization. Moreover, the needs form a hierarchy of development so that only after a lower, prepotent need is satisfied does the next need gradually become a motivating force. Therefore, if a person is severely deprived of a basic need in the first few years of life, he is likely to become relatively fixed at that need level for years to come. This study has emphasized the dichotomous distinction between insecure persons (those deprived of physiological and safety needs) and secure persons (those located at need levels three to five) as opposed to the ordinal distinctions of the need hierarchy.[5]

Jeanne Knutson's (1972) discussion of the behavioral and psychological correlates of the need syndromes contains an insightful profile of the insecure individual. Persons deprived of physiological needs become preoccupied with satisfying these needs later in life, being characterized by a single-minded concern with material well-being, as well as passivity and fatalism (Knutson, 1972: 25–28). If physiological needs are largely satisfied, an individual becomes motivated by his needs for safety and security, which may stem from either an unstable emotional or physical environment. Full of anxiety about the chaos perceived to surround them, insecure individuals may become preoccupied with a concern for predictability and control. Knutson has hypothesized that the need to impose a pattern or design on the phenomena surrounding him moves the individual toward rigid and dogmatic beliefs and a general intolerance of ambiguity (1972: 28–29).

Safety also becomes a central concern to insecure individuals as reflected in their special sensitivity to environmental cues that can be perceived as threatening. Further, feeling his environment to be hostile and unresponsive to his needs for order and safety, persons with unfulfilled security needs are likely to be characterized by feelings of helplessness and dependency. In Maslow's words, safety needs are likely to "find specific expression in a search for a protector or a stronger person on whom they can depend" (1970: 42).

Unlike the measure of self-esteem, attempts to locate individuals on Maslow's need hierarchy have not been guided by consistent, reliable, or valid measures. The scale used in the Twin Cities survey was devised by Sullivan and associates. Respondents were asked to choose from a list of eleven values[6] the one that was the most important to them. In keeping with our emphasis on the distinction between security and insecurity, the need hierarchy was collapsed into a dichotomous scale.

DEPENDENT VARIABLES

The measures of candidate evaluation used in the Twin Cities study were based on questions that asked the respondent to rate their least-preferred presidential candidates. Recall that in 1976 the field of possible candidates, before the party nominations, consisted of two Republicans—Ford and Reagan—and six Democrats—Carter, Harris, Humphrey, Jackson, Udall, and Wallace. Respondents were asked which candidates they "would *least* want to become president" and "would make the *worst* president (author's emphasis)." Subsequently, subjects were asked to rate their last-choice candidates on a series of nine seven-point semantic differential scales which were designed to capture the connotative aspects of candidate image related to personal, not party or issue, factors.

Our measures of candidate evaluation contain a number of advantages that recommend their use as well as several disadvantages that recommend caution. Most important among their benefits is that our measures are capable of producing more general results. Findings of studies which require subjects to rate each individual candidate are severely limited to specific candidates in specific election years. Our generic measures, on the other hand, are more generalizable to "anti-ideal" presidential candidates, regardless of the particular election or participants.

Our generic measures are not without their drawbacks, however. First, it may be difficult to assess the impact of image determination on anti-ideal candidate ratings. If, for instance, one or two candidates are over-represented in the last-choice categories, it is not always possible to determine the extent to which the ratings are truly generic or actually depend on a particular candidate. Second, and more importantly, these generic measures could minimize the extent of individual differences in candidate perception. Respondents are more likely to agree in their ratings of their least preferred candidates (for example, by alloting uniformly negative ratings) due to cultural uniformities in their judgments of the candidates they select. This means that because our measures should suppress the incidence of individual differences, any variation which we do find is significant.

Last-choice ratings contained substantial variation, indicating marked individual differences in the way anti-ideal candidates were perceived. The category frequencies for the good-bad scale are representative of the pattern of responses for the other eight differentials.

Category	Good	1	2	3	4	5	6	7	Bad	$\overline{X} = 4.3$
Frequency		17	23	25	68	39	33	30		$SD = 1.7$
Percentage		7	10	11	29	16	14	13		

The distribution is clearly skewed toward the negative end of the scale, with 43% of the responses falling in "bad" categories (5 to 7) and only 28% falling in favorable categories (1 to 3). These findings are in contrast to Sears and Whitney's (1973) studies which reported a "positivity bias" in the evaluations of most political figures. Apparently, when respondents are free to choose from a broad range of candidates, they are not nearly so generous in their evaluations. One immediate benefit of studying last-choice candidates is that the wide variation in ratings enhances the statistical properties of our dependent measures of candidate evaluation.

HYPOTHESES

The review of the literature leads us to expect a voter's self-estimate and security needs to figure importantly in his perception and evaluation of anti-ideal presidential candidates. Before stating the hypotheses, it is important to note that these personality traits can affect our measures of candidate evaluation in two general ways. A voter's personality may either motivate him to *select* systematically particular types of candidates as his least-preferred choice or, once selected, candidates may be differentially *perceived* by various personality types.

Individuals with a poor self-estimate should be motivated by their feelings of helplessness, vulnerability, anxiety, and futility—feeling lost in the political world and powerless to change it. Wanting to be protected from both the world's and their own inadequacies, we might expect them to fault their last-choice for being too weak, inexperienced, or unimportant. Because they tend to project their self-contempt onto others, they are expected to be most critical of their last-choice, possibly describing a candidate who might take advantage of their vulnerability. They are thus expected to be more likely to attribute such traits as dishonesty and malevolence to their least-preferred presidential candidate, than will persons with high self-regard.

The dispositional makeup of insecure persons leads to similar hypotheses. Individuals typified by unfulfilled security needs are likely to extend their search for a protector to the political realm in an attempt to alleviate feelings of dependency and helplessness. The candidate who represents the "worst" president therefore is likely to be seen as weak, inexperienced, and unable to fulfill their needs for a strong and decisive leader. Candidates who are perceived to represent a threat to the insecure individual's social or political order on which they have come to depend are likely to be considered dangerous. Finally, candidate ratings are also expected to be influenced by this person's tendency to possess relatively dogmatic belief systems and to be intolerant of ambiguity. The need to establish cognitive order is expected to push him to make simplistic, "black-and-white" distinctions in judging his last-choice. The insecure individual is therefore likely to attribute consistently negative traits to his least-preferred presidential candidate.

The effect of personality is not hypothesized to be equally important under all conditions. In general, the prediction of an individual's behavior is most directly tied to his personality when he is psychically engaged (Knutson, 1972: 22–25). Consequently, certain political factors may either inhibit or enhance the involvement of the syndromes of low self-esteem and insecurity. For example, extensive involvement in the political arena may indicate the importance an individual places on the outcome of political contests and the extent to which they are aware of the stakes involved. Therefore, it may be expected that a voter's personality will tend to be more important in their perception of a candidate if they are highly interested in politics.

Party preference and ideology may also lead to an enhanced effect of personality by structuring the conditions of threat which activate an individual's psychological dispositions. For example, radical candidates are more likely to be politically and psychologically threatening to a conservative who is insecure. It can be seen that an additional reason for looking at anti-ideal presidential candidates is that an individual's personality should be especially relevant for perception, for it is exactly these candidates who are likely to be perceived as threatening.

SOCIAL AND POLITICAL CORRELATES OF PERSONALITY

Because political perception occurs in a broader social and political context, it is important to examine the ways in which the dimensions of personality interact with these variables. Both personality scales are expected to covary with various social and political variables. Sniderman (1975), McClosky (1958), and others have found that persons with lower self-estimates tend to occupy lower positions in the status hierarchy. Also, various authors have found that persons with low self-esteem tend to be less efficacious and less interested in politics as well as more conservative.

Similarly, Knutson (1972) has pointed out that persons fixated at lower need levels are more likely to be found in lower socioeconomic areas typified by economic deprivation and unstable family and environmental conditions. In addition, due to their inability to control their environment and fulfill their needs, these individuals are expected to be less efficacious and less involved in politics. Finally, based on Knutson's explication of the syndrome of insecurity, one would expect these individuals to share a general resistance toward change—a characteristic of many traditional conservative ideologies (1970: 28–30).

Pearson correlations (not presented) between the personality measures and political (party identification, interest in politics, and ideology) and social (education and age) variables for respondents in the Twin Cities survey are of moderate magnitude and in the theoretically expected direction.[7] These results indicate a degree of content validity for the personality scales. More importantly, the correlations clearly demonstrate the need to include social and political variables in a multivariate model to isolate the independent effects of personality on candidate perception. Most of our analysis employs a multiple regression technique which allows us to evaluate the relative effect of personality on candidate perception vis-à-vis social and political variables. In addition, when further analysis indicates that the independent variables exert an *indirect* as well as a direct effect on candidate evaluation, we employ a path analytic technique.

RESULTS

The least squares partial beta coefficients, which express the effect of the two personality measures on the last-choice candidate evaluation scales while controlling for social and political factors, are presented in Table 7.1. As can be seen, with very few exceptions, the relations are weak and lack significance, a finding which might imply that any association between personality and perception would be spurious and without theoretical importance.

TABLE 7.1   Partial Beta Coefficients for Personality Measures and Semantic Adjective Pairs for Least-liked Candidates (controlling for social and political variables)

Semantic Pairs	Self-esteem		Security	
	Beta	Sign.	Beta	Sign.
Democratic–Undemocratic	−.110	.145	.046	.539
Experienced–Inexperienced	.025	.741	−.104	.170
Good–Bad	−.094	.209	.101	.181
Honest–Dishonest	−.029	.707	.003	.971
Important–Unimportant	.153	.042	−.081	.280
Pleasant–Unpleasant	−.253	.001	.034	.644
Predictable–Unpredictable	.191	.011	−.057	.446
Safe–Dangerous	−.102	.177	−.009	.907
Strong–Weak	.207	.006	−.049	.509

Tentatively, we can offer several explanations. For one, the generic categories used in the Twin Cities survey have the property of maximizing the effect of candidate image and, conversely, of minimizing the individual differences btween perceivers. Since the last-choice group includes eight different candidates (stimulus objects), the perceivers are responding to a wide array of possibly conflicting cues which may attenuate the systematic effects of personality. Another explanation for the unimpressive findings can be derived from psychological theory. It was hypothesized that the effects of personality should be enhanced under conditions of threat. One potential disadvantage of our generic measures is that they allow respondents great leeway in selecting their perceptual objects. Therefore, a number of voters selecting candidates who pose little threat are not expected to be psychologically engaged. Thus, their psychological dispositions may have little bearing on their perceptions of the candidates.

Both of these difficulties can be at least partially remedied by disaggregating the last-choice candidates into categories that are homogeneous enough to reduce the effects of image determinism and that enable us to isolate those candidates (or clusters of candidates) that are of a potentially threatening nature to the respondents. Unfortunately, insufficient numbers of subjects selected most of the candidates to permit us to examine each attitude object individually; there is, however, sound theoretical justification for breaking last-choice candidates into party clusters.

There is a strong (albeit predictable) relation between last-choice selection and party identification. Consistently, respondents chose candidates of the opposite political party who may be threatening for policy or psychological reasons. In addition to the threat posed by candidates who adopt issue positions that are discrepant from a voter's own policy preferences, candidates of the opposite party may also challenge the psychological identifications and affective allegiances that bind many voters to a political party. It will be argued subsequently that individuals react adversely in different ways to candidates of the two parties and that by disaggregating the candidates by partisan affiliation, the interaction between personality, party, and perception can be discerned. It is for these reasons that the models discussed below are presented for Democratic last-choice candidates (without Wallace, whom we felt was sufficiently unique to warrant exclusion) and for last-choice GOP contestants.[8]

Before considering the causal models for these two candidate clusters, it is necessary to describe how the following examples have been selected. For many of the semantic scales used, the relation between personality and the dependent variable was reduced to insignificance when controlling for social and political variables. Because this research is primarily suggestive, it is our intention merely to demonstrate certain conditions under which personality factors may become operative. As such, our selection of illustrative models and the appropriate dependent variable (i.e., semantic adjective) was guided by both convincing statistical results and the theoretical importance of the stimulus cue to the psychological model. Fortunately, both of these considerations pointed to use of the same examples, for most theoretically predictable associations were also the most statistically impressive, a fact which enables us to place a reasonable degree of theoretical confidence in our results. Thus, Maslow's need hierarchy scale will be presented in conjunction with the "dangerous-safe" scale, a variable that we argued would be of central importance to those who lack certain basic security needs. The self-esteem inventory, on the other hand, will be illustrated via the "strong-weak" dimension, a cue to which those with a poor self-image and strong feelings of vulnerability should be especially sensitive.

The multiple regression equation for those respondents ($N = 51$) who designated Democratic candidates as their last choice (Wallace omitted) using the security scale and the safe-dangerous adjective pair is estimated below. The coefficients are standardized regression coefficients with respective t-values in parentheses.

$$\begin{array}{llll} \text{Evaluation} & = 2.58 & - \quad .50 \text{ (Security)} - & .08 \text{ (Age)} + & .13 \text{ (Education)} \\ \text{(Safe-dangerous)} & (1.33) & (-2.76) & (-.476) & (.384) \end{array}$$

$$\begin{array}{lll} - & .02 \text{ (Ideology)} + & .21 \text{ (Interest)} + & .25 \text{ (Party ID)} \\ & (-.013) & (.225) & (1.3) \end{array}$$

The most important point about this equation, for our purposes, is the healthy correlation between security and the dependent variable. The negative regression coefficient indicates that those who are insecure are substantially more likely to see the last-choice Democratic candidates as dangerous, regardless of age, education, party, or interest. As we expected, it appears that individuals lower in the need hierarchy are more threatened by these anti-ideal presidential candidates.

These findings are easily explained by Maslow's theory of psychic motivation. It will be recalled that insecure persons who resist change may be characterized by a traditional conservatism that is psychological. Naturally, these individuals have ample political and psychological motives for being critical of the liberal Democrats in this study. A majority of the candidates in their political careers have been associated with big spending, New Deal economic policies that call for higher taxation. In addition, many have been associated with progressive social reforms or "dovish" stands on foreign policy. Thus, in challenging the status quo, liberal Democrats may be perceived to be a disruptive threat to the stable social, economic, and legal order on which the insecure individual has come to depend. Political threats may constitute psychological threats to this person's most basic needs for security, stability, and material well-being. This psychological explanation is bolstered by the fact that insecure individuals, in rating these Democrats as dangerous, appear to be threatened by them, increasing the likelihood that their need for security will be activated.[9]

We find at least partial support for the hypothesis that persons motivated by security needs will tend to evaluate candidates in black-and-white terms. Insecure individuals are also more likely to see last-choice Democrats as being bad, unpleasant, dishonest, and undemocratic. There is little evidence, however, of an inclination to generalize these negative evaluations to perceptions of weakness or inexperience. Most likely, the imposition of the clear-cut image of political strength of some of the Democrats in the study—notably Humphrey in his home state—tends to discourage perceptions of weakness.

In conclusion, it is important to note that neither the political nor the social variables exert a significant direct impact on candidate evaluation. Moreover, this same pattern tends to hold for several other adjective pairs on which last-choice Democrats were judged. In other words, vis-à-vis more traditional explanations of candidate perception, psychological factors appear to be quite important determinants.

In Figure 7.1, we turn to an analysis of the effect of self-esteem on the strong-weak dimension for those selecting Republican last-choice candidates. The coefficients are path coefficients while their significance levels are in parentheses. The final model was specified by estimating an exactly identified model and omitting all paths which were both statistically insignificant *and* theoretically unimportant. Thus, the insignificant paths retained in our final model are those that our theoretical perspective had predicted to be important.[10] Age is an exogenous variable in the model; its impact on education is clearly generational, as younger respondents have received more years of formal education than older voters. The model assumes that the two social variables are causally prior to personality and that personality may determine partisan identification and political interest. This means that personality may affect candidate evaluation either directly or indirectly through political variables. It is necessary to note that path coefficients have been corrected for the measured unreliability of the self-esteem inventory (alpha = .756). Tangentially, it may be noted that the party variable does not appear in this model because of its lack of variation in this subsample; those selecting GOP candidates were overwhelmingly Democratic and, hence, no relations emerged between party and other variables within the model.

Age and interest significantly affect the dependent variable directly in such a way that those who tend to perceive the candidates as stronger are generally older and less interested in politics. These results are consistent with the generally naive conception with which these groups view the presidency—an exaggeration of the powers and capabilities of the office. Perhaps these impressions are carried over to the contestants as well. But what is remarkable about the dependent variable is the degree to which it is influenced by self-esteem. Individuals with low self-esteem are substantially more likely to perceive the last-choice candidates as weak than those with higher levels of self-regard. This relation is especially true of those with poor self-images who are also uninterested in politics, a finding which can be shown by comparing the positive direct relationship between personality and strong-weak with the negative indirect effect of self-esteem through the interest variable ($-.272$).

The relation between personality and perception is of sufficient magnitude to offer caveats regarding its interpretation. For one, we are dealing with only 44 cases, a sample size small enough to capitalize on chance relationships. Further, the reliability of the self-esteem inventory (as measured by alpha) is an estimate of the lower bounds of its true reliability. As such, adjustment of the path coefficients is a correction for the maximum possible level of unreliability and tends to overcorrect the measurement error. The product, in other words, may be betas which are slightly too high. It should also be clear that beta values are unbounded by ± 1.0 and that a coefficient of .923 in no way represents an almost perfect association. Finally, only those associations that included the psychological variable have been corrected, thereby inflating somewhat the importance of self-esteem vis-à-vis other variables.

Despite the caution with which the relationship must be interpreted, it is worthwhile to note that self-esteem clearly exerts the most powerful influence on perception. Not only is its direct effect far stronger than that of any other specified variable, but its total causal effect (see Table 7.2) of .632 is

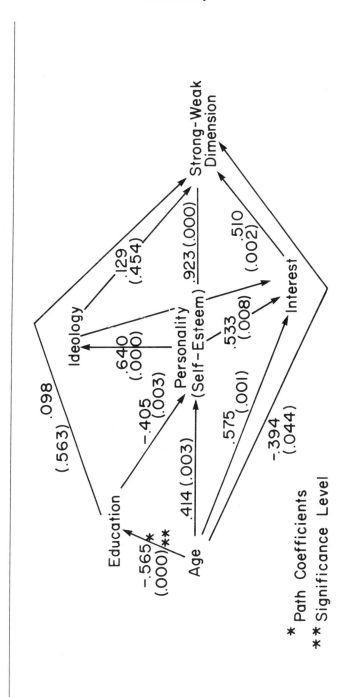

FIGURE 7.1 Path Model for Self-Esteem and Strong-Weak Dimension, Last-Choice Republican Candidates

substantially stronger than that of its nearest rival, age (.250). Moreover, Table 7.2 indicates that self-esteem also mediates the effects of the social variables in a nontrivial way. Despite the tendency for older people to perceive their candidates as stronger, the data indicate that those with low self-estimates, regardless of age, tend to perceive the candidate as weaker.

TABLE 7.2   Disaggregation of Path Effects for Self-esteem Model with Last-choice
Republican Candidates: Strong-weak Adjective Pair

Age	Indirect Impact	Direct Impact	Total Impact
Direct		−.394	
Indirect via S.E.	.406		
Total Indirect	.644		
Total			.250
Education			
Direct		.098	
Indirect via S.E.	−.256		
Total Indirect	−.256		
Total			−.158
Ideology			
Total			−.029
Interest			
Total			.510
Self-esteem			
Direct		.923	
Indirect via Ideology	−.019		
Indirect via Interest	−.272		
Total Indirect	−.291		
Total			.632

Figure 7.1, then, seems to support strongly the hypothesis that individuals with poor self-estimates tend to evaluate their last-choice candidates as weaker, perhaps because of their feelings of vulnerability and their preference for a protective figure.

Yet, Figure 7.2, which displays the self-esteem variable in the context of last-choice Democratic candidates, casts some doubt on a simple, monotonic relation between personality and social perception. Among those who liked Republicans the least, the relationship between personality and perception is positive, while among individuals who select a Democrat as least-liked, the tendency is for those with a low self-estimate to evaluate the candidates as stronger (i.e., a negative relation). It would appear that feelings of vulnerability, anxiety, and insecurity that characterize these individuals do not necessarily lead to perceptions of weakness in all perceptual objects which are disliked.

Several alternatives to the vulnerability hypothesis can be offered for the effect of personality that can adequately account for the seemingly contra-

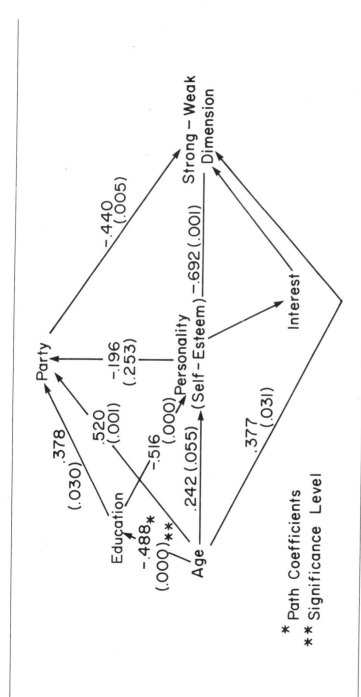

FIGURE 7.2   Path Model for Self-Esteem and Strong-Weak Dimension, Last-Choice Democratic Candidates

dictory evidence in the Democratic model. One explanation for the mirror-image pattern found for the weak-strong dimension is ideological. It is possible that many individuals attached policy connotations to the terms, such that strong is synonymous with concepts such as active, big government, strong federal executive, and New Deal liberalism. Weak, of course, would connote antithetical concepts. Thus, those selecting Democrats, most of whom are conservative Republicans, may dislike their choice because he is too strong and powerful as a political policy-maker. Conversely, the more liberal Democrats who selected Republicans may be criticizing these candidates for their weakness or restraint in policy matters. If the notion of psychic engagement or intimidation is valid, those who are lowest in self-esteem may be threatened most by those who are of an opposing ideology.

One final interpretation of the data can be deduced from McGuire's (1968) interactive theory of susceptibility to persuasion, which holds that self-esteem (due to its positive relation to intelligence) will be directly related to reception of a persuasive communication, but inversely related to yielding to the message (because of esteem's relation to ego strength). Thus, individuals low in self-estimate should be most susceptible to relatively simple and unambiguous messages—that they will be able to comprehend—and unsubstantiated and unconfirmed communications—to which they are likely to yield.[11] The tendencies of the culture—facilitated by the media—to typecast political figures in a way that is both simplistic and unsubstantiated may therefore be most effective on individuals with a lower-than-normal self-image. The popular image of the Republican party in 1976 was undoubtedly one of weakness and inexperience, especially in the Twin Cities area, then a bastion of Democratic liberalism. Further, Ford and Reagan, as the GOP candidates, were widely perceived as neither experienced nor effectual politicians, again especially in the Twin Cities area. In contrast, those who evaluated Democratic last-choice candidates (36% of whom selected Humphrey) were rating candidates with an almost objectively powerful image. Clearly, the popular image of Humphrey in his home state, even among his enemies, was of an experienced, well respected, and effectual legislator. In sum, it appears that those lowest in self-esteem are most likely to be susceptible to the popular, exaggerated images of the presidential candidates.

Thus, the data support the notion that personality can be a potent determinant of sociopolitical perception and, further, that its influence is not spurious with either social or political factors. Although we have had to exercise a degree of post hoc exploration, and although psychological theory is unable to specify the exact mechanisms by which these personality variables affect perceptual judgment, the results that we have obtained are theoretically plausible and even predictable, given the previous efforts of personality researchers.

SUMMARY AND IMPLICATIONS

At the outset, several goals were spelled out that we can now discuss with the benefit of our data. It has been our intention to ascertain the importance of the personality variable in last-choice candidate perception, vis-à-vis social and political factors and also to suggest various ways in which personality might operate in shaping candidate perception. From the preceding discussion of the findings, several generalizations are warranted. Most importantly, a voter's personality proved to be an important source of variation in the perception of presidential candidates. For both partisan clusters and for different adjective pairs, the impact of personality remained significant despite statistical controls for social and political variables. In fact, in all three of the models presented, personality had the most powerful direct impact on last-choice candidate evaluation, being more important than a variety of social and political variables that have traditionally concerned researchers in the area of political perception. In the case of self-esteem, personality also had the most powerful indirect impact on candidate evaluation.

Second, it is worth noting that the importance of the psychological variables is limited to a specific set of "threat" conditions and semantic scales. Although self-esteem and security appear to operate in fundamentally different ways, neither emerged as significant until the candidates were disaggregated into partisan clusters. While it is speculative to link ideological threat to psychological threat, it can be inferred that a candidate who offers to upset an individual's social, economic, or moral order has the capacity to activate a corresponding sense of psychological threat. Thus, the former may constitute one necessary but not sufficient condition for an individual's personality to influence his perception of political candidates.

It has been shown, too, that different stimulus cues are more important for different dimensions of personality. Even though personality is not significant across the board, the conditions under which it is important are both theoretically plausible and consistent with expectations. Although we cannot say, categorically, that personality is more important than other independent variables in all situations, it does appear to be an important form of perceiver variation that, in many cases, may help to paint a more lucid portrait of the causal processes which underlie candidate perception.

Further, although it has not been our intention to assess the relative merits of the stimulus versus perceiver debate, our findings shed some additional light on the controversy. The data tend to confirm the conclusion that both perspectives are important sources of the images that voters hold of the candidates. For example, it was suggested that a voter's low self-esteem did not lead him to perceive all least-liked candidates as weak. Rather, the disposition led to an acceptance of an exaggerated and simplistic image projected by the two parties. The images of the candidates thus appear to be the product of both the stimulus (what is "out there") as well as the perceiver's predilections (what is "in their heads").

Finally, it is of consequence that the "positivity bias" found by Sears is clearly not generalizable to all political stimuli, for we have encountered considerable negative evaluation in the perception of least-favored candidates. This finding undoubtedly reflects both the post-Watergate cynicism and the methodology employed, and the consequences for system legitimacy may be significant.

Our conclusions must be tempered with several methodological and theoretical caveats. Of particular consequence statistically, the path coefficients of the three causal models were estimated from samples containing as few as 44 to 51 cases with as many as five independent variables. As indicated, multiple regression analysis, with so few degrees of freedom, may inflate the estimates of the coefficients, so that the results must be interpreted with caution. There are also theoretical problems which, once again, should be noted. Most importantly, our use of data which were originally collected with other research goals in mind naturally hampered our ability to test definitively many of our hypotheses. Consequently, many of the explanations affixed to our findings were necessarily post hoc and somewhat speculative, often making it difficult to choose decisively between several competing explanations of a single finding. Given, however, the lack of prior theoretical and empirical work in the area, this research has covered fresh ground in an important but neglected area of candidate image. As such, the approach to the problem and the analysis reported here constitute a promising basis for future studies in candidate image and personality.

NOTES

1. Psychological scaling analyses have replicated these results. See, for instance, Nygren and Jones (1977) and Shikiar (1974).

2. It has also been reported (DeSoto et al., 1960) that high-F scorers are more likely than low scorers to attribute threatening characteristics to others. Further, there exists a literature which deals with the relation between authoritarianism and the ability to predict another's F-scale scores (Crockett and Meidinger, 1956; Rabinowitz, 1956; Scodel and Friedman, 1956; Scodel and Mussen, 1953; Simons, 1966).

3. Unfortunately, there has not been sufficient research to establish the linkage between the self-esteem syndrome and person perception. Most of the work to date is largely suggestive and often contradictory. For a review of the literature, see Shrauger and Altrocchi (1964).

4. Sniderman (1975: 12–15) [including notes].

5. Among the most important reasons for making the scale dichotomous are Maslow's conclusions that: (1) There exists a major character difference between secure and insecure individuals (1970: 66–67); and (2) there exists a greater correspondence between character traits and resulting behavior for lower needs because they are more imperative for sheer survival and are less confounded by associative behavior and non-basic needs (1970: 78–83).

6. The eleven values and their correspondence to need levels are: (1) Wealth and comfortable life correspond to physiological needs; (2) family security and national security to safety and security needs; (3) affection and true friendship to affiliative needs; (4) self-respect and social recognition to esteem needs; and (5) independence, wisdom, and beauty to actualization needs.

7. Education is measured in years; ideology is measured as self-placement along a liberal-conservative dimension; and political interest response categories are: "not very interested," "somewhat interested," and "very interested" in politics.

8. Unfortunately, omitting respondents who selected Wallace ($N = 128$) from the analysis diminished the size of the sample considerably. It should be mentioned that personality differences did emerge on several semantic scales for those who selected Wallace as their least-preferred candidate. These results, however, were considered less representative of the general trend found for the other candidates and, thus, are not presented, due to space limitations.

9. It might also be argued that insecure persons are responding to a purely political threat, since security, as measured here, might connote social and political conventionalism. Insecure respondents were those who tended to choose more conventional life values (wealth, physical comfort, family security, or national security). This explanation, however, is less plausible in light of the low correlation between the personality measure and the ideological self-placement scale in the full sample ($r = -.157$) and for those who selected Democrats ($r = -.18$).

10. An additional reason for including the insignificant paths to the dependent variable was to allow the examination of the relative importance of various direct paths to the dependent variable.

11. This literature on self-esteem and susceptibility to influence is reviewed by Sears and Abeles (1969).

PART IV: THE SUBSTANCE OF PUBLIC OPINION

8

POLITICAL TOLERANCE: AN OVERVIEW AND SOME NEW FINDINGS

James Piereson
John L. Sullivan
George Marcus

THE CONCEPT OF POLITICAL TOLERANCE

Tolerance implies a willingness "to put up with" those things that one rejects. Politically, it implies a willingness to permit the expression of those interests or ideas that one opposes. A tolerant regime, then, like a tolerant person, is one that allows a wide berth to those ideas that challenge its way of life.[1]

In a narrower political sense, tolerance is associated with procedural fairness. An important element of liberal political theory is its emphasis on the distinction between the substantive issues of political conflicts and the procedural rules by which they are resolved. Though liberal regimes may be divided by fierce conflicts, they can remain stable if there is a general attachment to the rules of democratic or constitutional procedure, which are assumed to be above the normal give-and-take of politics. Tolerance in this sense implies a commitment to the "rules of the game" and a willingness to apply these rules on an equal basis to all, regardless of their opinions. A person is therefore tolerant to the extent that he is prepared to extend such procedural guarantees—the right to speak, to publish, to run for office—to those with whom he disagrees. Similarly, a fully tolerant regime would be one in which such norms are in fact applied equally to all.[2]

We should observe at the outset, then, that tolerance implies opposition or disagreement. If there is no opposition or disagreement, there is no occasion for tolerance. The problem does not arise, since it is pointless to ask someone to tolerate a doctrine toward which he is indifferent or of which he approves. The problem of tolerance only arises when there are grounds for real disagreement; what one proceeds to do at this point determines whether or not he or she is tolerant or intolerant.

It follows that tolerance means something different than the mere absence of prejudice. The terms intolerance and prejudice are often used interchangeably, as if a prejudiced person must necessarily be intolerant. This need not be so. Such a person may in fact be very tolerant, if he understands his prejudices and proceeds to permit the expression of those ideas or interests toward which he is prejudiced. As Bernard Crick (1973: 64) observed, "Toleration need not imply the absence of prejudice but only its constraint and limitation." The attempt to eliminate prejudice in society is thus not an attempt to create a tolerant society, but rather an attempt to create one in which certain kinds of disagreements do not arise. In a sense, tolerance is applicable to a political situation that is something less than ideal. Controversies exist and people disagree for whatever reasons. Since these cannot be eliminated without calling other values into question, people are urged to be tolerant. They are urged to agree to disagree.

We will not address the questions of whether tolerance is desirable or undesirable and whether or not it is a "fundamental" principle of democracy. These questions are already sufficiently controversial, and were made even more so in the past few years by the debate surrounding the attempt of Nazis to march on a Jewish suburb of Chicago.[3] There is no doubt that citizens in a democracy must be prepared to tolerate some degree of opposition, since democracy is defined to some extent by the existence of a legitimate opposition. Thus, in the United States, Democrats, when they are in power, must tolerate Republicans, and vice versa. But how tolerant are citizens obliged to be of extremist groups on either the right or the left, such as Nazis or communists?

There are different and conflicting answers. Some believe that while citizens are obliged to tolerate groups and ideas that fall within the liberal consensus, they are not obliged to tolerate groups that deny the principles upon which this consensus is based. If successful, such groups would proceed to dismantle the apparatus of procedural liberties by which they came to power. There is thus a "paradox of tolerance," so to speak, which suggests that some degree of intolerance is required to defend the principle of tolerance. Others, contesting this view, argue that democracy requires procedural neutrality toward all political groups, so that citizens, as well as the government itself, should be tolerant of all groups so long as they follow legal and constitutional methods of opposition. The test of any group's legitimacy is its ability to mobilize a significant following through the "free market of ideas." Advocates of this view fear that if extremist groups are denied procedural rights that are given to groups in the mainstream, the majority in power will eventually define all opposition to its wishes as illegitimate. Thus, in the long-run, the existence of *any* opposition requires a high degree of tolerance for *all* opposition.

As these arguments are highly normative and ideological, they cannot be settled through an empirical inquiry of the kind that will be undertaken below. This being so, the abstract questions of the desirability or undesirability of tolerance and of the relation between tolerance and democracy must be left open. What, then, can we learn from an empirical study of tolerance? First, we can learn something about the levels of tolerance and intolerance in the society and about the kinds of groups that citizens are or are not prepared to tolerate. Second, we can uncover those factors which contribute to a tolerant or an intolerant outlook. Finally, from such findings we can draw inferences about how the political process either maintains or undermines tolerant attitudes and practices.

POLITICAL TOLERANCE AND AMERICAN POLITICS: THE EMPIRICAL LITERATURE

Because of the theoretical importance of tolerance, it has been the subject of several empirical studies since the development of survey research a generation ago. These studies, insofar as they deal with the United States, have tried to assess the extent to which Americans support the principles of tolerance and, on the basis of these findings, to assess the condition of American democracy itself. Three seminal studies were conducted during the 1950s: Stouffer's (1955) study of attitudes toward communists, socialists, and atheists; the Prothro-Grigg (1960) study of support for the "fundamental principles of democracy"; and McClosky's (1964) study of the differences between political elites and nonelites in their support for democratic norms. More recently, owing to a renewed interest in the subject during the 1970s, Davis (1975) and Nunn et al. (1978) published studies updating Stouffer's original findings and traced the changes that have occurred in the levels of tolerance in the society since the 1950s.

There is a sense in which these studies represent a single tradition of research in the area, since all incorporate in one way or another the assumptions originally made by Stouffer in his seminal study. Hence, one tends to find common problems of conceptualization in all of them. The most serious problem in these studies, from our standpoint, is that all tried to measure tolerance in relation to extremist groups on the left, usually communists, socialists, or atheists. Thus, by preselecting the targets for respondents, these investigators did not guarantee that all respondents were able to select groups to which they had a real objection. We shall develop the consequences of this procedure as we proceed.

The earliest systematic study of tolerance in the United States was Stouffer's (1955) analysis of public attitudes toward communism and communists, titled *Communism, Conformity, and Civil Liberties.* Based on a large national survey conducted in 1954, the study was designed to measure public attitudes toward communism and the extent to which Americans were prepared to extend procedural rights to communists and suspected communists, as well as to other "fellow-travellers" on the left. Although his study purported to study tolerance of "nonconformity," all but fifteen items used to measure tolerance listed communists or suspected communists as points of reference.[4] The conclusions of his study, therefore, bear more closely upon tolerance of communists than upon tolerance more broadly understood.

Nonetheless, his findings were important and quite disturbing. Clear majorities said that an admitted communist should not be permitted to speak publicly or to teach in high schools or colleges, or, indeed, to work as a clerk in a store (Stouffer, 1955: Ch. 2). Majorities also agreed that communists should have their citizenship revoked, that books written by communists should be taken out of public libraries, that the government should have the authority to tap personal telephone conversations to acquire evidence against communists, and that, withal, admitted communists should be thrown in jail. These attitudes softened considerably when the same questions were posed in relation to socialists, atheists, and those merely suspected of being communists. However, large proportions of respondents were also intolerant of these targets. The results undermined the assumption held by many that there exists a consensus in the society around procedural norms that allows extremist groups access to political institutions.

In addition to mapping these public attitudes, Stouffer also attempted to discern those factors most closely associated with the acceptance of tolerant or intolerant norms. Two of the most important were education and political involvement. Education, in particular, was strongly related to his measure of tolerance, so that the higher one's level of education, the more likely one was to be tolerant. Education, he argued, exposes citizens to a greater range of opinions and gives them the ability to evaluate information (1955: Ch. 4). Hence, to the extent that intolerance is based on fear of the unknown and conclusions drawn from false information, education forms a more tolerant outlook. This conclusion has been replicated in virtually every subsequent study of tolerance (see Prothro and Grigg, 1960; Jackman, 1972; Nunn et al., 1978: Ch. 4).

Perhaps Stouffer's most important finding from the standpoint of democratic theory was that political elites tended to be more tolerant than a national cross-section of nonelites. By nearly every measure, political influentials were more likely than rank-and-file citizens to recognize the procedural claims of these dissenting groups. This finding implied that the functioning of a democratic system may depend more on the acceptance of the "rules of the game" among elites than among citizens at large, since the latter do not participate in the day-to-day life of politics.

In addition to education and political involvement, Stouffer also discovered several other variables that were related to tolerance of nonconformity (as he understood it). Women, for example, tended to be less tolerant than men (1955: Ch. 6), and this relation between gender and tolerance held up when controls were introduced for education, occupation, place of residence, and religiosity. Despite the strength of this relation, however, Stouffer was unable to explain these consistent differences between men and women. Religiosity, or the strength of religious attachments, was also related to tolerance (1955: Ch. 6), as those who attended church regularly tended to be much less tolerant than those who did not. Stouffer did not investigate the relation between religious affiliation and tolerance, but Nunn and his associates (1978: 129) have reanalyzed Stouffer's data and have found that, in 1954, Jews and the religiously unaffiliated were more tolerant of these particular groups than either Catholics or Protestants.

Stouffer acknowledged at several points throughout his book that he was not studying tolerance as a general attitude but rather tolerance for the particular groups mentioned in his questionnaire. For example, he says at one point:

> Let us continually keep in mind the fact that we are not here measuring tolerance, in general. Rather, we are measuring willingness to grant certain rights to people whose views might be disapproved, such as the right to speak, the right to hold certain kinds of jobs, etc. The kinds of people used as test cases are Socialists, Atheists, Communists, and people whose loyalty has been criticized but who avow they were never Communists. We are not measuring willingness to tolerate other kinds of people whose views may be disliked [1955: 111].

This caveat was certainly warranted. Nevertheless, his warning has been generally ignored by those who have tried to build upon his study. Thus, many people have interpreted his conclusions as bearing on tolerance as a general phenomenon rather than tolerance for these particular groups—an error for which Stouffer perhaps should not be blamed. It is well to remember, however, that Stouffer claimed that he was studying "tolerance for nonconformity," seemingly a more general attribute than that suggested by the quotation above.

Stouffer tried to assess the extent to which Americans were prepared to extend procedural liberties to unpopular political groups. In subsequent studies, Prothro and Grigg (1960) and McClosky (1964) formulated the problem somewhat differently. They tried to find out if there existed a consensus in the United States around general procedural norms of democracy and minority rights and if citizens were prepared to apply these abstract principles to specific situations involving unpopular groups or individuals. In formulating the problem in this way, they were attempting to test a central proposition of modern democratic theory, which holds that a popular consensus for procedural norms is required for democratic systems to survive. Their investigations thus addressed three related though theoretically separable questions: (1) whether a consensus for abstract procedural norms existed in the United States; (2) whether citizens were prepared to apply these abstract norms to concrete situations involving controversial political groups or ideas, and (3) whether in fact a consensus for the abstract norms and some degree of consistency between these norms and actual practice are required to sustain a democratic polity.

The Prothro-Grigg study was based on samples drawn from two cities— Ann Arbor, Michigan and Tallahassee, Florida. The authors first presented respondents with a series of statements designed to abstractly express the "fundamental" principles of democracy, majority rule, and minority rights. For example, respondents were asked if they agreed that "democracy is the best form of government" or that "public officials should be chosen by majority decisions." These were then followed by a series of statements describing specific situations to which respondents were given the opportunity to apply these abstract principles. Among such statements were these: "If a communist were legally elected mayor of this city, the people should not allow him to take office." "If a person wanted make a speech in this city against churches and religion, he should be allowed to speak." As the authors put it, "these specific propositions are designed to embody the principles of majority rule and minority rights in such a clear fashion that a 'correct' or 'democratic' response can be deduced from endorsement of the general principles" (1960: 283).

As expected, they did find a general consensus on the abstract principles, but this consensus broke down on the specific applications of the norms, especially when they were applied to communists. On each of the abstract statements, over 90% of the respondents supported the democratic principle. However, with respect to the specific applications, the authors found very little consensus among their respondents. On all but three of the ten items designed to incorporate the abstract principles to specific situations, fewer than 75% of the respondents provided the democratic response. The authors also examined the relations between education and responses to these statements, and they found, as did Stouffer, that support for democratic principles increases with the level of education. In other words, the more highly educated respondents were most likely to apply the abstract norms to the specific situations. All told, then, their findings substantiated Stouffer's conclusion that there is an alarming lack of support for democratic procedural norms in the mass public and, to the extent that there is support for these norms, it comes from an elite segment of the population.

In a related study, McClosky (1964) compared political influentials and rank-and-file citizens in levels of support for the abstract principles of democracy and for the application of these principles to specific situations. He was thus concerned with a problem that Stouffer had initially raised—that of the difference in levels of tolerance between elites and nonelites. However, in focusing on the consistency between abstract principles and specific applications, he formulated the problem in a way similar to Prothro and Grigg. Among other propositions, he expected to find empirical support for the following:

That . . . the electorate exhibits greater support for general abstract statements of democratic belief than for their specific applications.

That the constituent ideas of American democratic ideology are principally held by the more "articulate" segments of the population, including the political influentials; and that people in these ranks will exhibit a more meaningful and far reaching consensus on democratic and constitutional values than will the general population.

That whatever increases the level of political articulateness—education, S.E.S., urban residence, intellectuality, political activity, etc.—strengthens consensus and support for American political ideology and institutions [1964: 362].

In testing these propositions, McClosky relied on data from national surveys of elites and the general electorate conducted in 1956 and 1958. As did Prothro and Grigg, he found a substantial gap between the proportion of respondents that endorsed the abstract principles and the proportion that was prepared to apply them in specific situations. In addition, the political influentials were more likely than the general electorate to support the application of these general principles to the specific situations that were described on the questionnaire. In short, he found substantial support for his initial hypotheses. He therefore concluded that "a large proportion of the electorate has failed to grasp certain of the underlying ideas and principles on which the American political system rests" (1964: 362).

There are several difficulties with these two studies that render their conclusions questionable. First, it seems unreasonable to declare that citizens are intolerant or undemocratic simply because they do not apply these abstract norms to concrete situations in a one-to-one fashion. These norms are meant to be general standards of action, not hard and fast rules. In addition, the questionnaire items that were used in these two studies often bring into play competing values, so that citizens are forced to choose among them. For example, one of the items that McClosky used as a "specific application" of the principle of free speech was the following: "A book that contains wrong political views cannot be a good book and does not deserve to be published." Presumably, one should disagree with this statement. However, it appears to contain at least three themes—whether or not there are "wrong" political views, whether a book that contains such views could be a good book, and whether or not such a book deserves to be published. Given its ambiguity, responses to this item are open to multiple interpretations. The following is one of the "specific applications" from the Prothro-Grigg study: "In a city referendum, only people who are well-informed about the problem being voted on should be allowed to vote." Again, respondents are required to disagree with this statement in order to consistently apply the abstract principle of majority rule and equality of access to influence. Yet the historic battles over literacy requirements and registration indicate that the principles expressed in this statement are controversial. Again, it is unfair to label respondents who disagree with this statement as "intolerant" or "undemocratic."

In addition, it is possible that their results would have been even more alarming, in their own terms, had they used a broader range of political groups as points of reference against which to measure support for democratic principles as they understood them. As in Stouffer's study, most of the groups specifically mentioned were leftist. McClosky's items tended to be very general even when he was trying to describe specific situations. Thus, his items rarely mentioned any specific political groups, and in the single case in which this occurred, "Communists" were referred to. Among the 5 items used to measure tolerance of minority views in the Prothro-Grigg study, 1 referred to a person making a speech against churches and religion, 1 to a person speaking in favor of government ownership of industry, 2 to a communist either making a speech or running for office, and 1 to a Negro running for mayor. Thus, 4 of these 5 items made reference to groups on the left and none made reference to comparable groups on the right. Had such groups been mentioned, the levels of tolerance found in their samples might have been much lower, since those hostile to the right but not the left would have been given a chance to express their intolerance. In a sense, then, their methods may have led them to overestimate the level of tolerance in the society, though they did not recognize this problem because they were concerned largely with the consistency between abstract beliefs and a few of their specific applications.

CHANGING LEVELS OF TOLERANCE, 1954-1978

The above studies were carried out and written during the peak of the cold war when the denial of procedural rights to communists and related groups was a major concern of those interested in civil liberties. In the meantime, the dimensions of political conflict have grown more complex, and challenges to the political consensus have come from varied sources, including civil rights activists, feminists, opponents of the war in Vietnam, advocates and opponents of legal abortion, and radicals and reactionaries of various persuasions. As the potential targets of intolerance have proliferated, it is no longer appropriate to consider tolerance solely by the treatment afforded communists and associated groups. At the same time, the ferment of the 1960s and 1970s may have created a more tolerant environment for dissent by broadening the range of political opinion in American society. For these reasons, the conclusions of these earlier studies have been reconsidered and updated.

The question of whether or not tolerance has in fact increased since Stouffer conducted his study in 1954 has been addressed in two recent studies. Davis (1975) attempted to test Stouffer's prediction that tolerance would increase as levels of education in the society increased and as the average age of the population declined. Drawing on a survey conducted by the National Opinion Research Center in 1971 that repeated several of Stouffer's items, he found a significant increase in levels of tolerance in the intervening seventeen years.[5] He attributed some of this to higher levels of education in the society and some of it to cohort replacement, but at the same time he found significantly higher levels of tolerance in 1971 among all cohort and educational groups. Thus, he concluded that the bulk of the change was due to unspecified "general trends" and a changed "climate of opinion" in the society that strengthened tolerant political norms.

Similarly, Nunn et al., (1978) measured changes in levels of tolerance by analyzing data from their own survey, conducted in 1973, that repeated the Stouffer items. Like Davis and others, they found a considerable increase in levels of tolerance between 1954 and the early 1970s. In their survey they found a 24% increase in those classified as "more tolerant" on an overall tolerance scale (see Nunn et al., 1978: Ch. 3). They concluded that while only 31% of the public could be classified as tolerant in 1954, fully 55% could be so classified by 1973 (Nunn et al., 1978: 51). These results are essentially the same as those reported by Erskine and Siegel (1975) who relied upon NORC surveys. According to Nunn and his associates, "the most important finding from our efforts to track trends in American tolerance is that citizens who are most supportive of civil liberties have emerged as the majority in our society—and they are not a 'silent majority' " (1978: 2). Nunn and colleagues go so far as to conclude that "Given the substantial increase in public support for democratic principles, the risk of demogogic takeover or the undermining of civil liberties is now less than it once was" (1978: 159). In drawing this conclusion, they go well beyond their empirical findings that there is now greater political tolerance for communists, socialists, and atheists. They have argued that tolerant norms are now more widely accepted and that support for democratic principles has increased as well.

As we have noted throughout this discussion, these generalizations rest on the assumption that tolerance for these particular groups is equivalent to tolerance as a more general belief, an assumption that Stouffer himself rejected. Given the dubious nature of this assumption, these conclusions regarding the changing levels of tolerance in America, as well as those arrived at by Stouffer, Prothro and Grigg, and McClosky regarding the determinants of tolerance, need to be reconsidered in the light of a more comprehensive understanding of the concept. In the next section, we shall set forth an alternate measure of political tolerance, one that is more consistent with the meaning of the concept as spelled out earlier in this paper. We shall then proceed to re-examine, in the light of this measure, some of the conclusions reached by this earlier tradition of research on tolerance.

A "CONTENT-CONTROLLED" MEASURE OF POLITICAL TOLERANCE

As was noted at the beginning of this chapter, tolerance refers to a willingness to put up with those ideas that one rejects. The problem with using generally unpopular groups, such as communists, socialists, or atheists, as points of reference against which to measure tolerance is that not everyone is hostile to these groups. An investigator cannot satisfactorily measure tolerance unless everyone in his sample is asked to respond to a group that he or she truly dislikes. This was certainly not the case in the earlier studies, since the groups mentioned in the questionnaire items were generally left-wing. Hence, we can assume that the tolerance of conservative respondents was sorely tested, but that this was not necessarily the case with more liberal respondents. It is likely, therefore, that this method exaggerates the true level of tolerance in the society and, in addition, may produce spurious relations with other variables, such as education, participation, religion, and sex.

The problem that we face, then, is this: tolerance can only be measured with reference to groups that people strongly dislike, but these groups are bound to vary from person to person. Smith may be hostile to communists, while Jones may be hostile to the Ku Klux Klan, while both may approve of, or be indifferent toward, the group disliked by the other. If we tried to measure tolerance strictly with reference to communists, it is likely that Smith would appear to be more intolerant than Jones. In effect, Smith would be given a more difficult test than Jones who might in fact be equally intolerant but of a different target. The solution to this problem is to devise a measurement that would enable us to measure the degree of Smith's tolerance of communists and Jone's tolerance of the Ku Klux Klan. Such an approach would enable us to hold their evaluations of their target groups constant, since each would be asked to respond to groups toward which he is hostile.

In an attempt to obtain such a measure, we developed and tested a self-anchoring measurement allowing the respondents themselves to select the group or groups they most strongly opposed. Each respondent was presented with a list of extremist groups that ranged from communists, socialists, atheists, the Black Panthers, and the Symbionese Liberation Army on the left to fascists, the John Birch Society, and the Ku Klux Klan on the right. We also included two other groups on the list, "pro-abortionists" and "anti-abortionists", which represent positions that are orthogonal to the left-right dimension. Respondents were then asked to identify the group they like the *least,* after which they were presented with a series of statements in an agree-disagree format that elicited their views about a range of peaceful activities in which members of that group might participate or about steps that might be taken by the government against that group. Some of these statements were as follows:

(1) Members of the _____ should be banned from being President of the United States.
(2) Members of the _____ should be allowed to teach in the public schools.
(3) The _____ should be outlawed.
(4) Members of the _____ should be allowed to make a speech in this city.
(5) The _____ should have their phones tapped by our government.
(6) The _____ should be allowed to hold public rallies in our city.

These statements were read as they appear above with the blanks filled in with the name of the group selected by each respondent. It should be emphasized that the activities referred to in these questions—such as running for office, teaching in the public schools, holding a rally, and making a public speech—are all peaceful and otherwise perfectly legal and constitutional. There was no sense in which respondents were asked to approve or to disapprove of violent or illegal activities by these groups, some of which have a substantial reputation for such activities.

The advantage of our procedure is that it creates a situation holding constant the evaluation of each respondent toward the group in question. This strategy generates "content-controlled" responses, and allows us to put general procedural norms into a specific context without completely predetermining the context. It prevents respondents from expressing agreement with general norms which they then fail to apply to specific groups. Clearly, our measures are not "content-free" since there is a context and a specific group toward which each respondent is asked to react. We therefore call this a content-controlled measure to emphasize that we are controlling for the contents of group beliefs by allowing respondents to select functionally equivalent targets.

We have shown elsewhere (Sullivan et al., 1979: Table 2) that this measurement procedure results in vastly different aggregate results than the more traditional Stouffer questions. For example, using the Stouffer questions in 1978 in a national sample, we found clear majorities giving the tolerant response on almost every question. Most of the majorities were in the 60% range. Using our questions in the same survey, we found a range of tolerant responses of 16% (banned from the Presidency) to 59% (phones tapped). Most of the content-controlled questions elicited an intolerant majority and a tolerant minority. It is difficult to escape the conclusion that the Stouffer items generate larger proportions of tolerant respondents than do the content-controlled questions. Since the latter is the more valid approach, these results raise questions about the claims made by the writers cited above that levels of tolerance in the American public are now very high relative to the 1950s.

A related and equally important question, which we shall address in the remainder of this chapter, is whether the content-controlled measurement strategy alters the patterns of correlations between political tolerance and various background and political variables when compared with the more traditional measures of tolerance. We shall examine three variables and their relation to tolerance: education, religion, and urbanization. We shall first describe the dependent variable further.

The levels of tolerance and intolerance for the different groups were measured by an overall tolerance scale, which was based on responses to the content-controlled items listed earlier. The responses to these 6 questions were summed to create a scale ranging from 6 to 30 (the scores on each item ranged from 1 to 5), with the lower number representing the intolerant end of the scale and the higher one representing the tolerant end. Respondents with scores between 22 and 30 were classified as "more tolerant" (16%), those with scores from 15 to 21 were classified as "in-between" (45%), and those with scores lower than 15 were classified as "less tolerant" (39%). These classifications are similar to those used by Stouffer in his study, but since the scales are based on different principles, our percentages cannot be compared meaningfully with his. The average score for all respondents on this scale was 16.1. Since the midpoint of the scale is 18, most respondents fell on the intolerant side.

SOME SOCIOLOGICAL DETERMINANTS OF TOLERANCE: EDUCATION, RELIGION, AND URBANIZATION

The studies of tolerance that were conducted during the 1950s produced a number of durable generalizations concerning the determinants of tolerant and intolerant attitudes. As noted earlier, education and political involvement were closely associated with tolerance in all three of the early studies reviewed above. In addition, Stouffer's findings suggested that sex, religion, urbanization, and region of residence, among other variables, were related to tolerance. These earlier conclusions have been confirmed by more recent studies of tolerance, such as that conducted by Nunn and his associates (1978).

We shall review some of these conclusions using our own measure of tolerance. To provide the reader with an adequate indication of the consequences of different measurement strategies—while at the same time limiting our discussion to a manageable length—we have chosen three independent variables which illustrate the range of impact that our measurement strategy has on the correlations between political tolerance and various independent variables.

EDUCATION AND TOLERANCE

Stouffer (1955) found a very strong relation between tolerance and level of education. In his sample, 66% of the college graduates were classified as "more tolerant" on an overall scale of political tolerance, while the corresponding figure among those with a grade school education was just 16%. His findings suggested that the relation was linear, since those in the intermediate educational categories were located between these two extreme points on the tolerance scale. Stouffer offered the following explanation:

> Schooling *puts a person in touch with people whose ideas and values are different from one's own.* And this tends to carry on, after formal schooling is finished, through reading and personal contacts. Now, we can plausibly argue that this is a necessary though not the only, condition for tolerance of a free market place for ideas. To be tolerant, one has to learn further not only that people with different ideas are not necessarily bad people but also that it is vital to America to preserve this free market place, even if some of the ideas traded there are repugnant or even dangerous for the country. The first step in learning this may be merely to encounter the strange and the different. The' educated man does this and tends not to flinch too much at what he sees or hears [1955: 127].

So Stouffer's argument is cognitive. The citizen must *learn* that a free market of ideas is vital to American democracy and that nonconformists are not necessarily bad. Learning these things is essentially one of being exposed to these nonconformists and their ideas, which the process of higher education does quite well. Stouffer, therefore, does not relate tolerance to the conditions of work and alienation or to the broader social structure, rather he sticks closely to the purely cognitive functions of education. One learns the abstract principle that a free marketplace of ideas is needed and one learns that to be different is not necessarily to be bad and dangerous.

Nunn et al., (1978) show that the relation between tolerance (as measured by Stouffer's items) and education not only held up in the 1970s, but that it now appears to be much stronger than it was in the 1950s. In their 1973 survey, 84% of the college educated respondents were classified as "more tolerant" (using the same items and category definitions) while only 19% of those with grade school educations were so classified. Thus, the gap between these two groups widened in the intervening years.

We have already criticized the use of Stouffer's questions because they measure tolerance solely in reference to left-wing groups. In this connection, it is possible that the strong relation between tolerance and education found in these earlier studies was an artifact of the Stouffer methodology. This would be the case if there happened to be a relation between education and the political groups by which people are threatened. Thus, the more highly educated may be less threatened than the less educated by the particular groups mentioned in the Stouffer items, while on the other hand, they might be more threatened by comparable groups on the right, such as Nazis and the Ku Klux Klan.

We were able to test this suspicion with our content-controlled items, since respondents were asked to identify the group that they liked the least. The figures in Table 8.1 show the relation between education and the groups selected as targets. The clearest pattern in the table is that those with the most education are the ones most likely to select target groups on the right, while those with the least education are the ones most likely to select target groups on the left. Thus, among those "high" in education, 26% selected communists or socialists as targets, while 43% selected one of the groups on the extreme right (fascists, the John Birch Society, and the KKK). Conversely, among those "low" in education, 41% selected either communists or socialists as a target, while 29% selected one of the groups on the radical right.

TABLE 8.1   Groups Selected as Those "Liked the Least": By Level of Education (1978 NORC)

Groups:	Low (Grade School)	Education Medium (High School)	High (Some College)
Communists and Socialists	41%	38%	26%
Atheists	7	11	6
New Left Groups (Black Panthers, Symbionese Liberation Army)	13	13	17
Radical Right Groups (Fascists, Ku Klux Klan, John Birch Society)	29	28	43
Pro-Abortionists	8	6	3
Anti-Abortionists	1	2	2
Others		2	3
N	150	698	507

These differences remain about the same when the proportions selecting atheists (the third group mentioned in the Stouffer questions) are added to these calculations. Thus, the three groups listed in the Stouffer questions were precisely the ones by which those with the least education were most threatened. Meanwhile, the political groups about which those with high levels of education are most concerned (that is, radical right groups) did not appear in these items.

Obviously, this kind of pattern might have inflated the relation between education and tolerance when the Stouffer items were used as measures of tolerance. In fact, we do find that the relation between education and tolerance is stronger when the Stouffer items are used as measures of tolerance than when our content-controlled items are used. In our data, the simple correlation between education and a tolerance scale based on four of Stouffer's items was .41. The corresponding relation using a scale based upon our content-controlled items was .29. The relation between education and tolerance persists with our measure, but it is much weaker than that produced by the Stouffer items.

This relation, using the content-controlled items, is presented in a more simplified form in Figure 8.1, which shows the proportions who were "less tolerant" and "more tolerant" on our overall scale by level of education. It is evident from the figure that the proportions of respondents who were "more tolerant" increase with education, though the largest increase occurs with those with some college experience. Conversely, the proportions of those who were "less tolerant" decline steadily with education. We may conclude, therefore, that education is related to tolerance, but that the strength of this relation has been overstated in the literature because of the way in which tolerance has been measured.

RELIGION AND TOLERANCE

Although Stouffer did not analyze Jews, he found that Protestants living in the South were significantly less tolerant than northern Protestants or Catholics. Nunn et al. (1978), however, reanalyzed Stouffer's data and found that in 1954, the percentages more tolerant were 28 for Protestants, 31 for Catholics, 71 for Jews, and 49 for nonreligious people. Thus they concluded that Jews were more tolerant in 1954, followed by nonreligious people, and then Catholics and Protestants roughly tied as least tolerant. By 1973, they discovered, these percentages were approximately 46 for Protestants, 59 for Catholics, 88 for Jews, and 87 for nonreligious people. The rank order remains about the same, except now the nonreligious are as tolerant as the Jews, and Catholics have become more tolerant than Protestants.

It occurs to us that, again, some portion of these religious differences is due to the content-bias of the questions asked. First, to find that Jews and

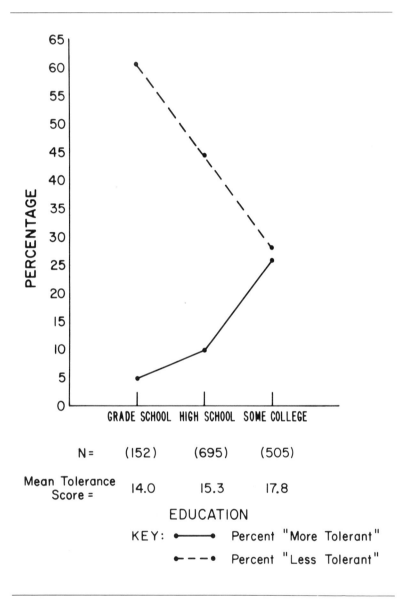

FIGURE 8.1   Education and Tolerance

nonreligious people are most tolerant of communists, atheists and socialists may not prove the point at all. Certainly, one expects nonreligious people to be most tolerant of atheists, since many nonreligious people are themselves atheists. In addition, Jews have historically been sympathetic to left wing groups, particularly compared to Protestants. A much stronger test, of course, is to examine the degree to which Jews are tolerant of fascists and Nazis, as witnessed by events in Skokie, Illinois. In Table 8.2 we find that Jews and nonreligious people are much less likely to select the traditional left-wing targets, and much more likely to select right-wing targets, than Catholics or Protestants. Fully 51% of Jews and 56% of nonreligious people selected a right-wing group as their least-liked while only 32% and 31% of Protestants and Catholics did so. Conversely, 47% of Protestants picked one of the Stouffer groups, while 42% of Catholics, 16% of Jews and 19% of those with no religion did so. There is plenty of opportunity for content-bias to play a role in the relation between religion and tolerance.

Again our results are somewhat mixed, although they continue to demonstrate the usefulness of the content-controlled measure (See Figure 8.2). In terms of the percentage "more tolerant" we find almost no difference among the Protestants, Catholics, and Jews, and even their mean tolerance scores are similar. Thus the argument of the content bias of the original Stouffer questions is undoubtedly valid, since, using our measure, Jews are not more tolerant than Protestants or Catholics. In fact, their mean score is lower than the Catholic's mean score. We continue to find, however, that people who adhere to no particular religious faith are more tolerant than the more religious respondents, and in fact, the differences are quite large. Although only about 12% of Protestants, Catholics, and Jews are in the more tolerant category, fully 44% of the nonreligious respondents are more tolerant; the means range from 15.4 for Protestants to 19.6 for the nonreligious group. And, for the first time, we discover a group of respondents for whom the more tolerant group outnumbers the less tolerant group; it does so for both the "other religions"and the "no religion" groups. Unfortunately, we have no measure of the religiosity of our denominational respondents, but our two main conclusions are clear: Prior research finding that Jews are more tolerant than Protestants and Catholics is artifactual, due to the content-bias of the questions asked; and, as suggested by Nunn et al. (1978), less religious respondents are considerably more tolerant than those with some denominational affiliation.

When the various Protestant religions are broken out for separate analysis there are few significant differences among them. Traditional wisdom is that the Presbyterians and Episcopalians should be more liberal, as their religious doctrine is less fundamentalist than their Baptist, Methodist, and Lutheran counterparts. Hence, the former two ought to be more likely to select right-wing targets than the latter. This is generally not true, although there is some weak tendency for the Presbyterians to be less likely to select the traditional left-wing targets and more likely to select right-wing targets. This is not true for the Episcopalians, however, as they differ little from the more fundamentalist religious groups. The only major difference in tolerance scores among

TABLE 8.2   Groups Selected as Those "Liked the Least": By Religious Affiliation
            (1978 NORC)

	Religion				
Groups:	Protestant	Catholic	Jewish	Other Religions	No Religion
Communists and Socialists	35%	37%	13%	40%	17%
Atheists	12	5	3	0	2
New Left Groups (Black Panthers, SLA)	15	16	11	10	15
Radical Right Groups (Fascists, Klan, Birch Society)	32	31	51	40	56
Pro-Abortionists	4	8	5	5	0
Anti-Abortionists	2	2	8	0	4
Others	1	1	8	5	6
N	851	357	37	20	97

the Protestant denominations is that the Baptists are less tolerant than the others. The mean score on the 6-item scale is 14.2 for the Baptists and very close to 16 for each of the other denominations.

URBANIZATION AND TOLERANCE

Stouffer found that city size was an important variable in understanding political tolerance. In metropolitan areas, 39% of respondents could be classified as more tolerant; in other cities, 30%; in small towns, 25%; and finally, on farms, only 18%. This finding held up under controls for region, and to a lesser extent, for education. Stouffer explained this as a function of contact with diverse ideas, an explanation similar to that put forward to explain the educational relation. As he put it:

Owing to the relatively high rural birth rate and to changes in technology which shrink the percentages of rural population with every successive Census, the population flow is mainly from the country to the city and the city suburb. Consequently, many city dwellers have lived in two worlds of values—those of their childhood in the country and those of their adulthood in the city. The reverse is rare. The shock of exposure to two value systems could have an effect on tolerance not unlike the effect of formal schooling as described above. It is precisely in those parts of the country where most people are natives of their type of community, if not actually of the same country in which they now reside—such as farm areas, especially in the South—that tolerance of "dangerous" ideas seem to be most difficult [1955: 127].

In their updated survey, Nunn and associates found that the percentage more tolerant had increased in each category but that the differences among city

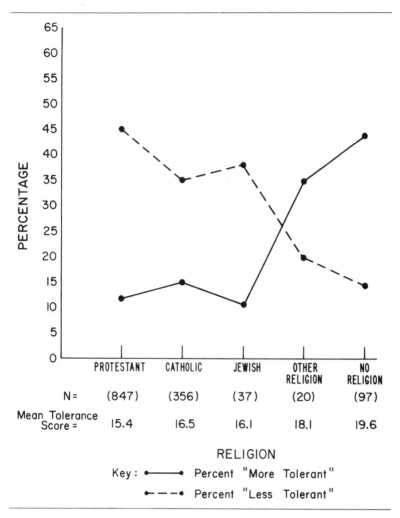

N =	PROTESTANT (847)	CATHOLIC (356)	JEWISH (37)	OTHER RELIGION (20)	NO RELIGION (97)
Mean Tolerance Score =	15.4	16.5	16.1	18.1	19.6

RELIGION

Key: •———• Percent "More Tolerant"

•— —• Percent "Less Tolerant"

FIGURE 8.2   Religion and Tolerance

size categories held strong. In metropolitan areas, 66% were more tolerant in 1973; in other cities, 50%; in small towns, 42%; and in farm areas, 30%. Following the familiar pattern, the differences among categories increased somewhat between 1954 and 1973. In their analysis, they controlled for the effects of education, region, exposure to mass media, gender, and occupation and still found what they called "persisting relationships" between city size and tolerance. Unfortunately, they do not specify how strong these persisting relations were, and we suspect that they were greatly diminished in comparison with the zero order relations. Their explanation was similar to Stouffer's, relying primarily on the notion of "incongruent experiences."

Our own results are presented in Table 8.3 and Figure 8.3 They are striking. Only in large cities over 250,000 do more respondents select right-wing than left-wing targets; in the very small towns and the open country-side, our respondents are overwhelmingly concerned with left-wing groups—the traditional ones studied by Stouffer (1955) and by Nunn and his colleagues (1978). Just on the basis of content bias, one certainly expects the residents of smaller locales to be less tolerant on the Stouffer items. People in large cities are not so concerned with the left-wing groups, and in fact even people who live in suburbs around these large cities are evenly divided between left- and right-wing targets. As we travel from the center city to the suburb and toward smaller and smaller towns, we find more concern with the traditional left-wing targets and less concern with the right-wing targets.

In Figure 8.3 we have collapsed several of the categories presented in Table 8.3 for ease of presentation. It is clear that although the residents of towns of less than 2,500 are less tolerant than the rest of our respondents, there are no significant differences among the remaining groups. The mean 6-item tolerance score ranges from 16.2 in towns of 2,500–50,000 up to 16.9 in unincorporated SMSAs, and 4 of the 5 groups have means of 16.2 or 16.3. It is remarkable that, given the strength of earlier findings, for our respondents it makes no difference whether they live in cities of 2,500 or cities over 250,000; they are equally intolerant. They do, of course, differ in the particular target groups they select.

TABLE 8.3 Ideological Groups Selected as Least-Liked by Size of City (1978 NORC)[a]

City Size	Percent Selecting Communists, Socialists or Atheists	Percent Selecting Birch, Klan, or Fascists	N
Over 250,000	23	47	279
50-249,000	42	24	146
Suburb of Large City	36	33	290
Suburb of Medium City	41	23	74
SMSA Unincorporated	37	27	166
10–49,000	47	29	80
2,500–9,999	48	24	94
1,000–2,499	50	23	75
Open Country	50	17	153

[a]We have not presented the full-blown table here, for purposes of simplicity.

SUMMARY AND CONCLUSION

In this brief chapter, we have criticized past research on political toler-ance, we have presented an alternate conceptualization of political toler-ance, and we have analyzed some data which were collected using a mea-surement strategy consistent with our alternative conceptualization. The following may be concluded from our analysis:

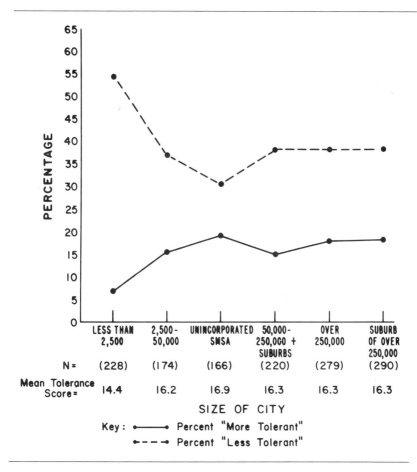

FIGURE 8.3   Size of City and Tolerance

(1) The traditional measures of political tolerance have relied too exclusively on left-wing target groups in their measurement procedures. The result is an overstatement of the current level of political tolerance in the American electorate.

(2) Our content-controlled measurement procedure shows that many of the current findings—about the background variables which correlate with political tolerance—are largely a result of the content-bias of the traditional measures. The relation between education and tolerance is smaller than current findings suggest, and the relations between religion and urbanization on the one hand, and tolerance on the other, are almost totally vitiated using our content-controlled measurement strategy. Although nonreligious respondents continue to be more tolerant, the differences among Jews, Catholics, and Protestants disappear; although those who live in towns of less than

2,500 continue to be less tolerant than everyone else, the "everyone else" includes almost the entire population of the United States. Differences among other cities, by size, are virtually nonexistent.

We may safely conclude, therefore, that it makes considerable difference how tolerance is conceptualized and measured. Both the pattern of aggregate results and the pattern of the correlates of tolerance are vastly affected by issues of conceptualization and measurement. Although the implications of this for democratic theory and for broader conclusions about the American electorate are important, we cannot explore them here. We can merely accomplish the narrow objective of demonstrating the usefulness of our measurement approach, and hope to whet the appetite of the reader for more detailed analyses presented elsewhere (Sullivan et al., forthcoming).

NOTES

1. This definition, and the discussion that follows, owes a good deal to Crick's thoughtful analysis of tolerance (1973: Ch. 3).

2. This approach to the status of "the rules of the game" in democratic systems has dominated previous research on political tolerance. See, for example, Prothro and Grigg (1960) and McClosky (1964).

3. As will become apparent as we proceed, much of the debate on tolerance in the postwar period has concerned the political rights of communists and related groups on the left. The provocative attempt by Nazis to march in Skokie in 1977 and 1978, along with the responses to this attempt by the Skokie city council, raised the issue of the extent to which groups on the extreme right should be tolerated. In this case, many of those who had previously defended the rights of communists found themselves opposed to the procedural claims of the Nazis, for reasons the legitimacy of which we will not consider. The whole controversy raised once again an old debate over whether pure tolerance is necessarily good or desirable. For those who are interested, see George Will's (1978) column on this issue, as well as Aryeh Neier's (1978) response to it, which represented the position of the American Civil Liberties Union.

4. The items used to construct the cumulative scale of "willingness to tolerate non-conformists" are listed in Appendix C of Stouffer's book (1955). Of the 15 items used to construct the scale, 11 referred to communists or suspected communists. The other 4 referred to atheists and those advocating government ownership of "railroads and big industries." See Appendix C, pp. 262–269, as well as Stouffer's discussion of the scale in the text (pp. 49–54).

5. For example, Stouffer asked 3 questions—whether the group in question should be allowed to make a speech, teach in college, and have a book written by them in the library—about 3 groups: communists, socialists, and atheists. We have repeated some of these questions about communists and atheists, and for these questions, we find increases in percentage tolerant between 1954 and 1977 ranging from 25% on the atheist-book question to 35% on the communist-teach question. For these data, see Sullivan et al. (1979), Table 1.

9

SUPPORT FOR POLITICAL WOMAN: THE EFFECTS OF RACE, SEX, AND SEXUAL ROLES

Marjorie Randon Hershey

Predicting election results in the United States is a hazardous job. But there is one prediction that any election-eve analyst could offer with supreme confidence—a prediction that would prove correct a dazzling 96 times out of 100 in Congressional races and even more often in the case of presidents. The reason is that the social-demographic composition of the American political leadership has remained very stable. And the prediction is that the newly elected official would be male (see Krauss, 1974: 1711; Lynn, 1979: 413–424).

In recent years, however, a growing number of women candidates have begun to make inroads in the long-standing male dominance of elective offices—particularly in state and local posts where the underrepresentation of women has been at least as dramatic as in higher offices (Johnson and Carroll, 1978: 4A–7A). Some writers speculate that this trend will have a major impact on the direction of American politics.[1]

But where will women candidates find electoral support and for what reasons? Other disadvantaged groups—blacks, white ethnics, and Jews—often first gained representation in politics by putting together a group-based coalition of supporters, combining their own numbers with members of other identifiable social groupings (see Pettigrew, 1972). Similarly, support for the Democratic and Republican parties is often measured in group terms (Nie et al., 1976: chs. 13, 14; Axelrod, 1972; these findings have provided valuable clues about the interests to which each party must respond with implications for the kinds of alliances and appeals it will be able to make.

This chapter will ask whether the potential support for women in politics also comes disproportionately from certain social-demographic groups, such as women, blacks, or particular income or occupational levels, and if so, whether these are the same groups that have distinctly supported black and other minority candidates. If a coalition of supporting groups can be identified, then the makeup of that coalition may constrain the actions and policy positions of women in politics, since it is reasonable to expect that women candidates and officeholders will try to attend to the concerns of their supporters.

But it is possible that the traditional aggregation-of-groups method will not work for women candidates. So this study will also look for attitudes and beliefs—especially attitudes toward sexual egalitarianism—that may form an alternate basis for the development of support for women in politics. Such a finding could have interesting implications. If potential supporters of women candidates can be identified more readily by their sexual-role attitudes (or other attitudes and beliefs) than by their group membership, this might suggest that women as a group face different hurdles in politics than blacks and other minorities do—that the process by which women are gaining some measure of political power differs in kind from the experiences of other disadvantaged groups with the political system.

Previous research in this area is limited. Ferree (1974) has reported that potential support for a woman presidential candidate is greater among the better-educated (see also Schreiber, 1978: 177), the young, and those also willing to consider a black candidate for president. And she finds that men and women expressed equal levels of support for a woman presidential candidate in 1972, although men had been more supportive than women during the previous decade. But these Gallup data are limited to a single-item measure of support that allows only a yes-or-no answer and does not deal with women running for offices other than the presidency. More important, we know little about the attitudinal basis for such support. Without considering why certain group ties or sets of attitudes should predispose an individual to support women, Democrats, or blacks, and the implications of these patterns for the political system, the empirical findings have little meaning.

CONCEPTUAL APPROACHES: WHY SEX, SEXUAL ROLES, AND RACE SHOULD AFFECT ATTITUDES TOWARD WOMEN IN POLITICS

Whether or not sex is "the most intractable basis of human inequality" (Turner and Turner, 1974: 161), it is unquestionably a major basis for social, political, and economic stratification. The tendency for males to monopolize positions of power in most societies may reach back to the origins of those societies. One study (Sanday, 1973) posits that if a society's means of subsistence (which stem from the ecology of its area) were compatible with its women's child-bearing and child-raising activities, as in societies that depend primarily on horticulture, then women could gain access to accumulating resources and thus sources of economic and political power. In most societies (e.g., those dependent mainly on hunting or plough agriculture), this was not the case. Male dominance has been maintained by myths and stereotypes justifying the differentiation of roles on the basis of gender, in the family, at work, at leisure, and in politics (Krauss, 1974).

This differentiation of roles suggests that, potentially, American women may have a distinct set of interests as a group. American blacks and French-speaking Canadians have developed distinctive political interests in part because the society has treated them as groups, closing certain roles to them and opening others on the basis of their group membership. Similarly, many types of opportunities in American society—political office, for one—are much more available to persons of one sex than to the other.

Further, several important political issues can affect women and men differently, such as war policy, abortion laws, and affirmative action programs. These differences in impact may lead to sexual differences in attitudes. And, in fact, men and women differ moderately but consistently in their attitudes toward war and violence, abortion, social welfare, and issues of personal morality (Hershey, 1977).

The existence of a potentially distinct set of women's interests does not by itself mean that women are aware of their mutual concerns, their agreed on preferred solutions, or that they are likely to identify politically with other women and support women candidates. This sense of identification may be inhibited because women are a very heterogeneous group, differing in other politically relevant characteristics such as race, party, and socioeconomic status (SES). However, Ferree's data (1974: 393) do show a recent, dramatic increase in women's willingness to support a woman for president. It is possible, then, that gender may become an important determinant of attitudes toward women in politics. If women of different races and statuses do come to share a distinctive willingness to support women candidates, then it seems likely that future women officeholders will be conscious of their debt to women voters, and interested in public policies that affect women especially, such as sexual discrimination, abortion, and childcare.

A second potential determinant of reactions to women in politics are sex-role orientations. We will look at two types of these orientations. The first, sex-role *attitudes,* are evaluations of what is "appropriate" and "inappropriate" for men and women to do, think, and seem. People with traditional sex-role attitudes are those who believe that certain activities are appropriate only for men and others only for women, while flexible sex-role attitudes are those which do not stereotype tasks by sex.

Sex-role *identities,* on the other hand, are self-ratings in relation to the society's definition of masculinity and feminity. Researchers (see Bem, 1974) have found that while many people rate themselves high on traditionally masculine characteristics and low on feminine ones (or the reverse), the dimensions of masculinity and femininity are not mutually exclusive. Some people, termed "androgynous," describe their sex-role identities as combining highly-valued masculine and feminine characteristics.

And there is increasing evidence (at least in studies of whites) that persons with more flexible sex-role attitudes and those with androgynous sex-role identities are much more supportive of increased political activity by women and of the symbols and goals of the women's liberation movement, than are more traditional people (Hershey and Sullivan, 1977; Tavris, 1973: 192–195). If the people with flexible sex-role orientations are the nucleus of a coalition supporting women candidates and officeholders, then greater support for women in politics would be linked with approval of change in the climate of opportunities for women and men at work, in the family, and elsewhere. The implication is that greater political participation by women would require profound changes in American society.

A third possible determinant has often been assumed but rarely if ever tested. The achievements of Barbara Jordan, Shirley Chisholm, and Patricia Harris are prime examples of the accomplishments of black women in politics; these achievements are often taken as evidence that blacks in American society are more willing than whites to grant leadership roles to women.

This contention is related to findings that black women play a more influential role in their families and communities than white women do in theirs (Kandel, 1971: 1004, 1016–1017)—or, put differently, that the relations between black men and women are more egalitarian than are those among whites (Epstein, 1973: 918; but see Hyman and Reed, 1969). Central to the argument are reports that black women are brought up to be more independent, self-reliant, distrustful of the reliability of men and marriage, and prepared to take on roles that white society often stereotypes as masculine, than white women are (Ladner, 1972; Turner and Turner, 1974: 157–160).

Black women also hold a larger portion of blacks' professional positions than do white women of whites' professional positions (Almquist, 1975: 137–138). That may provide more black women with the interpersonal skills that contribute to political success, while their disadvantage in income (Blau, 1979: 280) may motivate black women to enter politics. All these factors are thought to promote egalitarianism between black men and women and to make blacks more supportive of women's political activity than whites are.

In fact, some studies find that black women are at least as likely to participate in politics as black men are (see Pierce et al., 1973: 425; Lansing, 1974: 13–14). And one study reports (Orum et al., 1974) that sexual differences in political attitudes among black children are not as pronounced as among white children. If blacks are an important source of support for women in politics, then it is likely that black women will constitute a large part of the increase in women's participation, and that the concerns of black communities will affect the goals and styles of future women candidates.

This argument implies that blacks are more supportive of women in politics *because* blacks' sex-role orientations are more egalitarian. Similarly, any differences between men and women in support for women candidates and officials may be due to differences in sexual roles, just as sex-role attitudes and identities are reported to account for part of the difference between men's and women's attitudes toward issues such as abortion reform and the Equal Rights Amendment (Hershey, 1977). These causal pathways will be tested here in addition to the hypotheses that women, blacks, and people with flexible sex-role orientations will be major sources of support for women candidates and public officials.

METHODS AND MEASURES

SELECTING CASES FOR STUDY

At this time there is no national data that includes sophisticated measures of sex-role orientations, questions on support for women candidates and officeholders at several levels of office, *and* a substantial portion of black respondents. So this study must be smaller; it uses random samplings of college students to obtain comparative racial data.

Sampling in a college population offers the advantage that there should be ample numbers of cases on the nontraditional end of sex-role scales (Mason et al., 1976: 581–582) to test the hypothesis that flexible sex-role orientations increase support for women in politics. The disadvantage is that the findings should not be generalized beyond well-educated young adults. But the study can be adapted to take this limitation into account: In a population that should be especially likely to accept women in politics, how important are race, sex, and sex-role orientations as causes of that support, compared with support for black and other minority political candidates?

Two random samples of the Indiana University student population were taken in February and March, 1976. In the first, a 1/100 sample of the student body, lengthy questionnaires were filled out by 187 persons (or 63% of the sample). The second random sample included one-third of the university's black student population. After 3 waves, 50% of this sample completed the same questionnaires (N = 118).

Comparing these random samples with the known population parameters, the all-university sample contains a higher proportion of women (53%)

than does the student body (44%); this does not pose a problem, since the findings of this analysis will be checked within each sex. Otherwise, the two samples vary from population values by no more than 5% with respect to marital status, year in school, and grade point average. To obtain an all-white (N = 175) and an all-black (N = 122) sample, responses from the four blacks in the all-university sample were combined with those of the black sample, and the remaining nonwhites dropped from the analysis. These two samples differ in socioeconomic status, as would be expected (See Table 9.1).

TABLE 9.1   Measures of Socioeconomic Status in the Black and White Samples[a]

Indicator		Blacks	Whites
Father's Occupation:	White Collar	32%	77%
	Blue Collar	44	14
	Absent/No Paying Job	24	10
Mother's Occupation:	White Collar	54%	46%
	Blue Collar	14	9
	Absent/No Paying Job	32	45
Family Income:	Under $15,000	47%	21%
	$15,000–20,000	30	28
	$20,001–30,000	14	27
	Over $30,000	9	25
n =		117	175

[a]Percentages do not always add up to 100% due to rounding error.

MEASURING ATTITUDES TOWARD WOMEN IN POLITICS

To measure the respondents' willingness to give equal consideration to women and men candidates[2], they were asked, "Would you be *just* as likely to vote for a qualified woman as a qualified man to be president of the U.S.?"; the item was repeated referring to the office of district attorney of the respondent's county. To provide a standard, the same question was asked about black vs. white and Jewish vs. Christian candidates for president. Each item was followed by a 5-point scale ranging from "definitely yes" to "definitely not." Respondents' scores on the 4 items were summed, with higher scores indicating greater egalitarianism. The 4-item scale is quite reliable among whites (Cronbach's alpha = .82, mean inter-item correlation = .54). Among blacks these statistics are weaker (.65 and .32). The responses of black women are just as internally consistent as whites', but black men's interitem correlations are lower. Thus, each use of the 4-item scale was checked by breakdowns into the 4 component items.

Willingness to support women candidates may differ conceptually from having confidence in women officials. A member of an underrepresented group who wins an election may gain greater legitimacy in the eyes of the public—may be seen as having valued qualities that other members of the group are thought to lack. So respondents were also asked, "When you consider the responsibilities of the office of president of the U.S., would you be more confident with a woman as president, equally confident with either a man or woman as president, or more confident with a man as president?" This item was repeated to ask about other offices: mayor of a big city, state legislator, governor, and Supreme Court justice. Scores on the 5 items were summed; again, higher scores indicate more egalitarian attitudes.[3]

SEX-ROLE ATTITUDES AND IDENTITIES

Attitudes toward traditional sex-role norms were gauged by an index of sex-stereotyping. The index was constructed by asking whether each of 7 activities commonly stereotyped by sex—playing football, taking care of children, cleaning house, repairing highways, teaching nursery school, studying ballet, racing cars—was more appropriate for one sex than for the other or appropriate for either sex. Higher scores indicate greater flexibility—less stereotyping of activities by sex. When scores on all 7 items were summed, Cronbach's alpha = .79 for whites and .76 for blacks; mean interitem correlation = .35 for whites, .31 for blacks.

Sex-role identities were measured using the Bem Sex Role Inventory (Bem, 1974). The BSRI includes 20 traits judged to be positively valued for men and 20 judged positively valued for women in American society. Each respondent indicates how well each trait characterizes him- or herself on a rating scale from 1 ("never or almost never true") to 7 ("always or almost always true"). The respondent's mean self-rating is calculated separately for the masculine and feminine items, becoming his or her Masculinity and Femininity Scores. After reliability testing, the Femininity Scale was whittled to 15 items (such as "gentle," "warm," and "sympathetic") and the Masculinity Scale to 19 items (central are "assertive" and "strong personality"; see Hershey, 1978: 586–587).

The difference between a respondent's Masculinity and Femininity Scores represents the balance between the two sets of characteristics in his or her sex-role identity. The more negative this value, the greater the predominance of traditionally masculine qualities, and the more positive the score, the more traditionally feminine traits dominate the individual's self-image. Scores close to zero indicate a balance of masculine and feminine qualities. Reliability data show that the traditional dimensions of masculinity and femininity provide meaningful structure to the self-ratings of both blacks and whites (for the Femininity Scale, alpha = .84 for whites and .86 for blacks; mean interitem correlations = .31 and .34). For the Masculinity Scale, alpha = .89 and .87; mean interitem correlation = .31 and .26).

FINDINGS

RACE AND SEXUAL DIFFERENCES IN ATTITUDES
TOWARD WOMEN AND MINORITIES

Table 9.2 presents the proportions of black and white women and black and white men who say they would definitely give equal consideration to a woman or a minority candidate. The data indicate some hesitance to support women in politics. Except for white women, these groups would be more willing to consider a black or a Jew than a woman as a candidate for president. All four groups are more willing to support a woman in a local contest (for district attorney) than in a presidential race.

TABLE 9.2 Racial and Sexual Differences in Willingness to Support Women and Minority Political Leaders

	Women		Men	
Willingness to Support	Black	White	Black	White
n =	58	94	61	79
Woman for President	55.2[a]	55.8	31.7	25.3
Woman for District Attorney	67.2	68.4	48.3	35.4
Black for President	86.2	54.3	73.8	34.2
Jew for President	72.4	64.9	60.7	38.0

[a]Cell entries are the percentage of each group responding that they would "definitely" be just as likely to vote for the woman or minority candidate named as for a man or majority (white or Christian) candidate.

Sexual differences in attitudes toward women in politics are readily apparent in Table 9.2. Regardless of race, women are about 20% more likely to support women candidates than is either group of men. According to Ferree (1974: 393), there was a sharp increase between 1969 and 1972 in women's willingness to vote for women candidates. The present results may mean that this trend has continued into the mid-1970s (or it may simply reflect differences in the populations sampled, how the questions were worded or the larger range of response options used in this study).

As would be expected, black men and women are more favorable toward a black presidential candidate than whites are. But it is interesting that, even here, black women are more supportive than black men. The same sexual difference is found among whites and appears again in attitudes toward a prospective Jewish candidate for president.

T-tests for the difference of means among these groups (see Table 9.3) demonstrate that among whites, women's greater egalitarianism toward women and minorities in politics is statistically significant on all five scales. Among blacks, women are significantly more supportive of women presidential candidates and also score significantly higher on the summary index of support for women and minority candidates than men do.

The differences in attitudes between blacks and whites are much less pronounced. The only significant racial difference is found in attitudes toward a black presidential candidate. On the other items, racial differences can be seen only within categories of gender. Among men, blacks' attitudes *are* more egalitarian than whites' on every question, but among women this pattern appears only in relation to black and Jewish candidates for president.

TABLE 9.3   Difference of Means in Attitudes Toward Women and Minority Political Leaders by Sex and Race

Scale	Women			Men			t Value for the Sexual Difference Among	
	Black	White	t	Black	White	t	Blacks	Whites
n =	58	95		61	79			
Confidence in Women Officials	9.20 (1.31)	9.58 (1.01)	−1.93	8.82 (1.47)	8.68 (1.48)	0.56	−1.50	−4.77*
Woman for President	4.28 (.93)	4.31 (.96)	−0.19	3.63 (1.26)	3.46 (1.23)	0.83	−3.14*	−5.13*
Black for President	4.83 (.46)	4.29 (.94)	4.74*	4.66 (.66)	3.86 (1.11)	5.30*	−1.64	−2.75*
Jew for President	4.57 (.78)	4.37 (1.00)	1.35	4.38 (.95)	4.08 (.94)	1.86	−1.20	−1.99*
Support for Women and Minority Candidates	18.22 (2.29)	17.59 (2.77)	1.53	16.98 (2.45)	15.46 (3.37)	3.11*	−2.85*	−4.59*

*p < .05. All significance levels are based on two-tailed tests. Cell entries are mean scores for each group with standard deviations in parentheses.

CONSTRUCTING A MODEL OF SUPPORT FOR POLITICAL WOMAN

Since there are both sexual and racial differences in these preliminary findings, what are the relative strengths of sex and race as predictors of support for women in politics once other relevant factors have been accounted for? This can be determined by the use of multiple regression equations that include sex-role attitudes and identities and measures of socioeconomic status as well as race and sex.[5]

Regression is an especially effective tool when one can posit a causal order among the independent variables. Two such causal pathways have been suggested here: (1) that blacks are more supportive of women in politics because blacks' sex-role attitudes and identities are more egalitarian than whites'; and (2) that women's greater support for women candidates and officeholders is mediated by the effects of sexual roles.

The causal ordering of the first hypothesis dissolves immediately upon testing. The zero-order correlation between race and attitudes toward women candidates and officeholders, as well as the partial correlations controlling for sex-role attitudes and identities, are all less than $r = .08$. The hypothesis fails because, as Table 9.4 shows, when racial differences in sexual roles do appear, it is usually the whites who are more flexible in sex-role attitudes and more androgynous in sex-role identities. Black women identify more strongly with traditional feminine qualities to the BSRI than white women do, and black men's scores are more sex-typed masculine than white men's are. And within each sex, blacks are more likely to stereotype activities by sex (see also Hershey, 1978; Bayer, 1975: 393). So the contention that sexual roles are more egalitarian among blacks, and that as a consequence blacks are more likely to accept women in traditionally "masculine" roles such as political leadership, does not hold up.

Table 9.4 does show clear sexual differences: regardless of race, women's sex-role attitudes are more flexible than men's, and their sex-role identities more feminine. And there is some evidence that sexual roles act as a mediating variable in support for women in politics. The amount of variance in attitudes toward women officeholders that can be attributed to sex is reduced by half when the effects of sex-stereotyping are removed ($r = .25$, partial r $= .17$) and by one-third in the case of attitudes toward a woman presidential candidate ($r = .33$, partial r $= .28$).

Path analysis, however, provides evidence that both sex and sexual roles have direct effects on attitudes toward women in politics rather than that sex has an indirect effect only, mediated by sexual roles. When sex-stereotyping, Masculinity and Femininity Scores are all included in a path model (and assumed to have a noncausal relation with one another), about half of the total effect of sex on confidence in women officeholders ($p = .248$) is found to be direct ($p = .120$) and the rest is mediated by sexual roles (Figure 9.1a). When this path model is simplified, so that sex-stereotyping is

TABLE 9.4 Mean Sex-Role Identity and Sexual Stereotyping Scores by Race and Sex

Scale	Women			Men			t Value for the Sexual Difference Among	
	Black	White	t	Black	White	t	Blacks	Whites
n =	60	96		59	79			
Androgyny	.63 (.95)	.54 (.89)	.57	-.55 (.80)	-.32 (.84)	-1.62	-7.28*	-6.50*
Masculinity	5.10 (.74)	4.93 (.78)	1.37	5.43 (.63)	5.15 (.69)	2.47*	2.59*	1.97*
Femininity	5.73 (.69)	5.47 (.62)	2.37*	4.88 (.69)	4.83 (.61)	0.40	-6.70*	-6.78*
Sex Stereotyping	17.18 (3.13)	18.72 (2.52)	-3.19*	16.77 (2.88)	16.94 (2.84)	-0.33	-0.75	-4.38*

*p ≤.05. All significance levels are based on two-tailed tests. Higher scores indicate greater androgyny, masculinity and femininity, and *less* sex stereotyping.

the only mediator (Figure 9.1b), the direct effect of sex ($p = .143$) is more important than its indirect effect through sex-stereotyping ($p = .105$); this model explains almost as much variance in attitudes toward women officials (28%) as the more elaborate model does (29%).

Another reason to treat the two variables as independent predictors is that while sex-stereotyping is a good predictor of attitudes toward women officials ($p = .508$, explaining 26% of the variance), sex is not a good predictor of sex-stereotyping; 95% of the variance in stereotyping remains unexplained. So although the tendency for women to be more supportive of women officials can be explained partially by the greater flexibility of women's sex-role attitudes (see also Hershey, 1977), most of the difference between women's and men's attitudes on this issue cannot be so attributed.

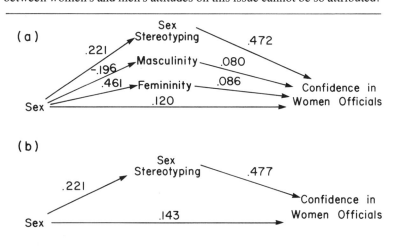

FIGURE 9.1 Path Diagram of the Relation Between Sex and Attitudes Toward Women Officials

The final standard multiple regression equations are shown in Table 9.5. As the previous analyses have suggested, sex is much more important than race in predicting support for women officeholders and attitudes toward women presidential candidates as well (not shown: $B = .19$ for sex, $-.01$ for race). But both sex and race are statistically significant influences on the combined scale of attitudes toward women *and* minority candidates. Race is more important in this second equation because of one component: Being black accounts for 11% of the variance in attitudes toward a black presidential candidate ($B = -.38$), while sex explains very little ($B = .03$). Race is also somewhat more important than sex in attitudes toward a Jewish presidential candidate.

These findings demonstrate that blacks do *not* distinctively support women in politics, even though blacks *are* distinctive in their support for

TABLE 9.5   Multiple Regression Equations Predicting to Attitudes Toward Women
and Minority Political Leaders: All Respondents

Independent Variables	Confidence in Women Officials Scale	Willingness to Support Women and Minority Candidates
n=	277	277
Sex Stereotyping	.47*	.43*
Sex (Female)	.11	.13*
Race (White)	−.00	−.19*
Masculinity Score	.09	.08
Femininity Score	.08	.13*
Mother's Occupation—		
White Collar	.04	.04
Blue Collar	−.01	−.06
Father's Occupation—		
White Collar	−.09	−.10
Blue Collar	−.10	−.08
Family Income	.00	.01
Women are Better Represented by Women Leaders	.05	.07
Respondent Has Run for Class or Club Office	−.00	.05
$R^2 =$	.30	.34

*F ratio significant at $p < .05$. Entries are standardized regression coefficients.

candidates from racial and religious minorities. In fact, the supporters of
women in politics cannot be distinguished from opponents on the basis of
race, economic level, or occupational status. Even sex is not a very powerful
predictor of attitudes toward women in politics; women are not as uniform in
their support for women candidates as are blacks in support of black candidates.

But the most important finding is that respondents' levels of sex-
stereotyping are the best predictors of their attitudes toward women in
politics. Recall that the items in the sex-stereotyping scale are far removed
from politics: cleaning house, repairing highways, playing football. It is
entirely plausible that someone might consider housecleaning equally appropriate for men and women while reserving the Supreme Court for men.
Yet the sex-stereotyping scale accounts independently for 22% of the variance in the women officeholders scale and 16% (B = .40) in attitudes toward
a woman presidential candidate. Even more surprising, sex-stereotyping
also accounts for 10% of the variance (B = .32) in attitudes toward a black
candidate and 5% (B = .23) in attitudes toward a Jewish candidate.

The Masculinity and Feminity Scores are much weaker predictors of
support for women in politics. Yet, a stronger identification with femininity
and with masculinity promotes acceptance of active political roles for
women. Androgyny in sex-role identities is the combination of positively-
valued feminine and positively-valued masculine qualities. Apparently each
of these components contributes to support for women in politics. This
further strengthens the finding that nontraditional sex-role orientations are

linked with greater acceptance of women in leadership roles.

Another belief that might seem to be a logical basis for the development of support for women in politics—that American women are better represented by women officials than by men—has very little impact when sexual and sex-role attitudes are in the question. The most important contributor to support for political woman is flexibility in sex-role attitudes.

These regressions were also run within racial/sexual groups, to make sure that the attitudes of white women, who are overrepresented in the sample, have not skewed the results (see Table 9.6). The equations show some interesting differences in the importance of the predictors. Sex-stereotyping is clearly the best predictor of white women's and white men's attitudes, accounting for 30–34% of the variance in attitudes toward women officials and 12–22% of the variance in attitudes toward black and Jewish candidates as well. The contribution of SES is much less important.

For black women, as for whites, sex-stereotyping is strongly related to attitudes toward women's opportunities as presidential candidates (B = .39, R^2 = .25) and as officeholders (see Table 9.6). And as with whites, SES measures are less important on these questions. But in attitudes toward black and Jewish candidates, the resemblance between whites' and black women's responses ends. Although black women's attitudes toward women and black and Jewish candidates are strongly intercorrelated (see Table 9.7), their support for black and Jewish candidates depends much less on sex-role attitudes (accounting for only 3% of the variance) than on having higher family incomes and working mothers. The SES variables account collectively for 19% and 25% of the variance.

Black men's attitudes provide the greatest contrast. These equations account for a substantial amount of variance in whites' and black women's attitudes, but the responses of black men are not well accounted for. In fact, when R^2 estimates are adjusted to reflect the sample size and the relatively large number of variables (see Nie et al., 1975: 358n), the amount of "explained" variance in black men's attitudes drops to nil. Although black and white men are equally likely to hold stereotyped sex-role attitudes and similar in their level of willingness to support women candidates, sex-stereotyping has little effect on black men's reactions to women officeholders and no effect at all on their attitudes toward women, black, or Jewish presidential candidates, while white men's responses show these links clearly. Further, SES does not predict well to black men's responses.

The evidence does not suggest that black men responded randomly or capriciously to the questions. Their attitudes toward women officials and women candidates are highly consistent (as Table 9.7 shows), and there is also a strong relation between their attitudes toward woman candidates for president and district attorney (r = .52). But there is a striking lack of correlation between black men's reactions to women in politics and their

TABLE 9.6 Multiple Regression Equations Predicting to Attitudes Toward Women and Minority Political Leaders: by Race and Sex

| | A. Confidence in Women Officials Scale | | | | B. Willingness to Support Women, Minority Candidates | | | |
| | Women | | Men | | Women | | Men | |
	Black	White	Black	White	Black	White	Black	White
Sex Stereotyping	.42*	.59*	.26	.49*	.39*	.61*	.02	.47*
Masculinity Score	.13	.04	.05	.13	.26*	.01	.08	.08
Femininity Score	.01	.13	.11	.14	.10	.15	.16	.21*
Mother's Occupation—								
White Collar	-.22	.00	-.04	.25*	.15	-.02	-.04	.10
Blue Collar	-.08	-.05	-.04	.10	.21	-.07	-.29	-.03
Father's Occupation—								
White Collar	.10	-.08	-.25	-.11	-.04	-.06	-.15	-.12
Blue Collar	-.13	-.13	-.12	-.09	-.27*	-.14	.03	.07
Family Income	.22	.02	-.06	.03	.35*	-.05	-.02	.14
Women are Better Represented by Women	.17	-.04	-.04	.15	.18	.02	.15	.08
Respondent Has Run for Class or Club Office	-.05	-.10	.10	.03	-.26*	.09	.11	.06
R^2 =	.30	.38	.15	.41	.53	.38	.18	.38
Adjusted R^{2+} =	.15	.30	<.01	.32	.42	.30	<.01	.29
n =	56	91	53	77	56	91	53	77

*F ratio significant at $p < .05$. Entries are standardized regression coefficients.

R^{2+} adjusted for the number of independent variables and the number of cases. This is a conservative estimate of the amount of variance explained when the n is not large.

TABLE 9.7   Relationships Among Measures of Attitudes Toward Women and
Minority Political Leaders

Correlations Relating Supportive Attitudes Toward	Women		Men	
	Black	White	Black	White
n =	56	91	53	77
Women Officials × Woman Presidential Candidate	.54	.78	.52	.64
Woman Presidential Candidate × Black Presidential Candidate	.47	.49	.09	.48
Women Officials × Black Presidential Candidate	.34	.29	.02	.39
Woman Presidential Candidate × Jewish Presidential Candidate	.53	.44	.20	.49
Women Officials × Jewish Presidential Candidate	.22	.30	.15	.34
Black Presidential Candidate × Jewish Presidential Candidate	.61	.57	.15	.65

reactions to black and Jewish candidates—and, again, this lack of correlation is found only among black men.

It is apparent that black men's attitudes toward women in politics are isolated from their reactions to other minority candidates and to women's roles more generally, while the attitudes of other respondents are not. The variables measured in this study cannot explain this anomaly. But there is at least the hint in these data that black men do not regard the underrepresentation of women in politics, or other forms of sex-based discrimination, as problems in the same league as racial discrimination.

In summary, potential supporters of women in politics are most likely to be people with flexible sex-role attitudes. Support does *not* come disproportionately from certain social-demographic groups. Blacks are no more supportive of women in politics than whites are. Even women, who come closest to providing group support, are not as unified on behalf of women political leaders as are black respondents on behalf of black candidates.

IMPLICATIONS

Several writers (see Hochschild, 1973: 1018–1020) have pointed out parallels between the status of women and that of blacks in American society, and implied that the two groups' progress in gaining political representation will also be parallel. But the findings of this analysis indicate that the dynamics of attitudes supporting women candidates and officeholders are quite different from those of attitudinal support for black candidates, and that gaining electoral support for women is likely to be the more difficult task.

The respondents in this study are young college-educated people, who would be expected to be more likely than the average American to accept women and blacks as political leaders. But we have seen that in most cases these respondents are less willing—and black respondents are *markedly* less willing—to support prospective women candidates and officeholders than to support black and Jewish candidates, especially when the presidency, rather than a local office, is at issue.

One possible explanation can be found in a penetrating analysis by Stern et al., (1976: 670–671). They show that while blacks have made measurable gains in occupational status relative to whites in the last 30 years, women have not made comparable gains relative to men. The difference is due in part, they feel, to the effects of group size: To attain occupational equality for women would require a much greater restructuring of the social system than to achieve occupational equality for blacks in a continuing system of sexual stratification. Similarly, in politics, a great increase in the proportion of political leaders who are women would inevitably displace many male officeholders and redistribute a great deal of power.

Male dominance in politics reflects the unequal distribution of power between men and women in society. Traditional sex-role norms are designed to justify this inequality by teaching that women "naturally" belong in some roles and not others, rather than that women are usually limited to supporting roles because they are a disadvantaged group. Thus it is understandable that an acceptance of women as political leaders would require a reduction in the power of these traditional sex-role attitudes more generally. And, clearly, this would mean a pervasive social change, involving greater acceptance of new opportunities for women (and therefore for men) throughout American society.

As sexual roles become less restrictive, more women are likely to perceive that they have the aptitude for becoming candidates and the chance to win political leaders' support. Studies show (Karnig and Walter, 1976: 607–608; Darcy and Schramm, 1977) that women who do run for office are successful about as often as men candidates are. So the major hurdle for women seems to be recruitment and candidate-selection; it is at this stage where women are excluded or become discouraged from running. Part of the problem may be the sex-role attitudes of party leaders, activists, and contributors. More flexible sex-role attitudes among political power-holders might help to convince prospective women candidates that they have at least a shot at gaining campaign funds, volunteer workers, and other specialized services that spell the difference between a contender and a sacrificial lamb.

Another difference between women and blacks as candidates is signalled by the finding that supporters of women in politics are not as readily identified in group-terms—and especially that women as a group are less favorable toward women candidates than black respondents are toward black candidates. Consequently, women lack the cohesive voting patterns (so often found among blacks) that can warn political leaders that a social grouping has become a force to be reckoned with, requiring inclusion of its members on party slates and attention to its special concerns.

The spatial concentration of blacks in American society has facilitated the growth of black consciousness and cohesion—the sense of shared identity and destiny, the communication of group aims, and the organizing of group members. In contrast, the spatial dispersion, large numbers, and variation in personal opportunities among American women make such consciousness much harder to achieve. So as Miller and associates (1978: 15) found, there is much less group identification among women than among blacks in American society. One likely result is that many women political leaders hesitate to call themselves "women's candidates" or to direct their campaigns to women's rights issues (see Mezey, 1978: 374); without distinctive support from women voters, candidates would gain few points for doing so.

The time-honored coalition-of-groups methods by which ethnic and racial minorities have gained some measure of political power do not yet seem available to women. But there is evidence that a coalition receptive to supporting women in politics can be built on less traditional moorings: among individuals, groups, and communities with more flexible sex-role .attitudes.

NOTES

*It is a pleasure to acknowledge the contructive comments of Ted Carmines, Jim Kuklinski, Austin Ranney, Gina Sapiro, W. Phillips Shively, and especially Howard V. Hershey, and the capable assistance of Jonathan Hurwitz, Barbara Allen, and Jill Baker.

1. There is some evidence to suggest that policy outputs would change if a higher percentage of public offices were held by women. Several studies show that women legislators have given somewhat greater attention than their male colleagues to issues of health, education, social welfare, and "good government"—areas traditionally seen as "appropriate" for women in politics (see, for example, Diamond, 1977: 45, 49–50; Kirkpatrick, 1974). But other research finds women legislators no more favorable to various issues of interest to women (such as abortion policy) than men are, nor more likely to give these issues high priority (see Mezey, 1978). It is risky, however, to try to predict the characteristics, policy preferences, and effect of future women political leaders by making a linear extrapolation from the findings of current studies. Present women candidates and officials have faced great obstacles in running and an overwhelmingly male environment in office. This political environment has probably selected for certain types of women candidates and affected their behavior. We might expect to find different distributions of attitudes and behavior among women in politics when political leadership is no longer an unusual role for a woman.

2. Note that potential support for women in politics is operationalized as giving "equal consideration" to men and women candidates. This wording is designed to measure androgyny in attitudes (an egalitarian orientation) rather than feminism (defined as the commitment to give preference to women). Androgyny and feminism are often confused, as Heilbrun points out (1973: 58), because they are blocked by the same force in a patriarchal society: the view that

roles should be assigned according to sex, and leadership roles are properly assigned to males. But given the public's limited experience with women officeholders, it seems preferable to conceptualize "support" as attitudes receptive to more female leaders, rather than limiting our concern to those who actively prefer women to men as public officials.

3. Only 2–5% of the respondents expressed greater confidence in a women than a man official on any item. Treating this response as a separate value results in a skewed scale due to zero- and small-N cells in the higher values. So this response was combined with that of equal confidence in women and men officials; the resulting scale had greater internal consistency (alpha = .78 for whites, .76 for blacks; mean interitem correlation = .42 for whites, .38 for blacks). To examine the implications of this decision, regressions were run using both versions of the scale. The beta-weights were virtually unchanged; combining the two responses increases the scale's reliability without altering the substantive findings.

4. Socioeconomic status measures included data on family incomes and dummy variables for the respondent's mother's and father's occupations (one variable for white-collar jobs and a second for blue-collar, with absent/unemployed as the residual category). The intercorrelations among these measures, and between SES measures and race, are low (range = .06 to .34), except for high correlations between father's occupation (white-collar) and income (r = .55) or race (.46) and between white-collar and blue-collar father's occupations (r = .68). In these cases the beta-weights are best interpreted as a joint effect of both variables. When hierarchical regression was used, varying the order in which variables were added to the equation, the minimal changes in coefficients suggest that multicollinearity is not a serious problem here.

10

THE RACIAL REORIENTATION OF
AMERICAN POLITICS

Edward G. Carmines
James A. Stimson

It was arguably the case that issues of race were not partisan issues as
recently as 1960. Advocates of racial liberalism were to be found about
equally among northern Democrats and Republicans. Hostility to the aspira-
tions of black Americans was almost exclusively the province of the southern wing of the Democratic party. For the mass electorate, race was a
regional concern; on this question the union halls and country clubs were in
easy agreement. Neither party found it advantageous to stake out distinctive
positions on this potentially volatile issue, and citizens responded accord-
ingly. Except for the Dixiecrats, race was an irrelevant cue for the development of party attachments.

None of these assertions would now be true. The Democratic party has
become the home of racial liberalism. The strident Dixiecrats of old have
nearly vanished from the American political scene; one of the few who
remains is now a Republican. Gone also are most of the racially liberal
Republicans who played a key role in the early legislative victories for civil
rights. Time is the principal explanation for the passage of these actors from
the scene, but it cannot account for their nonreplacement by others of similar
stripe. For that we need to postulate an issue realignment.

Substantial changes of long duration at the elite level could not occur
without influencing (or being influenced by) mass policy attitudes. And we
shall see that this is the case with regard to race. All partisans, in the

AUTHOR'S NOTE: This material is based upon work supported by the National Science
Foundation under Grant No. SOC-7907543.

aggregate, are more liberal on questions of racial desegregation now than in the past (largely, it would appear, from cohort replacement over time). But within the secular movement of mass opinion is a smaller partisan reorientation. In no individual year but 1964 is the change of notable magnitude, but the mass public, like the political elites, has undergone an apparent sorting, leaving the racial attitudes of the two aggregate parties different now—when that was not earlier the case.

The goal of this chapter will be to highlight the distinctive elements in racial attitudes that appear to be working a continuing reshaping of American politics in the 1970s. Toward that end we will need to come to terms with "issues" in general and race as a special case; that is the focus of section 2. We then examine the dimensional structure of racial attitudes (section 3), evidence of race/party realignment (section 4), and finally the belief structuring role of racial attitudes.

One theme of this chapter is that race is not just another issue, that including it in that analytic category is likely to distort our understanding both of issues and "racial issues." An issue typology is a useful device to lay the groundwork for that separation.

A TYPOLOGY OF ISSUE EVOLUTIONS

We begin with a fundamental assumption that the New Deal party system is the backdrop for the origin, evolution, and resolution of policy issues in American politics. New issues develop within that old framework. Some are natural extensions of the old party system. Some emerge but never develop in an inhospitable political environment. Some emerge as a response to a temporary opportunity. And some emerge, persist, and modify the environment from which they were created. Defined by their duration and relation to their party system environment, issues can be classified into one of four types.

I. ORGANIC EXTENSIONS

Our type I issues have an organic relation to the New Deal party system. These issues form the political agenda for the fulfillment of the New Deal promise; they are direct evolutionary descendants of the New Deal issues. While not a focus of concern during the New Deal itself, these issues nonetheless represent the logical culmination of the increased domestic, social welfare role of the federal government undertaken during Roosevelt's presidency.

Federal aid to education, for example, an issue that occupied a prominent place on the political agenda of the 1950s and early 1960s, posed the same kind of questions and invoked the same sort of reactions as did the New Deal. From its very inception, federal aid to education was a party-cleavage issue (Page, 1978: Ch. 5), separating Democrats from Republicans. Other examples of this type of issue include government provision of health care and government guarantee of full employment, both of which also reflect the underlying issue-party cleavage that has its roots in the New Deal (Carmines and Gopoian, 1978). Because issues of this type develop fully within the boundaries of the pre-existing political environment, they do not have the capacity to alter the political system. They are instead a source of continuing stability.

II. NONSALIENT POLICY CONFLICTS

Those issues that never capture the public's attention compose type II. These issues may have important objective consequences. They are, however, too complex, technical, and nonsalient to form an effective communication link between citizens and elites. For this reason, they tend ultimately to be resolved by the political elites themselves with very little guidance from the mass public (Matthews and Stimson, 1975). Perhaps the best contemporary illustrations of "nonsalient issues" are the host of conflicts involved in national energy policy. Genuine policy disputes of unquestioned importance, these conflicts have so far failed to exert substantial influence in electoral politics for lack of shared referents between masses and elites.

III. SHORT-TERM ISSUES

Some issues have great impact in the short term, but do not leave a permanent mark on the political system. These issues are linked typically to political events that cause disturbances in the existing political environment. The public may become aroused about these issues, even to the point of decisive electoral impact. These issues do not, moreover, reinforce the bases of the existing party system, but instead can be a source of strain in one or more of the political parties.

But while type III issues can be important in a particular election, their effects are short-term. They may influence system outcomes, but they do not change the system. These issues have the important limitation of being unable to sustain themselves beyond the events that brought them into being. Thus, as the events fade in public memory, the issues lose their salience and with it their ability to shape public opinion. The dramatic short-term electoral importance of these issues is thus counterbalanced by their inconsequential long-term partisan effects on the political system. Contemporary examples of this issue type include Vietnam and Watergate.

IV. LONG DURATION ORTHOGONAL ISSUES

Type IV issues are those that have the capacity to alter the political environment within which they originated and evolved. These issues have a long life cycle; they develop, evolve—and sometimes are resolved—over a great number of years. The crucial importance of this issue type stems from the fact that its members can lend to fundamental and permanent change in the party system. These are "realigning" issues in the weak connotation of the term. They do realign the coalitional basis of the party system. But that does not imply realignment in the stronger sense, the creation of new majority parties.

This issue type possesses the key characteristics absent from each of the other three. Thus, unlike organic extension issues, realigning issues do not merely continue the existing party system. They cut across the direct line of evolutionary development. They emerge from the old environment, but once having emerged they introduce fundamental tensions into the party system and are inconsistent with the continued stability of old patterns. These issues capture the public's attention for more than a short span of time; they tend to be salient for a number of years. They are distinctive, finally, in their unique combination of short-term and long-term effects. Thus, they may result in voting defections among partisans, but more importantly, they also alter the fundamental link between citizen and party. They have the ability to alter the party system from which they emerged.

Realigning issues are likely to be underestimated within the limits of the cross-sectional research design, because their important long-term consequences can be hidden by modest, short-term effects. Since they develop and evolve slowly, the snapshot given of them in cross-sectional designs is bound to underestimate their effect, a problem that concerned the authors of *The American Voter* (Campbell et al., 1960) early in the history of mass behavior research. Only a longitudinal perspective can capture the long-term consequences of realigning issues.

The number and effect of realigning issues are restricted by the stability of party attachments. Race, we believe, is the only issue of this type since the formation of the New Deal (for a discussion of the New Deal realignment see Andersen, 1979). It has a nearly full evolutionary cycle, developing from partisan obscuring during the New Deal itself, to dramatic significance during the 1960s, to lessened (but still strong) salience during the 1970s. It is an issue with deeply felt preferences. Like few issues in American history, race touches a sensitive nerve.

Race, in sum, is not merely one issue among many that have crowded the political agenda since the New Deal. It is the single manifestation of the issue type that has the greatest implications for the long-term development of the political system. And it is a useful vehicle for understanding the more general phenomena of issue evolution.

Before we can proceed with analysis of racial attitudes, we need to determine their structure. The 1972 Center for Political Studies (CPS) National Election Study provides unusually rich materials for the task.

THE STRUCTURE OF RACIAL ATTITUDES

To argue that "race" is a long-term influence on electoral behavior presumes, among other things, that race is a durable attitude dimension. Its influence may come and go, but the attitude itself is thought to persist. The emotional intensity of the racial issue also leads us to expect a consistency between the various subdomains (housing, jobs, busing, or whatever) forming the attitude dimension.

But the racial struggle in American politics has tended to be a series of skirmishes, some of which have resulted in cumulative victories (integrating the armed forces, outlawing de jure school segregation, and the like), while others—equal employment opportunities, for example—remain on the agenda year after year. The centrality of the various subdomains would consequently be expected to change over time as some issues leave the agenda to be replaced by others.

What then is the structure of response to racial issues in the 1970s? Only school busing achieved major public notice in the "benign neglect" Nixon years. Is it now the central racial issue? As the only specific racial issue assigned a seven-point proximity scale in recent CPS national election studies[1] and the only racial issue given more than fleeting attention in most analyses, busing seems a prime candidate for that role.

The 1972 CPS study, particularly rich in racial items, allows mapping of patterns of association among a number of "old" racial issues, varied black images (through "feeling thermometers"), and, of course, busing. A factor analysis (principal axes) of the correlations among these items (Table 10.1) indicates that they measure two fairly distinct dimensions of racial attitudes.[2] Factor 1 will be referred to as the "segregation/integration" dimension; the items that load most strongly on it are key elements of the traditional civil rights program (e.g., desegregation, school integration, and neighborhood integration). This factor is an indicator of the extent to which respondents felt the federal government should promote racial desegregation. The items that load most strongly on factor 2, on the other hand, tap feelings toward images of black leaders and activists. The difference between these factors suggests that respondents discriminate between the content of the civil rights program on the one hand and its public advocates on the other.[3] And where policies and advocates are most clearly linked, in the case of (traditional) civil rights leaders, so too are the two factors.

The two CPS seven-point scales—one on school busing, the other on government aid to minority groups—do not load cleanly on either factor. And this must question the assumption that these issues are the new exemplar of racial politics in America. These measures, the subjects of so much analysis, appear to have dubious validity as indicators of racial liberalism or conservatism. Response to busing particularly is not strongly correlated

TABLE 10.1   The Dimensions of Racial Attitudes: A Principal Factor Analysis (with
              varimax rotation)*

Variable	Factor 1 "Segregation/ Integration"	Factor 2 "Affect toward Black Activists"
Equal employment	.480	−.244
School integration	.535	−.268
Public accommodations	.577	−.137
Neighborhood integration	−.594	.037
School busing	.385	−.344
Aid minorities	.459	−.391
Civil rights too fast	−.504	.335
Blacks violent	−.478	.167
Blacks helped/hurt cause	.461	−.228
(De)segregation	.615	−.141
Prefer (de)segregated neighborhood	.460	−.211
Same intelligence	.399	−.098
Feeling thermometers		
Black militants	−.151	.791
Urban rioters	−.120	.776
Civil rights leaders	−.490	.528
Eigenvalue	5.16	1.42
(Percent explained variance)	(34.4)	(9.5)

*The sample consists of 2191 respondents who were interviewed in both pre and postelection waves.

with the rest of the racial program, including school desegregation. This seems to reflect the simple fact that nobody likes busing. It is a sort of inverse apple pie, so uniformly disliked that it is a valence issue. However important it may be in its own right, the busing issue is not an important component of more general racial policy attitudes. To measure racial attitudes for our analysis we have abandoned the CPS seven-point scales and instead use our two factor scales.[4]

That brings us to the question of whether "race," in any of its forms, is a continuing influence on the political behavior of the American electorate.

RACE AND THE REALIGNMENT OF PARTY IDENTIFICATION

Issues that matter in the evolution of American politics go beyond influencing the outcome of a single election; they leave their mark on the identification of citizen with party. Boyd has elaborated the point in contrasting the electoral influence of candidates and issues:

> In short, the impact of a candidate is substantial but of short duration. The impact of issues, while rarely great at any moment, accumulates over a period of time. Overall, issues may outweigh candidates in affecting the outcome of the elections, for issues have the capacity to alter the greatest single determinant of a vote, Party Identification [1969: 510].

The large cluster of policies known as "the New Deal" had that effect. Much of that conflict is long since forgotten, but the evidence of a four-decade-old polarization is still clearly visible in the 70s.

Race is not of the order of impact of the New Deal. But we will see that racial more than economic conflicts now seem central to ideological thinking. Might they be central for developing party identifications as well?

Party identification is resistant to change. Once formed, identifications tend to persist, and that limits the possibilities for realignment largely to those with weak or nonexistent identifications. The evidence of realignment in progress would then be expected to be slim. Inertia limits the pace of realignment, but when overcome, promises by the sheer weight of demography to carry it into the future.

To trace race-related change in party identification over time, we have used the 1972 data on racial attitudes, along with personal histories of party identification, to reconstruct the partisan divisions of racial attitudes for those segments of past electorates still present in 1972. The electorate for each presidential contest back to 1952 is recreated by reclassifying 1972 respondents according to their reports of party identification change and by eliminating those not old enough to vote in each reconstructed year.[5]

The recreated electorates *cannot* be taken as representative of actual electorates for any given year, but only of those young enough to be sampled in 1972. They do not accurately tell us what past electorates were, but they do, within the limits of recall, tell us where the 1972 electorate came from.[6] Apparent evidence of secular change in racial liberalism particularly should be ignored, for it may well be an artifact of the biased age distributions of the simulated electorates.

Figure 10.1A traces the 2 dimensions of racial attitudes from 1952 through 1972 for 3 categories of party identifiers: Democrats, Republicans, and the white subcomponent of Democratic identifiers. Figure 10.1B suggests that the dimension we have called "Affect toward Black Activists" separates Republicans and Democrats and has always done so. The slight widening of the gap between partisans appears to reflect the infusion of young voters into the Democratic ranks. However, because the partisan differences are nearly constant—the lines nearly parallel—this attitude dimension cannot explain race/party realignment.

The trends of Figure 10.1A are not so easily dismissed. We have already noted the danger of inferring secular trends from these data, but the observed trends do establish a baseline against which changes among subgroups can be judged. That baseline highlights the one major instance of aggregate change in racial attitudes contrary to the trend, a move to racial conservatism by Republican identifiers in 1964.[7] That movement created a gap between the parties that has never been closed. After at least a decade of similarity to the Democrats, Republican identifiers moved to the racial "right" in 1964

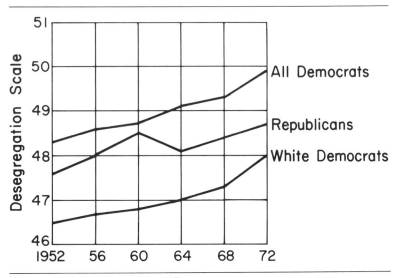

FIGURE 10.1A   Desegregation and Party

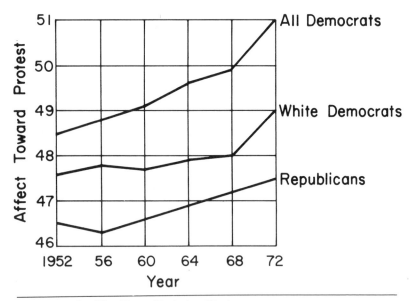

FIGURE 10.1B   Affect Toward Protest and Party

and stayed more or less in that track while other elements moved uniformly to the "left." By 1972 the GOP rank-and-file was only slightly more liberal than white (disproportionately southern) Democrats.

The divergence of the parties on the traditional segregation/integration dimension is not large. Neither party can accurately be called the party of segregation or integration. But a divergence did occur, and it went against the grain of a century of association of racism with the Democratic Party.

Because we can trace the flow of new party identifiers over time, we can highlight the larger changes among *new* partisans that are considerably diminished when aggregated with the old. In Figure 10.2 we plot the aggregated racial attitudes for new identifiers, by year and cumulatively since 1952. New identifiers are in the main newly eligible voters, but the category also includes a very much smaller group that reports movement from either independence to a party or from one party to the other.

After attracting new identifiers slightly more liberal than the Democrats in the period through 1960, the Republican party not only moved to racial conservatism in 1964 but did so quite dramatically. Those who report first identifying with the GOP in that year are strikingly more segregationist than any other group of identifiers. About two-thirds of those new identifiers were newly eligible voters; their attitude distribution is, in any case, almost identical to the previously eligible who report a new Republican identification. Movement away from the GOP contributed virtually nothing—contrary to much speculation at the time—to the new look of Republican identifiers.

The 1964 presidential election thus appeared to mark a sharp and durable change in the racial policy preferences of party supporters, leaving Democrats more supportive of using the federal government to insure the rights of black Americans. This is preliminary evidence that the 1964 election was a "critical" election, reorienting the attitudinal base of the two major parties (Key, 1955).

What is interesting about the 1968 new identifiers is not what did happen but what did not. The appearance of George Wallace on the electoral scene in 1968 appears to have stopped for a time the racial polarization of party identification. Although the causes are no doubt multiple and messy, it seems reasonable to assume that Wallace delayed the normal development of identification with party for his young constituency. By removing a large number of racial conservatives from the ranks of new identifiers, those remaining are slightly more liberal than would be expected and, more importantly, undifferentiated by party. Ideologues of the left may also have been slow to identify in that year because of the McCarthy and Kennedy insurgency in the Democratic party. But the number of new identifiers is too small to permit systematic analysis of these speculations.

Whatever was the case in 1968, the alignment of racial attitudes with party identification began again in 1972. Considerably less dramatic than the 1964 alignment, the Democratic party again went against its southern heritage to recruit distinctively more liberal new identifiers and the Republican party moved slightly rightward from its 1968 recruitment.[8] That rightward turn is less slight in contrast to the attitudes of other new identi-

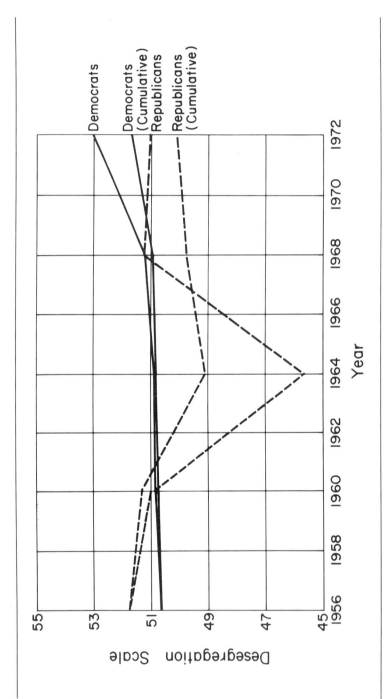

FIGURE 10.2   New Identifiers

fiers; a small move to the right is stark against a trend in the other direction.

The net effect of adding new identifiers is shown in the cumulative portion of Figure 10.2. Since the Republican party has attracted both more liberal (before 1964) and more conservative identifiers over the twenty-year span, the net effect—an average of both trends—is not large. But the inter-party differences in racial attitudes in 1964 and beyond are so large that they easily outweigh the earlier pattern. And the new identifiers (Figure 10.2) are now about half of each party's base. Thus we have a change of some perma-nence, for even if race now ceases to be a salient aspect of partisan divisions, the changes already effected will be carried into the future by the inertia of established loyalty.

In summary, our analysis through 1972 reveals that race has affected the relation of citizenry with party. No longer similar in racial attitudes, as they were from at least 1952 until 1964, party identifiers are now distinguishable, with Democrats being more firmly committed to using the federal govern-ment to establish and maintain the rights of black Americans. Particularly when set against the historical positions of the parties, attitudes toward racial integration appear to have provoked an issue realignment.

It is a strange sort of realignment, however, for it appears to work to the detriment of the minority party. Not a new issue cleavage to balance the scale of party strength, it appears rather to add further imbalance.

1976 AND BEYOND

The 1972 contest has been the centerpiece of this analysis for a number of reasons. It was the first presidential election subsequent to the electoral period when race was generally believed to be salient. Thus, it was impor-tant to speak to the contention that 1972 marked the end of racial politics. The quantity and diversity of racial attitude materials that the 1972 CPS study offers also are unsurpassed in the national election study series. And with neither Nixon or McGovern closely identified with the racial politics of the 1960s, it offered an opportunity to study the long-term effect of race relatively free from short-term disturbances.

The 1976 election, on the other hand, is clouded by Jimmy Carter's identification with southern regional pride, culture, and politics side by side with appeal to, and support from, black voters. This election-specific confu-sion makes 1976 a bad candidate for the study of realignment. The 1976 CPS measures of racial attitudes also are not the equal of the earlier study. But to assert an issue realignment compels us to look at the newest evidence.

Because we regard the 1976 contest with some suspicion, it is treated as an independent test of the issue realignment thesis.[9] Our method is as before: a scale of contemporary (i.e., 1976) desegregation attitudes[10] is projected backward (to 1972) by reclassifying respondents who report shifts in party

identification or who were not old enough to vote at the earlier time. There
are three possible outcomes of this analysis:

(1) Interparty differences in desegregation could decline over the 1972–1976
period. That would undercut the realignment thesis, leading to the conclusion
that the observed realignment was either weak or transitory.
(2) Interparty differences could stay about the same over the period. That would
be evidence of a consolidated realignment; the effects of the past would
endure, but not increase.
(3) Interparty differences could increase. That would be evidence of intensifying
realignment.[11]

The outcome reported in Table 10.2 comes closest to the "consolidated
realignment" interpretation. Although the desegregation attitudes of Republican and Democratic identifiers are significantly different in both years,
the slight *increase* in the gap between the two sets of identifiers is not
statistically significant.

TABLE 10.2   Desegregation Attitudes of 1976 and (reconstructed) 1972 Identifiers*

	All Identifiers		"New" Identifiers
Party	1972	1976	1976
Democrat	50.44	50.81	53.58
Republican	48.16	48.42	50.36
Difference	2.28	2.39	3.22
	(P<.001)	(P<.001)	(P<.05)
N	1349	1506	158

*Entries are mean scores on Desegregation Scale. Higher scores indicate stronger advocacy of
desegregation measures (see n. 12).

Comparison of the 1972 and 1976 cross sections is muddied by the fact
that they are partially overlapping samples. A somewhat cleaner view of
change can be gained by looking only at new partisans, those who either are
newly eligible to vote or report a party identification change subsequent to
1972. That analysis, also reported in Table 10.2, shows that the Democratic
party continued to recruit new identifiers more favorably disposed to racial
desegregation than their Republican counterparts, a difference that is statistically significant. It is notable that this occurred in the face of Jimmy
Carter's evident appeal to white southerners of traditional inclination. The
"intensifying realignment" interpretation therefore also has some support.

The 1976 data offer one last indication of what may lie ahead in racial
politics. A good part of the issue realignment we have observed, particularly
in the 1960s, resulted from the shift of black voters from "mostly Democratic" in loyalty to a position of near unanimity. The Democratic party thus
became, in the aggregate, more liberal on racial issues than its opposition.
But the aggregate party differences obscured the "contradiction" of racial
attitudes within the Democratic coalition. White Democrats, disproportionately southern, have always been more segregationist in outlook than

white Republicans. This awkwardness of the Democratic coalition on issues of race, the preoccupation of many who observe American politics, has undoubtedly slowed the pace of realignment.

The slow realigning forces we have observed in the 1970s appear to be largely among white voters—there was no further room for movement among blacks. By 1976 this movement had led to a resolution of the contradiction: even among whites, Democrats more than Republicans now advocate desegregation. The margin of difference is insignificant, but the trend which brought us to this point is an indication of a slow but powerful reshaping of racial attitudes and party loyalties.

Table 10.3 is a verbal summary of the complicated changes we have observed. It displays a growing split that is by no means symmetrical, a result of one powerful move to the right by the Republicans and two later countermoves to the left by the Democrats—all of course superimposed on an apparent secular trend for the electorate.

TABLE 10.3   The Sources and Consequences of Racial Attitude Change: 1960–1976

Year	Source of change:		Net Partisan Effect
	New Democrats	New Republicans	
1960	No change	No change	None
1964	No change	More conservative	New inter-party difference
1968	No change	No change	Sustained inter-party difference
1972	More liberal	No change	Increased inter-party difference
1976	More liberal	No change	Increased inter-party difference

AN ISSUE EVOLUTION

The mainline racial issues reached their peak of public attention in the 1960s and have been much less discussed since then. But the evidence suggests a continuing impact of racial attitudes on identification with party several years beyond heated discourse. Converse and Markus (1979) have recently noted that "civil rights," marked by over time stability in the 1950s, has that same attribute in the 1970s—in contrast to all other old issues. That is consistent with the continuing issue realignment we see in the same data.

It is intriguing that the "effect" seems to occur in the absence of the "cause." That leads us to speculate about causal mechanisms other than the obvious. One is the possibility that race may have a surrogate in ideology, that it may continue to exert influence because it has changed the belief structures of the American mass public. We hypothesize, more specifically, that race has become central to the way Americans see the political world.

THE CENTRALITY OF RACE

With the publication of Converse's masterly study of belief systems in mass publics (Converse, 1964), a controversy was introduced into political science which, if anything, has grown more intense during the last few years. Examining a large collection of diverse data pertaining to mass political attitudes and issue preferences, Converse drew a most unflattering portrait of the American electorate. According to his analysis, most voters did not use ideological terms such as liberalism and conservatism to evaluate political parties and candidates; they did not even recognize and understand these terms when asked about them; their preferences on different policy issues were not related to one another, indicating a lack of "constraint" in their political belief systems; and in fact, the over time stability of their issue preferences was so low as to suggest that they really did not have meaningful political beliefs.

More recent studies have called into question at least one aspect of this now-familiar portrait. Nie and his associates (1974, 1976) have presented seemingly persuasive evidence indicating dramatic increases in issue constraint among the mass public during the last fifteen years. A 1950s electorate characterized by almost total lack of attitudinal consistency had apparently by 1964 given way to one which possessed substantial structuring of political beliefs. The tendency of citizens to structure their issue preferences along clear liberal-conservative lines—so long considered a benchmark of political sophistication by political analysts and journalists alike—had apparently become a reality for many American voters.

But even before this newer evidence could become part of our conventional wisdom about American politics, it too had been questioned. A series of recent reports (Bishop et al., 1978a, 1978b, 1978c, 1979; Brunk, 1978; Sullivan et al., 1978, 1979) have suggested that there has actually been very little increase in issue constraint since the early 1960s. Instead, it is argued that the increased constraint discovered by Nie and his associates was the result of changes in survey question formats.

Examining data for four issue areas (welfare, integration, welfare for blacks, and the Cold War)[12] collected from a series of SRC/CPS election studies and from two NORC surveys, Nie et al. argued that the data fall naturally into two periods. From 1950 through 1960, there were very low levels of issue constraint while the upsurge was dramatic in 1964, and the higher levels of attitude consistency continued through 1973.

Table 10.4 presents the average correlations for these 2 periods and for 3 issue types: nonrace issues (welfare and the Cold War), mixed issues (one of

TABLE 10.4   Levels of Issue Constraint, by Time Period and Issue Type (average gammas between issues)

	1956–1960 average	1964–1973 average
Nonrace issues	.15	.22
Mixed issues	.17	.33
Race issues	.54	.69

Source: These correlations were recomputed from those provided in Nie, Verba, and Petrocik (1976: 124).

the issues in the correlation is racial while the other is nonracial), and racial issues (integration and welfare for blacks). One important aspect of the table is immediately discernible. The racial issues have been highly related to one another throughout both periods. The 1956–1960 average correlation of .54 is especially noteworthy, for it suggests that even during the quiescent 1950s, there was substantial internal cohesion for the issue domain. A second revealing aspect of the table and one that bears more directly on our thesis involves the relative increases in average correlations for the nonrace issues and the mixed issues between the two periods. The increase is only .07 for the former issue type but more than twice that for the latter type (.16). This differential increase, unexplainable in the context of both Nie's interpretation as well as his critics', is quite consistent with the thesis developed in this chapter. It suggests, simply, that race has been relatively central to the increased levels of issue constraint found in the American mass public. Racial issues have perhaps provided a structuring principle for the political attitudes of a substantial number of American citizens.

The evidence is far from conclusive. But these data suggest an important role for race in the heightened internal consistency of mass belief systems.

RACIAL ATTITUDES AND ATTITUDE STRUCTURE

The 1972 presidential campaign provides a demanding test of our thesis. On the one hand, the campaign was, at least from a comparative perspective, preeminently an ideological and issue-oriented contest (Miller and Levitin, 1976; Miller et al., 1976). McGovern seemed in particular to represent the very personification of ideological choice in American presidential elections. Calling for major alterations in taxing and welfare policies, for immediate peace in Vietnam, and for massive spending to reduce unemployment among minorities and the poor, McGovern espoused policy positions of a consistently left/liberal ideological persuasion. The objective issue differentiation between the candidates had a predictable effect on mass perceptions: Across a variety of specific issues, McGovern was consistently seen as the more liberal candidate, with a considerable distance separating him from Nixon (Aldrich and McKelvey, 1977).

On the other hand, race—the issue which we have argued is central to attitude integration within the mass public—was conspicuously absent from the rhetoric of the 1972 presidential campaign. It was simply not an issue. Instead, Nixon concentrated on his foreign policy achievements, while McGovern emphasized Vietnam and income redistribution schemes. The civil rights movement, unable to compete for public attention with the war in Vietnam, Watergate, energy, and an ill-behaved economy, seemed to be a thing of the past. It was thus not surprising that the major study of the election found racial attitudes to be relatively unimportant in determining electoral behavior (Miller et al., 1976).

The inattention given to race, coupled with the heightened concern with other issues, makes 1972 a perfect test of our thesis. For if we find racial attitudes at the core of issue constraint in 1972, we have no reason to believe that it results from short-term stimulus factors associated with the presidential campaign. There were no overt racial cues provided in this election.[13] Instead, it would suggest that race has played a long-term and powerful role in shaping mass belief systems.

The strategy we adopt to demonstrate empirically that racial attitudes are central to belief structuring in 1972 is to examine the level of attitudinal consistency found among political issues without controlling for racial attitudes, as compared to that when controls are introduced. If the latter shows substantially less constraint than the former, then we have strong evidence for the centrality of race. Our approach is complicated somewhat by the fact that the degree of attitudinal consistency has been found to be positively associated with level of formal education as well as levels of political activity and information (Converse, 1964). Therefore, an index of cognitive ability is created which, in the ensuing analysis, will be used to classify the 1972 electorate into four groups.[14]

Table 10.5 presents the results of a factor analysis of the intercorrelations of a variety of political issues and 2 racial attitudes separately for each of the 4 ability groups.[15] The political issues are measured by the familiar seven-point self-placement scales (not proximity measures) and focus on attitudes toward guaranteed jobs, tax reform, legalization of marijuana, national health insurance, women's rights, withdrawal from Vietnam, controlling inflation, and protecting the rights of the accused. The two racial scales are the factor scores we have earlier discussed.

The evidence provided by Table 10.5 is clear. The lowest ability groups show almost no evidence of unidimensional attitude constraint. In fact, for the lowest ability group only 4 of the 10 variables have their highest factor loading on the first unrotated factor. Moving from those of low cognitive ability upward on the scale, there is clear evidence of increasing unidimensional attitude constraint. For example, all 10 variables have their highest loading on the first factor for the highest ability group. Moreover, this factor explains 33.4% of the total variance in the intercorrelation matrix, which is substantially higher than that explained by 2, 3, or 4. All of the evidence

TABLE 10.5 The Factor Structure as Evidence of Issue Constraint, by Cognitive Ability Group

Cognitive ability group	Average intercorrelation among issues	Eigenvalue of first factor	Variance explained by first factor	Number of issues with highest loading on first factor	Average loading of issues on first factor
1 (lowest)	.13	2.07	20.7%	4	.35
2	.13	2.19	21.9	8	.37
3	.18	2.88	28.8	9	.45
4 (highest)	.25	3.34	33.4	10	.51

TABLE 10.6 The Factor Structure as Evidence of Issue Constraint Controlling for Racial Attitudes, by Cognitive Ability Group

Cognitive ability group	Average intercorrelation among issues	Eigenvalue of first factor	Variance explained by first factor	Number of issues with highest loading on first factor	Average loading of issues on first factor
1 (lowest)	.10	1.66	20.7%	3	.28
2	.08	1.49	18.6	5	.25
3	.09	1.64	20.5	5	.30
4 (highest)	.13	1.85	23.2	4	.36

provided in Table 10.5 supports the same basic conclusion: Those of higher cognitive ability have more unidimensionally constrained belief systems. That is a baseline for further analysis.

Table 10.6 presents the results of a factor analysis of the intercorrelations among the political issues controlling for racial attitudes. That is, the factor analysis is based on an analysis of the partial correlation matrix. Among the lower cognitive ability groups, there is again a lack of attitudinal consistency. Whether one controls for racial attitudes or not has little effect on the levels of constraint discovered among those of lowest cognitive ability. In both instances, there is almost a complete absence of attitude integration.

The differences between the two tables, however, are quite striking with respect to the higher ability groups. When controlling for racial attitudes, the two highest ability groups show almost a total lack of issue constraint. For example, the first factor accounts for only 23.2% of the variance for those of highest ability. Similarly, only 4 of the 8 issues have their highest loading on the first extracted factor. The differences in the 2 tables can be seen in a simple comparison: there is no more issue constraint among the highest ability group controlling for race (Table 10.6) than there is among the lowest ability group not controlling for race (Table 10.5).

But while the higher ability groups look very different from one another in the 2 tables, the differences among ability groups in Table 10.6 are minimal. Indeed, those of lowest and highest ability look quite similar to one another in that they both display little evidence of attitudinal consistency. The overall conclusion seems inescapable: The higher levels of attitude integration found among the upper ability strata are almost completely nullified by controlling for racial attitudes.[16] Race does seen to have been at the core of the higher levels of issue constraint.

Our analysis thus indicates that racial attitudes were central to the level of attitude consistency found among the 1972 electorate. This structuring role has historically been associated with the use of the liberal-conservative dimension. Through the use of the abstract ordering dimension, specific political attitudes and issue preferences were to be determined by underlying ideological beliefs of great generality concerning government's role in society. The question naturally arises in this context whether racial attitudes are related empirically to liberal-conservative beliefs, especially among those segments of the 1972 electorate that displayed relatively unidimensional belief systems. In fact, the multiple correlations between our 2 racial attitudes and the liberal-conservative 7-point self-placement scale for the 4 ability groups are .27, .29, .55, and .58 (from lowest to highest). This suggests that racial attitudes are not only performing the structuring functions associated with the liberal-conservative dimension but that much of the meaning of this ideological dimension is also racial in nature. This is especially true among those upper ability groups that display the highest levels of attitudinal consistency.

A SUMMARY NOTE

Among the questions that might be asked to determine the role of any political attitude are whether it affects behavior, whether it is stable or transient, how it is related to the party system, and how it is aligned with other attitudes. The behavior question we have addressed elsewhere (Stimson and Carmines, 1977; Carmines and Stimson, 1979). The answer to the question is "yes" in every case we have examined. That is a continuation of a long train of research findings on both mass and elite behaviors. "Civil rights" was the empirically viable case for representational linkage for Miller and Stokes (1963); it remains viable in the 1970s.

Converse (1964) and Converse and Markus (1979) have examined over time stability. Race (or civil rights) is again unusual, showing some relative stability in the 1950s, when other issues—for whatever reason—did not manifest attitudinal stability. Race remains relatively stable in the 1970s, although it is now surpassed by new moral issues. Race alone is relatively stable in both periods.

We have seen that racial attitudes have become related to the party system after the momentous events of the early 1960s. Our evidence suggests small but pervasive impacts. The party of succession and the party of Lincoln and Reconstruction are switching sides in the struggle over black rights. We are impressed not with the size of the transition, but with its regularity. The evidence is much stronger on the question of attitude centrality. But why racial attitudes should lie at the core of structures of political belief is much less clear.

We know what we have seen in all these data; it is an issue evolution. Now we need to understand why issues evolve.

NOTES

1. The CPS studies also contain a 7-point item on governmental aid to minority groups which is quite diffuse and captures some nonracial content as well (Miller et al., 1976: 764).

2. Two additional factors with eigenvalues of 1.2 and 1.08 were excluded.

3. The apparent orthogonality of the two factors is not an artifact of the Varimax rotation. Oblique rotation also produces a near orthogonal solution.

4. To facilitate presentation, the two measures are rescaled to have means of 50 and standard deviations of 10. High scores in both cases indicate liberal response to racial integration and its public advocates. It should also be noted that racial policy conservatism is not necessarily racism. The primary referent of our measure is "government." Racism—not well measured in the survey tradition—is doubtlessly associated with racial policy conservatism, but

the degree of association is an empirical question. The distinction is particularly important in the assessment of attitude trends. The new Republican racial conservatism may, for example, be a considerably different species than the old Dixiecrat variety.

5. The alternate approach, to examine actual electorates with those measures of racial attitudes available in a given year, is dangerous on two counts. The lesser of them is that even perfectly comparable measures across time render the measurement of subtle change a dubious proposition; the greater is that comparable measures do not exist (Achen, 1975; Bishop et al., 1978; Sullivan et al., 1978). If tracing attitude change were our goal, the representativeness of simulated electorates could be improved by the simple expedient of age-weighting.

6. This is similar to the technique used by Andersen in Nie et al. (1976).

7. We use the term "move" loosely. We cannot discriminate between individual attitude shifts and aggregate shifts caused by the gain and loss of identifiers. We assume the latter process is the major one.

8. The pattern is obfuscated by the fact that new Republican identifiers, while racially conservative relative to other new identifiers, are liberal relative to "old" Republicans. Thus the party in aggregate became more liberal by recruiting the most conservative group of new identifiers.

9. It is a genuinely independent test in the important sense that our analysis to this point was completed before we examined the 1976 study. Our predictions are thus a priori in more than the normal connotation of the term.

10. The 1976 scale is composed of four items (school integration, neighborhood integration, "civil rights too fast," and [de] segregation) which were central to the 1972 desegregation scale (see Table 10.1) and continued in the later study. The scale is a sum of the four equally weighted items, expressed as a standard score with a mean and standard deviation of 50 and 10.

11. Interparty differences could also increase from the disappearance from the electorate of prealignment age cohorts, in effect, without continuing realignment. The separate examination of "new" partisans allows us to rule out this possible artifact.

12. We do not include the size of government item in our analysis because its meaning has changed dramatically during this period. See Nie and Rabjohn (1979).

13. By contrast, this would be a plausible alternate explanation for the centrality of race in structuring mass belief systems if we were analyzing the 1964, 1968, or even 1976 presidential elections.

14. For details about how this index was created, see Stimson (1975).

15. The method of factor analysis used is principal axes with squared multiple correlations placed in the main diagonal as an initial estimate of communality. The solution is interrated to reach convergence.

16. On the suspicion that *any* potent issue would produce a similar effect if partialed out of a factor matrix, we replicated this analysis for the two most likely alternatives to the centrality of race, the withdrawal from Vietnam, and "government responsibility to provide jobs" scales. Both dampened the overall appearance of structure, as expected, but left undisturbed the differentiation by cognitive ability.

11

THE NATURE OF PARTY IDENTIFICATION: A REVIEW OF RECENT DEVELOPMENTS

W. Phillips Shively

"Party identification," a psychological identification by which an individual adheres to a political party, was the glory variable of the 1950s and early 1960s. The discovery by the Michigan research group of Campbell, Converse, Miller, and Stokes that knowing an individual's party identification allowed one to predict that individual's vote fairly accurately; their finding that party identifiction was rather stable across individuals' lives; and, most importantly, their elaboration of the implications of this for a wide variety of political questions—all of these brought fame to the Michigan group, provided the basic structure for most studies of voting over a decade or two, and provided a key element in the revision of democratic theory which was produced by behavioral political science in the late 1950s and early 1960s (Campbell et al., 1954, 1960, 1966).

Why was this variable so important? It was, and is, important because it provides one of the few sources of electoral stability in a world filled with sources of electoral flux. Candidates come and go, issues appear and fade, yet election results are fairly predictable from one time to the next, even down to fairly small geographic units. For example, Key and Munger (1959) demonstrated considerable geographic stability of voting patterns by county over periods of up to 100 years. What had imposed such stable patterns? The two most likely explanations would be either something to do with individuals' propensities to choose a party (and indeed, with *families'* propensities, since Key and Munger demonstrated continuity over periods of time longer than any individual's adult life), or else the presence of enduring party organizations that could impose structure on the vote. In the United States, with our weak party organizations, the latter explanation appears unpromising. This leaves us with individuals' propensities to choose one or another party, and party identification has appeared to provide such a factor. As a result, party identification has been a central element in all sorts of analyses of political change and stability. Key's (1955) concept of a "critical election" was reinterpreted by the authors of *The American Voter* to be one in which patterns of party identification change, and this reinterpretation of critical elections has henceforth been generally accepted. Campbell (1960) used the contrast between the effects of party identification and of more transitory factors to produce an intriguing explanation for the differences between presidential elections and off-year congressional elections. The erratic electoral behavior of American farmers was explained at least in part through an examination of party identification (Campbell et al., 1960: Ch. 15). Party identification was developed as a baseline against which to measure variations in behavior (Converse, 1966). And most importantly, theories were developed which portrayed party identification as a systematic force protecting mature democracies against rapid political change (Converse, 1969).

In addition to the theoretic interest which party identification attracted, there is apparent in the literature of the 1950s and early 1960s an emotional attachment to party identification that went beyond the question of utility for theories. This was a period in which American social scientists were fascinated by stability. A conservative form of structural-functional analysis dominated political science, and homeostasis was king. In this context, few scholars were struck by the contradiction between party identification, under which voters are thought to give up a good deal of their political choice to party leaders, and the traditional, liberal democratic assumptions of political free will. Party identification was seen as a natural state, and "independence," its absence, was portrayed as characteristic of the politically unfit and immature. While the *presence* of party identification was not seen to be an anomaly, when the percentage of the population identifying with a party began to decline in the late 1960s after a decade and a half of stability, this *decline* was seen to be an anomaly requiring explanation.

That decline—unexpected by theorists of party identification—together with the general ferment and reconsideration of change and stability that characterized the late 1960s—has led to a reexamination of party identification on a variety of fronts. As a result, the nature of party identification has been found to be not as clear and simple as was once thought, and its role and its political importance have come under scrutiny. This chapter will review some of these new findings and their implications.

New critical work about party identification has primarily addressed two questions: (1) Is party identification as measured by the Michigan group unidimensional? (2) Just how stable is party identification, and to what may change in it be attributed?[1] The latter of these is the more important, so I shall deal with it first.

THE QUESTION OF DURABILITY, AND THE NATURE OF PARTY IDENTIFICATION

The American Voter presented party identification as a lifelong attachment to a party, originating in childhood, which could be expected to change only under fairly extraordinary conditions, such as those of a critical election; because it appeared often to originate in childhood—a time when people are little occupied with politics—party identification appeared to be relatively low in political content. Obviously this picture was not completely accurate, as there was a certain amount of continual shifting of identifications at all times. However, Dreyer (1973) provided evidence that much of what shifting did occur was random movement of the sort one might expect simply from the rough techniques of measurement being used. (But see Brody [1977] for contrary evidence.)

Above all, the aggregate level of party identification appeared to be very stable, indeed. As can be seen in Figure 11.1 the percentage of the population identifying with a party did not vary by more than a percentage point or two from 1952 to 1964.

Figure 11.1 also displays, however, the steady decline in party identification which first appeared in 1966. It was this unexpected drop that made us reconsider the basic nature of party identification. Party identification had been thought to be a "standing decision," not directly tied to immediate political events. In fact, it was often defined as the "long-term electoral force," which was contrasted with "short-term forces," such as the state of the economy, the presence of one or another candidate, or various political issues. However, the decline in party identification beginning in 1966 coincided so neatly with the upheavals of the civil rights movement and of protest against American involvement in the War in Vietnam, that it was hard to avoid the conclusion that the decline was a political response to immediate political events. (Recently Converse [1976] has demonstrated compellingly that the decline was in fact rooted in these events.) This not only cast dust on the image of party identification as the conservator of electoral patterns, but it also forced us to reconsider the nature of party identification. Was it in fact a more immediately political variable than we had thought?

In the wake of this surprising political response on the part of the electorate, scholars have reexamined the stability of individuals' party identification. Both Dobson and St. Angelo (1975) and Brody (1977) have identified movements of party identifiers between parties or in and out of strong identification which are pretty clearly politically based. In fact, changes in

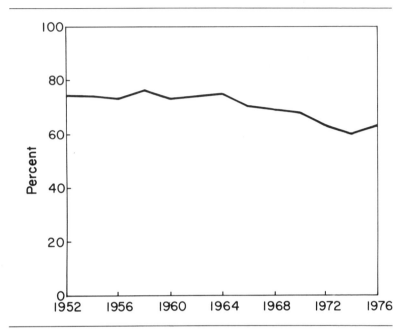

FIGURE 11.1   Percentage of Electorate Identifying with a Party, 1952–1976

party identification had always had political roots, even during the period of considerable partisan stability from 1952 to 1964. Within the overall stable level of party identification, there were hidden significant shifts in the percentage identifying with each of the two major parties. As is seen in Figure 11.2, those shifts were similar to shifts in the vote for the two parties and presumably reflected similar political causes. The changes from one election to another in the percentage of respondents identifying with a party are in the same direction as the changes from one election to another in the percentage of voters voting for that party in 8 of the 12 cases displayed; in 3 further cases, there was no change in the percentage identifying with the party; in only one case (the Republicans, from 1968 to 1972) did the percentage identifying with a party shift in a different direction (-1%) from the percentage of voters supporting the party ($+17\%$).

Thus it is apparent that party identification does respond to political stimuli. It is also apparent that it responds more sluggishly than does the vote. While the *direction* of change in party identification is generally consistent with the direction of change in the vote, the *magnitude* of its change is generally no more than half as great as the magnitude of change in the vote. The conclusion is inescapable that, while party identification is relatively viscous and thus acts to retard electoral change, it is not solely a

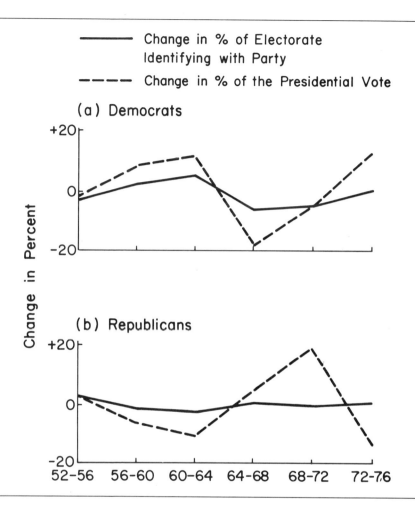

FIGURE 11.2   Change in Vote Share and in Percentage Identifying, by Party

"long-term force" or "standing decision." It changes, though relatively slowly, in response to day-to-day politics.

CHILDHOOD VS. ADULT SOURCES OF PARTY IDENTIFICATION

With the realization that party identification among adults changes—albeit sluggishly—in response to political stimuli, it has made sense to reexamine the established notion that party identification originates in childhood and is largely acquired from one's parents. We know that adults frequently identify with their parents' party, but it is not clear whether this is because of direct transmission or because the children share their parents' social situation and many of their basic values; either of these might eventually lead them to choose the same party as their parents, but in the latter case the identification—chosen by adults—would presumably have greater political content. Goldberg (1969) provides some evidence for the latter of the two processes.

Similarly, we know that children report party identification, and that their reports are fairly stable; and we know that adults report party identification, and that their reports are fairly stable. But no one has as yet been able satisfactorily to link childhood party identification with adult party identification—admittedly a massive problem of design and analysis. The best evidence on this question is that of Jennings and Niemi (1978) who followed a panel of adolescents aged 17–18 in 1965 through to 1973, when they were aged 25–26. Along with this panel, they followed a panel of the respondents' parents. Thus, they ascertained how thoroughly the party identification of people at what might be called their late childhood carried over into the early years of their adulthood. They found (1978: 349) that the relation between adolescent party identification and young adult party identification, over the 8-year span, was $T_b = .42$. By way of comparison, the stability of the parents' party identification over the same time span was $T_b = .67$. Though some of the adolescents may have in fact been "adult" at 17 or 18 years, T_b of .42 is large enough to show a relation between childhood party identification and adult party identification. However, it is also small enough, compared with T_b of .67 for the sample of adults, to suggest that much of the formation of adult party identification may occur during the adult years. Thus there is simply not as yet a clear verdict on how much of adult party identification can be traced to childhood.

NEW CONCEPTIONS OF PARTY IDENTIFICATION

From this general reexamination of the nature of party identification, it has become apparent that party identification is a more immediately political factor than had originally been thought. This has sparked a wide array of attempts to rethink the variable.

Antiparty identification. Maggiotto and Piereson (1977) have suggested that an important part of the identification with party A may consist, not of a positive attraction but of negative feelings about the alternate party B. Maggiotto and Piereson show that adding respondents' evaluations of the opposing party as a variable additional to the standard party identification measure improves substantially on our ability to predict how the respondents will vote. They prefer to keep hostility to the opposite party separate from party identification, arguing that absorbing it in a new measure would make measuring party identification too complicated. Weisberg (1978), however, proposed reconceiving party identification as a set of dimensions, one of which is hostility to the opposing party.

Hostility clearly affects voting strongly. Whether it should be included conceptually as part of identification with a party is another matter. One useful characteristic of party identification as a variable has been that it was *not* the same thing as the choice of how to vote, but rather was (apparently) the most long-term factor among a set of factors influencing the vote. Adding into it such things as hostility toward the opposed party might come dangerously close to transforming party identification simply into a bundle of important independent variables, which would predict well how people would vote but would not be sufficiently distinct from the vote itself to help much in the development of theory.

Party identification as a weighted sum of past satisfactions. A great deal of work on elections is based on models of rational political behavior; voters are assumed to make choices to further fairly specific goals. Party identification as a long-term factor or "standing decision" has always posed a problem for students using such models as it was not clear how such a standing decision could further any particular specific goal. Fiorina (1977) has presented a definition of party identification as a weighted average of past evaluations of the two parties—a definition which may help to address the problem of rationality.

He devises a factor he calls "past political experiences," that is the sum of all satisfactions (or dissatisfactions) a person has had in the past or that his or her parents or other forebears have had in the past, weighted in such a way that feelings whose sources lie far in the past do not count as much as those that are more recent. Thus, vivid experiences which one's parents gained regarding the Republican party during the Great Depression might still influence one's feelings about the two parties, though not as strongly as if the Great Depression had been more recent.

A voter will at any time, then, exhibit a weighted sum of past political experiences for both the Republican and Democratic parties. Party identification is thus defined as:

$$\begin{matrix} \text{Party identification} \\ \text{with Republicans} \end{matrix} = \begin{matrix} \text{Past political} \\ \text{experiences with} \\ \text{Republicans} \end{matrix} - \begin{matrix} \text{Past political} \\ \text{experiences} \\ \text{with Demo-} \\ \text{crats} \end{matrix} + \text{gamma}$$

where "gamma" is a fudge factor indicating the bias with which one first entered the electorate.[2]

With the exception of gamma, Fiorina's definition of party identification is consistent with rational models, since it presents party identification as a "rational" use of past experience to evaluate the parties. Note that it incorporates hostility to the opposite party, as Weisberg suggests we should do, although unlike Weisberg, Fiorina does not maintain such hostility as a separate dimension.

A definition such as this seems broadly consistent with earlier notions of party identification, except for its inclusion of hostility to the opposite party. It emphasizes the role of adult political experiences more than had been done, but that is clearly necessary in light of the fact that adults' party identification does respond to political stimuli. Casting the definition in a way which lets the variable be included easily in rational models is an important step forward, which may help to lessen the estrangement between theory and empirical research in this area.

Party identification purely as political response. We have noted that party identification must involve some element of response to immediate political stimuli. Some scholars, especially Europeans, have concluded that party identification consists solely of immediate political response—that it is, in fact, simply a restatement of how the respondent intends to vote—and that it should not be regarded as a standing decision at all. Measures of party identification in Europe typically do not show the same sort of stability as the measure shows in the United States (Budge et al., 1976). Thomassen (1976) provides good evidence that expressions of party identification among the Dutch should be treated as determined by respondents' choice of which party they plan to vote for rather than the reverse.

It does not appear, at least in the case of the United States, that party identification can be treated solely as an expression of how one will vote. We saw in Figure 11.2 that voting fluctuates much more than party identification does. In fact, voting choice would not be an especially good predictor of party identification.

Even in the European context, however, it may be a mistake to treat party identification solely as an immediate political response. I have argued elsewhere (Shively, 1979b) that peculiar historical circumstances have made it unnecessary for European voters to develop party identification as American voters had done, but that those circumstances are changing and that we might expect in the future to see European voters develop American style of party identification. Baker (1978) provides evidence that this may now be happening in Germany.

Party identification as a mix of "standing decision" and immediate response. A fairly obvious change in the original conception of party identification—in fact, a minimal change in the concept—is to note the presence in it of an element of immediate political response but to regard the concept as an amendable standing decision, with elements both of immediate response and of resistance to change. Converse (1976) takes such a tack, for instance, in his examination of the decline of partisanship in the 1960s.

Such an approach needs elaboration if it is to be helpful. Since it portrays party identification as much more an adult political act than it had previously been thought to be—an identification amendable by adults, and thus presumably rooted ultimately in adult political experience—it underlines the question of why adults would make such a standing decision, giving up a portion of their political individuality to the leaders of a party, rather than simply deciding for themselves at each election how they will vote.

I have attempted elsewhere (Shively, 1979b) to explain why adult voters might become or remain party identifiers. The explanation I use is simple—that voters who have difficulty handling the cacophony of varying political claims and arguments need some sort of guide in deciding how to vote, and that a standing decision to identify with one or another party may provide that guide.[3] Since the identification is then seen to be a tool serving a purpose, it is understandable that changed circumstances, such as the rise of a new and important issue, might cause a voter to change his or her tool to fit the changed conditions. On the other hand, because it is a useful tool for making decisions under ordinary circumstances, party identification would not be changed casually. This interpretation of party identification provides the political content that we obviously need while retaining for party identification the useful characteristic of resistance to change.

There is fairly strong empirical evidence to support this interpretation. I identify two groups of voters as being at opposite poles in their need for a guide to help them in choosing how to vote. On the one hand, voters without much formal education (who might have relatively great difficulty in handling complicated political information) and who feel it is important that they vote (thus, are driven to make electoral choices in spite of their difficulty in doing so) should need such a guide very much; on the other hand, well-educated voters who don't care much about voting should not need such a guide. For convenience, let us call the first type "earnest" and the second "cynical."

In the 1956–1960 CPS presidential election panel, (Shively, 1979b: Appendix A) fully 62% of earnests who did not identify with a party in 1956 shifted into party identification in 1960, while only 8% of earnests who identified with a party in 1956 moved the other way; by contrast, 40% of cynics who did not identify with a party in 1956 shifted to identification in 1960, while 12% of those who identified with a party in 1956 shifted out of identification. Thus, the probabilities of moves into and out of party identification for earnests were .62 and .08; for cynics they were .40 and .12.

Similar results are found for the 1972–1976 CPS presidential election panel. Over these elections, the probabilities of moves into, and out of, party identification for earnests were .53 and .13; for cynics, .25 and .15.

One implication of this interpretation is that, gradually, the U. S. electorate should shift toward less dependence on party identification as a guide, since the population is becoming more fully educated. For instance, the most vulnerable group—those with only grade-school education—composed 27% of the 1956–1960 panel, but only 17% of the 1972–1976 panel.

THE DIMENSIONALITY OF PARTY IDENTIFICATION

Let us turn now from our review of the basic conceptual discussion revolving around the nature of party identification to a more technical problem: Is party identification, as currently measured, a single dimension? And if not, how may it best be measured? The Michigan group developed a measure of party identification based on a central, first question, followed by one of two possible follow-up questions, the choice of which depends on the answer to the first. The interviewer first asks, "Generally speaking, do you usually think of yourself as a Republican, a Democrat, an Independent, or what?" If the answer to this first question is Republican, Democrat, or some other party, the interviewer then asks, "Would you call yourself a strong _____ or a not very strong _____?" If, however, the answer to the first question is Independent, the interviewer then asks, "Do you think of yourself as closer to the Republican or Democratic Party?" From responses to the two questions, investigators construct a 7-point scale of party identification: strong Republican ("Republican," "strong"); weak Republican ("Republican" "not very strong"); leaning Republican ("independent," "Republican"); independent ("independent," "neither"); leaning Democrat ("independent," "Democratic"); weak Democrat ("Democrat," "not very strong"); and strong Democrat ("Democratic," "strong"). This 7-point scale has been taken to measure party identification, from extreme "Republican-ness" through "independence" to extreme "Democratic-ness." It is this scale that has figured in one form or another in almost all work on party identification.

Petrocik (1974) first raised the question whether this scale actually represents a single dimension, or whether in fact the scale represents a mix of various dimensions. In the latter case, any results reached using the 7-point scale must be ambiguous, as one would not know for certain which of the dimensions, in what combinations, were responsible for a relation. Petrocik showed that there were orderly relations between the 7-point scale and clearly partisan variables, such as one's intended vote or the evaluation of parties. However, a variety of other variables generally thought to be related to party identification did not show orderly relations to the 7-point scale. Participation, concern about the outcome of the election, interest in campaigns, regular voting, and other variables showed an irregular relation, with leaning partisans higher on the variable (and, thus, closer to strong partisans) than were weak partisans.

Katz (1979) reports another anomaly that suggests that the conventional scale may be multidimensional. He notes that of strong identifiers in the 1956–1958–1960 American panel study, strong identifiers who switched parties from one election to another were more likely to switch to *strong* identification with the new party than to weak identification or to independence leaning toward it. In other words, strong identification with the Republicans appears to have been "closer" for a strong Democrat (and thus an easier move for that Democrat to make) than was weak identification with the Republicans. From this and from further analysis, Katz concludes that the scale is actually a mix of two dimensions: the direction of one's partisanship and the intensity of one's attention to parties.

Should the party identification scale be broken down and treated as a set dimensions? Clearly there is evidence that it is not a straightforward scale, and a sense of neatness if nothing else would suggest that it should be broken up into clean scales. On the other hand, since we never have perfect measurement the question of how much error we will tolerate in a scale is to some extent pragmatic. There are benefits in working with a single scale rather than a set of scales if the single one identifies with reasonable accuracy unique combinations of the separate component scales. In other words, it might be that strong Republican measures a unique combination of the direction of one's partisanship and of the intensity of one's attention to parties, and that this is also true of other values on the 7-point scale. If this were the case, then the ease of working with a single variable (and the greater prospect of theoretic advances, which that ease would lend us) might lead us to stick with the single dimension as a simultaneous measure of the component dimensions. As a preliminary test, I ran the following test with an undergraduate class. I asked them to rate each party on a 7-point scale from "very good" to "very bad." And, I asked them "How importantly do the Democratic and Republican parties affect your decision when you are choosing how to vote?" (a 7-point scale from "not at all" to "very strongly"). The latter question may be taken to measure political independence. From the *difference* between the party evaluations and from the independence question, a 13×7 space can be constructed. A week later I asked the classic party identification questions of the same students. On Figure 11.3 I have indicated the incidence of various categories of party identification in the 13×7 space.

Notice that strong Republicans generally cluster in the upper right-hand corner of the table, while strong Democrats cluster in the lower right-hand corner. Weak identifiers fall more towards the center of the table, and independents towards the center-left. Thus, at least in a rough way, the standard party identification questions appear to have isolated groups of people who fall within specific regions of the two-dimensional space. How accurately do they accomplish this placement? In Figure 11.4 I have blocked off regions of the two-dimensional space which appear to correspond to the 7 points of the standard scale. (I have left out all cells for which the difference between the parties is zero, but for which some influence is ascribed to parties, as I assume these cases represent unresolved problems in the measures from which the 13×7 space is constructed.) The correspondence

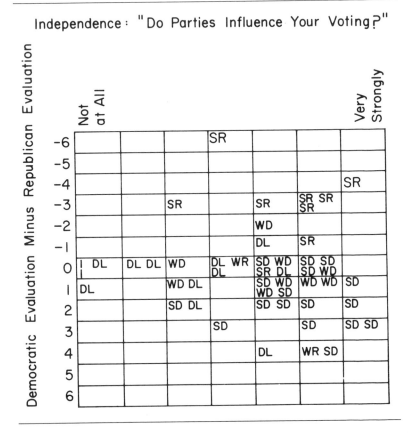

FIGURE 11.3   Party Identification at Various Combinations of Independence and Party Evaluations

between the standard scale and position in the 13×7 space is by no means perfect. Predicting scores on the 7-point scale from position in the 13×7 space as I have partitioned it here gives correct predictions 25 of 36 times. Remember, though, that asking the classic question twice with a week intervening might yield, perhaps, only 30 or so cases of perfect correspondence; it appears that the 7-point scale can locate individuals on the ordinally related regions of the two-space rather well.

Note that this is a miserable N, based on a sample with little external validity! It can provide only the most preliminary hint of an answer to our question. Assuming that this sort of thing holds more generally, however, what would it imply? Certainly, a two-(or more) dimensional measure of party identification is conceptually more appropriate than the old scale, and it lends itself more easily to interval measurement. On the other hand, it is more complicated, and therefore is not as easily used as the measure of

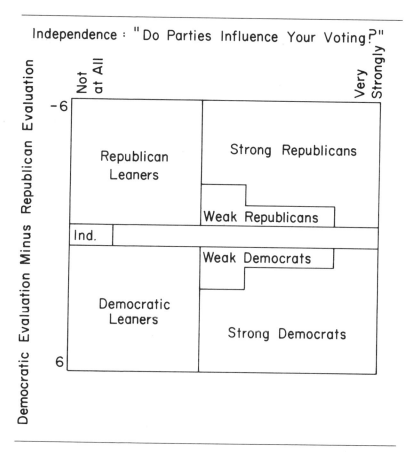

FIGURE 11.4   A Partitioning of the 7 × 13 Space, to Correspond to the Standard
Party Identification Scale

standing decision, which made the old party identification measure popular
in the first place. Thus, either way of measuring party identification might
be more or less good, depending on what one wants to use the measure(s)
for. Let me reemphasize, however, that this little preliminary test does *not*
produce sufficient evidence to conclude that the 7-point scale elicits unique
combinations of component dimensions of party identification. It only suf-
fices to suggest the possibility that that might be the case.

A FURTHER ASPECT OF DIMENSIONALITY: ACQUISITION AND STRENGTHENING OF PARTY IDENTIFICATION

The works cited above have emphasized the separate component dimensions of partisan direction and "independence," or the extent to which one
relies on parties. A somewhat similar body of work has focused on the

question of whether changes from independence to some sort of partisanship are the same sort of thing as changes from weak identification with a party to strong identification with a party. That is, scholars raise the question of whether the different points on the scale represent varying degrees of the same thing, or whether instead the comparison of "strengths" at the two ends of the scale is different than the comparison of independence with "partisanship" around the middle of the scale. In other words, does the process by which individuals acquire a party identification differ from the process by which that identification becomes weaker or stronger?

There is some empirical evidence that this is so. Brody (1978) found that shifts from independence to one of the parties, or shifts from one party to another, are relatively infrequent, but that shifts between various strengths of identification with the same party occur frequently and are apparently a result of satisfaction with the parties' nominees, policies, and so on. Elsewhere (Shively, 1979b) I have shown that a fairly simple model may account in large part for moves from independence (including leaners as independents) to identification with one of the parties, but that more complicated models—incorporating satisfaction with the parties and their policies—must be used to predict who, once identified with a party, will come to identify with it strongly.

Claggett (1979) has developed the same general notion more elegantly through simple logic. He notes that voters apparently become more frequently party identifiers, and party identifiers become stronger identifiers as they age (though there is some dispute about this; see n.1). The explanation generally offered for *both* processes in *The American Voter* and elsewhere is that party identification is self-reinforcing—once a person identifies with a party, that person becomes more attentive to the party and more receptive to favorable information about the party; thus, party identification produces its own reinforcement. However, as Claggett points out, this can only operate once a person already identifies with a party. How can what does not yet exist be reinforced? Reinforcement might account for a tendency to move from "weak" identification to "strong" identification, but it cannot account for moves from independence to identification. Therefore, if strengthening of party identification does occur through such reinforcement, the process by which party identification is acquired *must* differ from the process by which it is strengthened.

THE PROBLEM OF LEANERS

The two problems of dimensionality are intriguing questions that get to the very nature of party identification. A further question about the 7-point scale has attracted considerable attention recently, not because of its conceptual importance, but for practical reasons. Very often—in fact, whenever one wants to compare independence with partisanship—the 7-point scale is collapsed into a dichotomy—independents/"party identifiers." (For instance, this use of the scale underlies Figure 11.1 which displays "percentage identifying with a party" under varying circumstances.) When collapsing the 7-point scale into such a dichotomy, the investigator is faced with a problem: what to do with the independents who, on the follow-up question, admit to being "closer" to one of the two parties. Are these people independents, or are they party identifiers? Where the cut is made often affects, profoundly, the results of research. There is some evidence that leaning independents act rather partisan. Though Petrocik found all of the anomalies associated with leaning independents to be in characteristics not particularly related to parties—characteristics such as interest in politics, degree of participation, and so on—there is further evidence that shows a good deal of apparently partisan behavior on the part of the leaners. Brody (1977) found that over two-year panels from 1956 to 1958 and from 1972 to 1974, 70% of respondents who were independents "leaning" to a party at the first year were "directionally stable," that is, they indicated some sort of identification or "lean" to the same party two years later. About 90% of weak identifiers and 95% of strong identifiers are directionally stable, but still the 70% stability of leaners is enough to show that their lean is not a casual choice.

Further evidence of partisan behavior on the part of leaners is seen in Table 11.1. Averaging across elections from 1952 to 1972, independents who leaned to a party were actually slightly *more* likely to vote for that party's presidential candidate than were weak identifiers of that party.

TABLE 11.1   Percentage Voting Consistently with Party Identification, 1952–1972*

	Democrats	Republicans
Strong identifiers	86%	96%
Weak identifiers	66	84
Leaning independents	71	87

*Calculated from Asher (1976: 82–83).

Such evidence does suggest that the leaning independents are partisans in disguise, who on the initial question choose the socially acceptable answer of "independent," but who, when pressed, admit to a party preference. An alternate interpretation of the leaning independents, however, may also be reasonable. It might be that they are true independents who had already decided how to vote at the time of the survey. Such voters, having already identified themselves as independents, might interpret the follow-up question ("Do you think of yourself as closer to the Republican or Democratic party?") as asking them how they intend to vote. Under this interpretation, "leaning independents" would be true independents, but would be more politically involved and alert than "pure" independents. We might then expect them to show the various characteristics Petrocik describes, and we would also expect to see the relation shown in Table 11.1. If leaners defined the direction of their lean by their intended vote, it would not be surprising to find that their actual vote reflected their leaning fairly accurately.

An anomaly in the juxtaposition of Table 11.1 and Petrocik's findings adds plausibility to this interpretation of the leaners. As noted above, Petrocik found that on partisan dimensions of behavior (changeability of their vote and ratings of the two parties) leaners were less partisan than were weak partisans. It was only on dimensions of behavior that were not directly partisan that intransitivities appeared. His conclusion was that the leaners were indeed independent, but were a particularly participant and involved group of independents. Vote choice, however, is certainly a partisan dimension of behavior, yet Petrocik's intransitivities appear in Table 11.1. It is hard to think of any explanation of this anomaly except that independents of the sort Petrocik described have treated the CPS follow-up question as asking for their intended vote thus producing the relation seen in the table.

It is difficult to test which interpretation of the leaning independents is more appropriate, but at least one critical test suggests itself. If leaners are in fact partisans who call themselves independent, then they should act like other partisans when they decide to vote for the opposite party—they should generally retain the same party loyalty, while deviating from their expected vote. On the other hand, if their reported "leaning" is simply another statement of how they intend to vote, then a change in the party for which they intend to vote should bring a corresponding change in the party to which they lean.

The results of such a test are shown in Table 11.2; they support the interpretation of leaners as true independents. From 1956 to 1958 and from 1958 to 1960, "identification" appears to have moved with the vote for leaners in a way quite unlike the behavior of partisans. The numbers of cases available, however, is small. Also, the second interpretation of leaners would predict not that half the leaners who changed their vote would shift their identification but that all would. Even granted the usual problems of

TABLE 11.2   Probability that Direction of Party Identification Changed from First Election to Second*

	$Vote_2 = Vote_1$	$Vote_2 \neq Vote_1$	Difference
1956–1958:			
Strong	0 (234)	.182 (11)	.182
Weak	.008 (131)	.125 (32)	.117
Lean	.045 (66)	.500 (12)	.455
1958–1960:			
Strong	.003 (296)	.065 (31)	.062
Weak	.006 (173)	.116 (43)	.110
Lean	.065 (46)	.444 (9)	.379

*N's are in parentheses. For 1956–1958, all members of the 1956–1958 panel are used who identified with a party at both elections and reported a vote for both elections. For 1958–1960, all members of the 1958–1960 panel are used who identified with a party at both elections and who reported a vote at both elections. By Fisher's exact calculation of the χ^2, the chance probability of as great a difference as is observed among vote-changers between leaners on one hand, and merged strong and weak partisans on the other, is .015 for the 1956–1958 panel and .016 for the 1958–1960 panel.

measurement error, we should have expected a somewhat stronger relation than that in Table 11.2, if all leaners fit the second interpretation. My reading of the test is that, based on still scant evidence, it appears that most leaners should be considered independents who have used the follow-up question to indicate their intended vote. However, a minority of leaners may fit the disguised partisan or other interpretations. A test based on such small N's is chancy, but it does generally support grouping leaners and pure independents.

THE DIMENSIONALITY PROBLEM: SUMMARY

I have reviewed a number of questions which have been raised about the 7-point scale as a measure of party identification. Are the things captured in that scale a single dimension? Are basic processes of development the same for party identification at all points on the scale? Where should the scale be cut to separate independents from party identifiers when that is desired?

Evidence is scanty on all these questions. There is good evidence that the 7-point scale partakes of more than one dimension, and at the very least this should lead us to a fruitful reconsideration of the nature of party identification. There is as yet, however, little evidence on the pragmatic question of whether the 7-point scale is "good enough" for most purposes.

There is considerable evidence that processes by which party identification becomes stronger differ from those by which it is acquired in the first place. Finally, there is as yet not enough evidence to let us decide with confidence whether leaning independents should be grouped with independents or with party identifiers. The scant evidence available suggests that it is safer to treat them as independent.

CONCLUSIONS

I have reviewed two broad areas of controversy about party identification. Both controversies are heartening. The question of dimensionality has been raised because of apparent problems in the original measure. It is likely that a variety of solutions to the problem will be pursued—with different approaches dictated by varying applications of the concept—but the result should be that we measure party identification more appropriately and thus say more cogent things about it.

Concerning the basic concept, whatever thinking prevails, it is certain that party identification will have a more directly political flavor. This should lessen some of the apparent estrangement of students of elections from, on the one hand, "practical politicians" and, on the other, political theorists. Both have found the idea of a not-very-political party identification hard to swallow.

This has been a period of considerable questioning. It would be tempting to turn our attention away from party identification, partly because it has lost its simplicity, partly in reaction to what now appears to have been an exaggerated interest in it a decade or so ago. Yet party identification is still dominant in many people's decisions on how to vote, and is still one of the few factors transcending immediate elections. It is good that continuing and varied attention is addressed to it.

NOTES

1. A side issue that has attracted considerable treatment is the question of whether individuals become more partisan, and more strongly partisan, as they age, or whether the observed differences between different age groups in the intensity of their party identification are simply a matter of historical differences among the various generations in the population. (See Abramson, 1976; Converse, 1976; Abramson, 1979; Shively, 1979a.) This question has drawn scholars' attention partly because it is important to some theories of electoral development and partly because it is an interesting example of the methodological problems of cohort analysis (Mason et al., 1973). But it is not as basic a question as the two addressed here—party identification would function in much the same ways whether or not it developed individually across the life cycle—and I shall not deal with it in this paper.

2. I have taken some liberties with Fiorina's definition, making it less precise than it is in his statement to ease the narrative presentation.

3. This notion is obviously not original. It is developed in considerable detail in Downs (1957) and in *The American Voter*.

12

CANDIDATE PREFERENCE UNDER UNCERTAINTY: AN EXPANDED VIEW OF RATIONAL VOTING

Herbert F. Weisberg
Morris P. Fiorina

INTRODUCTION

Some two decades ago Anthony Downs (1957) presented his "economic theory" of democracy. Though Downs was primarily concerned with specifying optimal behavior for unified parties solely interested in winning elections, that concern presupposed a model of the voting behavior of a rational electorate. Downs postulated that citizens estimate their expected welfare level under each of the alternate parties then vote for the party associated with the highest estimated benefit. While Downs was quick to recognize that uncertainty permeated such calculations, he chose against the formal incorporation of uncertainty into his model.

Subsequent work on rational voting generally has followed Downs in admitting that uncertainty exists, but proceeding as if it did not. For example, in the Davis et al. (1970) spatial model, parties compete in multidimensional issue space. Citizens are assumed to know with certainty where each of the parties stands and where they personally stand in this space. To the extent that the certainty assumption fails, it is assumed that the consequences are random and thus of no import. Somewhat paradoxically, formal models of party preference are rather informal in their treatment of uncertainty.[1]

This paper examines how rational voters might choose between candidates under conditions of uncertainty. We shall emphasize two rational voting approaches—"defensive voting" and "credulous voting"—which have previously escaped notice. Additionally, we shall map out some of the implications of electoral uncertainty for empirical tests of the rational model. Election surveys have begun to ask the type of issue questions needed to operationalize the spatial model voting. Unfortunately, those questions assume certainty, so some of the errors in prediction with the usual proximity analysis may be due to uncertainty rather than to irrational voting.

Thus, our focus on electoral uncertainty leads us into an interconnected reconsideration of three areas of existing research: (1) the spatial theories of electoral competition; (2) the wording of questions designed to elicit information about voter preferences; and (3) the usual analysis of existing survey items such as proximity measures. The discussion moves back and forth among these concerns, but most important is our expansion of the conventional view of rational voting.

CHOOSING A CANDIDATE: THE IMPACT OF UNCERTAINTY

The behavioral literature on voting has focused on a variety of factors to answer why citizens prefer one candidate over another. Such factors include group allegiances (Berelson, 1954), party identification and short-term attitudes toward the candidates and issues (Campbell et al., 1960), and the relation between the citizen's issue positions and those advocated by the competing candidates (Nie et al., 1979). In contrast to the complexity of the empirical literature, the theoretical literature on candidate preference is simple and straightforward. Models of the voting decision have abstracted from the richness of the empirical literature and posited a party differential which neatly summarizes a citizen's candidate evaluations (Downs, 1957). The citizen imagines what his overall welfare level would be given the election of candidate A, compares this estimate with that given the election of candidate B, and prefers the candidate whose associated welfare level is higher. The *party differential* is the difference between these two estimates.[2]

This theoretical discussion of the party differential is neat and tidy—deceptively so. In passing from the rich complexity of the empirical literature to the stark simplicity of the theoretical, an important consideration is left behind: *the pervasive uncertainty facing the citizen.* No matter how calculated, the party differential is an estimate shrouded in uncertainty.

Uncertainty enters the voting act in a number of ways. There is first the uncertainty attributable to the voter—his lack of information or limitations on his information processing capacity.[3] A candidate might project a specific policy position on an issue only to have the citizen misperceive that position.

Statistically, the citizen perceives the true candidate position plus (possibly) an error term. Given such misperception, an inaccurate party differential may lead the citizen to vote for a candidate who actually would provide less utility than an available opponent.

Second, there is uncertainty which stems from the behavior of the competing candidates. Such uncertainty takes two forms. "Equivocation" occurs when the candidate says different things to different audiences, while "vagueness" exists when the candidate conceals his exact intentions. Equivocation produces a range of perceived candidate positions *across the electorate,* with different citizens perceiving different positions. The citizen, in effect, takes a sample of a single candidate position from the range of positions the candidate projects and then uses that position to calculate the party differential. In contrast, vagueness (such as Nixon's announcement in the 1968 campaign of a secret plan to end the war in Vietnam) produces a range of perceived candidate positions *within each citizen.* Note that in this latter case even the most informed, intelligent elements of the electorate will have party differentials that are uncertain estimates.[4]

Finally, there are uncertainties inherent in the electoral process. All citizens realize that future events and situations are inherently uncertain. Thus, they must choose their government without full knowledge of the agenda that government will face. Elected officials may justifiably abandon past promises in the face of changing circumstances and issues. Additionally, candidates have been known to lie or at least to give the appearance thereof; the electoral process does not bind candidates to their previously stated positions. Moreover, no candidate can enact and enforce a policy all by himself. Even if the candidate is clear and honest, he might have to accept compromises in order to have his programs made into public policy by the legislature, the courts, and the bureaucracy. As a result of these factors, citizens realize that situations change, that candidates may be lying, and that candidates eventually have to compromise their positions. Facing such strong uncertainties even the informed citizen knows that he can regard a candidate's stated positions only as rough indicators of some range of public policies which might eventually result from the candidate's election. Statistically, the citizen places an interval around the point location projected by the candidate, so that the citizen perceives a range of possible issue positions for a candidate even when the candidate projects only a single issue point.[5]

Note that the preceding forms of uncertainty are likely to occur in combinations. The candidate may project a point, but the citizen may both misperceive that point and construct a range around the misperceived point. The candidate may project a range, but the voter may misperceive its end points. The previous literature has recognized the possibility of misperception along with the uncertainty related to the electoral process. But once it is recognized that the uncertainty related to the electoral process cannot be eliminated from voting, the nature of the decision-making problem facing the citizen is fundamentally transformed.

The foregoing discussion is a prelude to a simple observation: A citizen's estimate of a candidate's position in an issue space is likely to be much less precise than typically assumed in electoral theory or typically measured in empirical research. As a consequence, spatial theories based on precise candidate locations are insufficiently general in that candidate strategies they deduce may be inappropriate when uncertainty is taken into more complete account. Correspondingly, the information obtained by empirical studies of candidate position-taking may not have the meaning that is generally assumed.

To address these contentions, consider the 7-point issue scales devised by the 1968 election surveys of Brody and Page and subsequently adopted by the Center for Political Studies (CPS). The respondent is shown a 7-point scale relating to an issue with the two end points labeled (such as seeking immediate withdrawal or military victory in the war in Vietnam), and the respondent is asked his or her own position on the scale along with the positions of the presidential nominees on the same scale. In attempts to operationalize the spatial model of voting, the differences between the respondent's position and the respondent's perception of the candidates' positions have been used to measure the party differential. But what happens if the respondent perceives the candidate as a range on the scale rather than as a single point?

When a citizen tells an interviewer that Hubert H. Humphrey is at position 4 on a 7-point scale, he *may* believe that Humphrey is exactly at position 4. A much more likely possibility is that he believes Humphrey is somewhere between 2 and 4, or 3 and 6, or wherever. He simply obliges the interviewer by settling on an exact point. But what does a point estimate of a candidate position really signify? And how do citizens use such point estimates to calculate their party differentials? These are separate questions which might have different answers.

We know of no way to answer the first question with data presently available. Are citizens intuitive statisticians who consistently reveal the mean of their judgmental distributions to the interviewer? We will make the standard assumption that this is the case, but we recognize it will not always be correct. Consider, for example, a citizen who believes that Richard Nixon will either pull out of Vietnam or escalate the war. His subjective distribution over a 7-point scale might appear as in Figure 12.1. Where will this citizen place Nixon on the scale? At the mean or median—about 4—even though he is certain that Nixon is not at 4? Or will he select one of the more likely modes—the end points 1 or 7? Assuming that citizens invariably respond with means may very well lead to error in some unknown fraction of cases, but there does not appear to be any more plausible initial assumption.

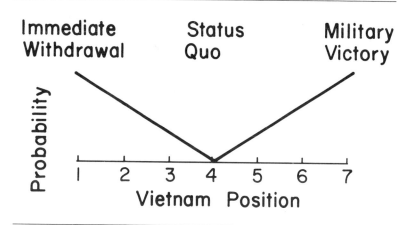

FIGURE 12.1   Hypothetical Nixon Policy Distribution on ICPR 7-Point Vietnam Scale

Having assumed that citizens reveal mean candidate positions, the next question is whether those means determine the party differential. The citizen who wants to pull out of Vietnam immediately might say that Nixon is at position 4 on the scale but still might compute his party differential based on the possibility that Nixon is at position 1 or on the possibility that Nixon is at position 7. Assume that our same citizen judges Humphrey's position on Vietnam as in Figure 12.2 with a mean of 4. Is the citizen's party differential on Vietnam then necessarily zero? Or do other parameters of his judgmental distributions come into play? The next section of this chapter explores the possibilities.

ALTERNATE CALCULATIONS OF THE PARTY DIFFERENTIAL

Empirical analyses have assumed that the citizen's calculation of the party differential is a decision made under certainty—perfect information about the positions of the candidates. Thus, researchers have employed "proximity measures" indicating how close the citizen is to the candidate, obtaining these measures by subtracting the citizen's position from his perception of the candidates' positions. This "standard proximity analysis" is inappropriate under conditions of uncertainty, since the citizen's decision-making rule, and possibly, his utility function must be considered when dealing with decision-making under uncertainty.

Most formal analyses likewise presume that the citizen's calculation of the party differential is a decision made under certainty. Only Zechman (1978) and Shepsle (1972) have performed analyses which explicitly include

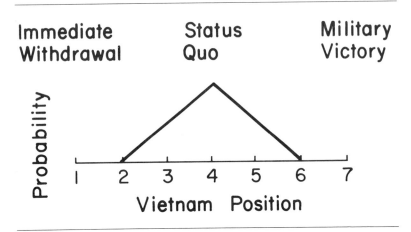

FIGURE 12.2   Hypothetical Humphrey Policy Distribution on ICPR 7-Point Vietnam
Scale

uncertainty in the candidate preference decision, analyses which build on strong simplifying assumptions.

Zechman adopts a Bayesian perspective. Before the campaign begins, the citizen has a "prior distribution" for the location of each party which can be modified by the "likelihood function" he develops about the location of the candidate as the campaign progresses. Based on the two, the citizen arrives at a "posterior distribution" concerning the location of each party and then votes on the basis of party differentials calculated from the posterior means. The use of the posterior means incorporates into Zechman's analysis the subjective expected utility approach, the most common, though not the only, theory as to how decision makers respond to uncertainty.

In Shepsle's (1972) model, each candidate presents himself as a lottery: a probability distribution over a policy space (one dimensional in Shepsle's analysis). This lottery is "objective" in the sense that every citizen perceives the same lottery, and this objective lottery is completely under the control of the candidate. Given these assumptions Shepsle carries out an analysis of electoral competition under uncertainty. But his results are relative to a particular model of decision making under uncertainty. The voters are expected utility maximizers: Their choices over lotteries satisfy the axioms of the Von Neumann-Morgenstern expected utility theory (Luce and Raiffa, 1957). Given an electorate that makes decisions in accord with some other theory of decision making under uncertainty, different conclusions may follow.

In this section we will illustrate with examples the voting decisions of citizens who follow different models of decision making under uncertainty. We also will discuss the kind of voter psychology which might suggest adoption of one model rather than another and the role of partisanship and candidate orientation for the different types of voters.

MODEL 1: VOTING AS (SUBJECTIVE) EXPECTED UTILITY MAXIMIZING

Consider the example in Figure 12.3. The voter's ideal point is at 4 on the scale. Assume he has a symmetric single-peaked utility function so that $u(3) = u(5)$, $u(2) = u(6)$, and so on. Assume candidate A is perceived as a discrete rectangular distribution over the range 2 to 4 on the scale, while candidate B is perceived as a discrete rectangular distribution over the range 1 to 7. Which candidate does the citizen prefer?

If the voter is a subjective expected utility maximizer,

$$EU(A) = \frac{u(2) + u(3) + u(4)}{3}$$

$$EU(B) = \frac{u(1) + u(2) + u(3) + u(4) + u(5) + u(6) + u(7)}{7}$$

$$= \frac{2u(1) + 2U(2) + 2U(3) + u(4)}{7}$$

(by the symmetry of the utility function)

so

$$EU(A) - EU(B) = \frac{7u(2) + 7u(3) + 7u(4) - 6u(1) - 6u(2) - 6u(3) - 3u(4)}{21}$$

$$= \frac{u(2) + u(3) + 4u(4) - 6u(1)}{21} > 0$$

(since $u(4) > u(3) \geq u(2) \geq u(1)$ by the single-peakedness of the utility function)

Thus, the subjective expected utility maximizing citizen prefers candidate A.

Note that the conventional spatial model of voting and the proximity measures based on that model which have been used by empirical researchers would lead to error in this example. If the citizen gives the interviewer the means of judgmental distributions of the positions of the two candidates, he would be recorded as closer to candidate B whose mean is 4 rather than A whose mean is 3. Yet we see that A is more preferred when the voter's preference function and decision rules enter the picture.[6] The proximity measures can be misleading if the citizen views the candidates as ranges rather than as single points.

What kind of a voter is a subjective expected utility maximizer? He is a voter with a complete transitive preference ordering over certain alternatives

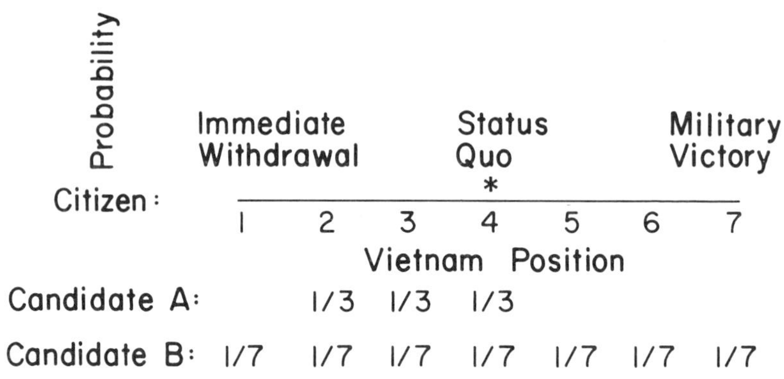

Probability							
	Immediate Withdrawal		Status Quo *			Military Victory	
Citizen:	1	2	3	4	5	6	7
			Vietnam Position				
Candidate A:		1/3	1/3	1/3			
Candidate B:	1/7	1/7	1/7	1/7	1/7	1/7	1/7

FIGURE 12.3   Illustration of Expected Utility Maximizing: Voter Ideal Point and
Perceived Candidate Distributions

and over lotteries formed from those alternatives. He satisfies a strong substitutability axiom, and he receives no utility or disutility from the uncertainty of his decision context. Less formally, the expected utility maximizer behaves as if he has a complete probability distribution (objective or subjective) over the positions each candidate might adopt. He is permitted to be uncertain, but his uncertainty is presumed to be of a rather precise nature. In the terminology of an earlier era, his uncertainty is reducible to *risk*—a condition in which ambiguity or uncertainty is quantifiable as probabilities.

On the normative level, expected utility and subjective expected utility models reign supreme.[7] On the experimental level, a considerable amount of negative evidence exists (Lichenstein and Slovic, 1971; Slovic and Tversky, 1974; Grether and Plott, 1977). And on the level of empirical political research, the little data that are available suggest similar doubts about the universal applicability of expected utility models (Ferejohn and Fiorina, 1975). If we keep an open mind, then, what are the alternatives?

MODEL 2: DEFENSIVE VOTING

Recall Figures 12.1 and 12.2 that portray a voter's judgments about the Vietnamese policies of Nixon and Humphrey as in Figure 12.4. Given that the means of his judgmental distributions are both 4, the standard proximity analysis would treat this voter as indifferent between Nixon and Humphrey on Vietnam (no matter what the characteristics of his utility function). But the voter might reason as follows: "There is a chance that Nixon will follow a policy further from me in either the more hawkish or more dovish directions than will Humphrey. Thus, I insure myself against the furthest deviation from my preferences by voting for Humphrey."

This is a kind of "minimax" decision-making. For each candidate, estimate the possible policy position furthest from your own, then support the

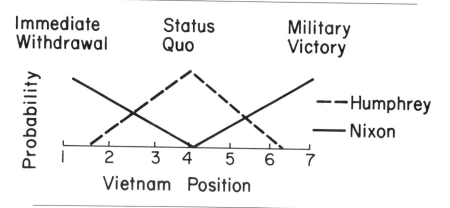

FIGURE 12.4   Hypothetical Candidate Distributions on 7-Point Vietnam Scale

candidate whose furthest policy is closer. Clearly, the minimax consideration might enter the voting decision given the very different judgmental distributions of candidate positions presumed in the above example. Would such a model of decision-making also enter the voting decisions when the judgmental distributions are of comparable shape, but of different mean? Perhaps not. But such a decision-making rule might be used when the voter is unable to form a distribution over a candidate's possible positions—when he considers himself to be in a classic uncertainty situation in which probabilities are unknown or not even meaningful. Perhaps he can pin each candidate to a range of policy positions but has little sense of what is likely within each range.

Again, the minimax decision maker might confound the empirical analysis of proximity measures. Consider the example in Figure 12.5. Assume the individual has a single-peaked preference function symmetric about an ideal point of 5. The mean of candidate A's positions is 5, the voter's ideal point, while the mean of candidate B's possible positions is 4. According to the simple proximity measures, a vote for candidate A results. But the minimax voter reasons that candidate B at the worst will be 1.5 units from his ideal point whereas candidate A could be 2 units away. Hence, he votes for B.

Minimax voting is defensive voting. The citizen goes through a worst-case analysis and defends himself against the worst.[8] Empirically, such behavior is not so foolish. Take the citizen who is highly uncertain about the exact policy positions of a candidate but who can use such devices as party identification and group endorsements to pin the candidate down in a certain area of the policy space. Why should some central point in this range count more than the point furthest from his ideal? Moreover, the candidates themselves may induce the voter to behave in such a manner. Faced with "shoot

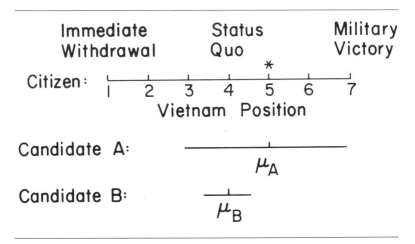

FIGURE 12.5   Illustration of Defensive Voting: Voter Ideal Point and Perceived
                      Candidate Distributions

from the hip" Goldwater, a worst case analysis makes considerable sense.
Goldwater *might* start a nuclear war. Were American voters saying that they
thought such actions *would* occur under Goldwater, or were they just expressing a nagging fear that such actions *might* occur?

MODEL 3: CREDULOUS VOTING

Real world elections have Eisenhowers running as well as Goldwaters.
Just as a voter might go through a worse-case analysis, so he might on
occasion go through a best-case analysis.[9] In the example used to illustrate
defensive voting (Figure 12.5), the decision would reverse if a voter were
engaging in a credulous or optimistic analysis. Candidate B is less uncertain,
but *at best* he will end up .5 units from the citizen's ideal point; candidate A
might end up exactly on the citizen's ideal, so he receives the citizen's vote.

We doubt that credulous voting is very common, at least in our more
recent elections. Still, the occasional widely loved and revered candidate
might stimulate such a popular response. At least the committed partisan
might engage in a best-case analysis for his party's candidate and a worst-
case analysis for the opposition candidate. And perhaps there are some
citizens in the electorate who generally take an optimistic, credulous attitude
toward politics. (Barnum believed such citizens were common.)

Notice that partisanship and candidate orientation would have a relatively
different role in credulous voting than in defensive voting. The credulous
voter is more strongly influenced by campaign promises and is more likely to
switch parties when the other party begins to make better promises. In
particular, the credulous voter may depart from his traditional partisanship
quite readily when the opposition candidate seems totally credible. Espe-

cially believable candidates (such as members of one's own religion, race, ethnic group, and region) might induce credulous voting.

MODEL 4: MIXED MODEL VOTING

An obvious possibility is that voters use some mix of the three decision models we have discussed. Perhaps the voter makes an estimate of a candidate's mean or most likely position then adjusts that decision by taking into account the best and worst he might receive at the hands of the candidate.[10] Or he might adopt a sequential strategy: eliminate from consideration any candidate who threatens a totally unacceptable position and then choose from among the remaining candidates (if more than one remain) on the basis of which provides the greater expected utility or the greater maximal benefit. In practice, using the mean or mode and extreme points of a candidate's position distribution might approximate the kind of comprehensive decision-making presumed by expected utility theories.[11]

SUMMARY

We can summarize these several models in terms of "The Voting Question" which the voter asks when deciding how to vote.[12] The expected utility rule asks: "On average, whose issue positions will provide me greater utility?"; The cynical defensive voting question is: "How can I best avoid getting screwed?"; while the credulous voter asks "If I am lucky, who might do the best for me?" The mixed model voter asks the most complex voting question: "How do I weight my expectations, my fears, and my hopes?"

Which of these models holds true for actual voting? We would suspect that each does for some citizens with respect to some candidates and at some elections. It is most unlikely that any single model would always prevail, but instead we should expect each to be of some importance.[13] The result is a considerable expansion of what we would term rational voting from the narrow view incorporated in models of voting as decision-making under certainty.

Unfortunately, the questions asked currently in surveys do not permit defensive voting and credulous voting to be identified. They do not obtain the respondent's judgments about the range of likely policy positions of the candidates, nor do they permit a test of whether the citizens view the candidates' positions as certain or uncertain. Furthermore, they obtain only the respondent's preference peak without checking the shape of his utility function. Thus, the surveys make a series of assumptions which are not very reasonable (certainty, and so on) and provide no means of testing their validity. As a result, we cannot estimate the extent of subjective expected utility and defensive and credulous voting. We would, however, urge some methodological experimentation with possible question wordings which would elicit more complete information to test rational voting models more fully.

Finally, it would be desirable to test some of the correlates of the models. Do the defensive voters tend to be cynical and the credulous voters trusting? Are partisans credulous about their own party's candidate and defensive about the other party's candidate? Are independents mean value voters? Are those who leave a party and become independents more cynical and more defensive voters than those who switch parties?

ELECTORAL IMPLICATIONS OF ALTERNATE VOTER DECISION RULES

Do different theories of individual voting behavior produce correspondingly different implications for the operations or outcomes of electoral processes? We cannot begin to make a comprehensive study of such questions at the present time. But we can present a few examples which show that the differing models advanced in the previous section have differing implications for candidate behavior and electoral outcomes in some simple electoral contexts.

It is well known that if electoral competition is confined to a single dimension of public policy over which voters have single-peaked preference functions (if all citizens vote), and if majority rule determines the outcome, then the median citizen's most preferred point is the equilibrium outcome of the electoral process. This is the substance of Black's (1958) "median dominance" theorem. Black's theorem is stated in the context of decision-making under certainty where candidates take exact positions that are communicated to the electorate without error or distortion.

Shepsle (1972) demonstrated that the introduction of uncertainty into the electoral process can upset the median dominance theorem. Specifically, if a majority of voters is "risk acceptant" in some interval of the policy space containing the median ideal point, then a risky strategy exists which can defeat the median in a majority vote. Shepsle's interpretation is that a relatively certain incumbent can be beaten by an uncertain challenger if voters are "gamblers." Risky strategies which defeat the median are never themselves in equilibrium, however. And if voters tend to be risk-averse, rather than risk acceptant (a common supposition), then the median defeats risky strategies pitted against it.

DEFENSIVE VOTING

What happens when voters are not restricted to expected utility maximizing behavior? What if, for example, we have an electorate of defensive voters? Generally speaking, Black's theorem would still hold. Consider Figure 12.6. Candidate A is at the median in the figure, while candidate B projects an uncertain strategy that includes the median. Assuming voters have single-peaked symmetric preference functions, and vote defensively, A not only wins, he wins unanimously. Every member of the electorate finds himself closer to the median than to the most distant point of candidate B's range.[14] This conclusion generalizes to all cases where the range of one candidate's positions lies completely within the range of the other's. The less uncertain candidate wins unanimously in all such cases. Thus, given an electorate of defensive voters, each candidate should try to cover a proper subset of the other candidate's strategy range. Clearly, if applied repeatedly, this candidate strategy leads both candidates to converge to a single point, and if that point is not the median, to jump to the median.

What if candidates' strategy ranges are not variables under their control as seems likely in the real world? After the primary process, for example, we might have a situation analogous to that outlined in Figure 12.7.

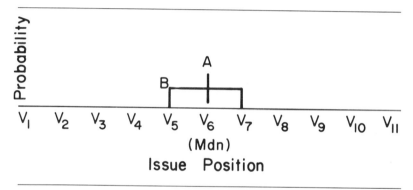

FIGURE 12.6   Uncertain Candidate vs. Median, Defensive Voting

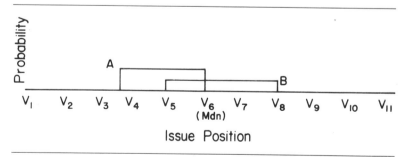

FIGURE 12.7   Two Candidate Election, Overlapping Uncertain Candidates

In this figure one candidate is perceived to be somewhat to the right side of the median, while the other is mostly to the left, but they each overlap in an area around the median. Who wins? Clearly, the determining factor in this instance is the maximum distance of each candidate from the median voter. Here, for example, the riskier candidate, B, wins. Where candidate ranges do not overlap at all, the election winner depends on the location and range of the candidate positions, much as in the case when candidates are locked into point strategies not at the median, or lottery strategies whose expected value is not at the median (as presumed by Shepsle). Generally, whichever candidate manages to get his entire range closer to the median wins.

CREDULOUS VOTING

It should be obvious that an electorate of credulous voters would produce implications precisely the opposite of those just enumerated. Take Figure 12.6, for example, Voters 7–11 choose candidate B since his rightmost point is closer to them than the median, while voters 1–5 choose B since his leftmost point is closer to them than the median. The median voter himself is indifferent. Thus, the riskier candidate B wins in this illustration. Moreover, optimal candidate behavior would continuously expand one's strategy to include the other candidate's strategy as a proper subset. Ultimately, both candidates would cover the entire policy dimension.

What of situations where the candidate's strategies are fixed, and one candidate's strategy is not a proper subset of the other's? (Figure 12.7 is one of an infinity of such situations.) In general, it is not better to be either more or less risky. The actual outcome in each such case will depend on the precise location of each candidate's position distribution. All we can be sure of is that a range including the median defeats one which does not, given an electorate of credulous voters.[15]

SUMMARY

The preceding discussion is artificial in two senses. First, it presumes that each voter perceives candidate uncertainty identically—that citizens agree on candidate ranges. Second, it presumes electorates composed entirely of defensive voters or entirely of credulous voters. Nevertheless, our examples do show that differing models of decision-making under uncertainty produce differing implications about electoral processes. Candidate behavior changes, and expected electoral outcomes change as voter decision models change. Thus, given no general agreement on *the* appropriate model of individual decision-making under uncertainty, we would be wise to consider a variety of possibilities in our larger theoretical models of electoral processes.

UNCERTAINTY AND CANDIDATE STRATEGIES

It may seem from the preceding section that the effects of uncertainty in real elections cannot be the objects of universal statements. However, we would prefer viewing the analysis as adding a new aspect to rational models of candidate competition. Previous studies have emphasized that candidates compete in spatial locations (Downs, 1957), the certainty of their positions (Shepsle, 1972), and their emphasis on different issues (Page, 1976). We find that they also could rationally compete by attempting to affect the rules citizens use in making their voting decisions.

Some candidates campaign on their credibility, trying to induce credulous voting. If the personality and background of the candidate make such an appeal successful, then he can afford to be ambiguous. His opponent may try to attack his vagueness, but such an attack would be to no avail if the electorate moves to credulous voting. Eisenhower provided the modern prototype of this strategy, with Carter's 1976 campaign attempting to emulate that model.

By contrast, the candidate who induces defensive voting could harm himself by uncertainty, since he can be defeated by a candidate who gets "inside" his issue positions. Thus, the candidate who seems insincere or aloof might find uncertainty counterproductive in his campaign. Uncertainty would be taken as a confirmation of his other undesirable characteristics.

Clearly a candidate who takes a centrist position with certainty should seek to foster defensive voting. He should attack the credibility of his opponent, so that any uncertainty would work to his benefit. Nixon's campaigns tended to be of this type—centrist campaigns which attacked the credibility of his opponents—and Ford's 1976 campaign followed the same pattern.

Given the nature of electoral politics, the incumbent running for reelection is likely to be viewed as a better known alternative than would a challenger running for the presidency for the first time. According to our previous results, this means that the challenger would want to be viewed credulously. Two factors that can destroy such a strategy are campaign blunders and continued opposition to the challenger within his own party. Both make him less credible while inducing some citizens to react defensively. Indeed, we would suspect that these factors are more important in inducing defensive voting than is the prevailing level of voter cynicism about politics. In our view the campaign blunders and intraparty rifts which characterized the Goldwater and McGovern campaigns induced a similar voter reaction—high levels of defensive voting—although the general level of voter cynicism was much lower in 1964 than in 1972.

There is a paradox here. The candidate with the broad range who wants to be viewed credulously might find himself labeled irresponsible and defeated by a defensive electorate. The candidate with a narrow range who wants to be viewed defensively might find himself outflanked by a broad candidate who can make a credulous appeal. As a result, the conflict over the definition of the situation is at least as important as the differing positions, probabilities, and emphases.

EMPIRICAL ANALYSIS OF ALTERNATING VOTER DECISION RULES

An empirical test between these models for a given election would require survey questions which obtain the respondents' views of the range of actions they consider possible if a given candidate is elected. Unfortunately, such questions are not asked, and, as a result, we have little empirical evidence on the degree of uncertainty in citizens' perceptions of candidate positions. Given that uncertainty assumptions seem more realistic than certainty assumptions, it would be very useful if surveys were modified to include this additional information.

However, we can make one test employing a suggestion from Zechman (1978). The CPS surveys ask the respondents to place themselves, the candidates, and the parties on a series of 7-point issue scales. The usual analysis (Miller et al., 1976) employs candidate proximity measures, based on how close the citizen was to the two candidates, though the initial analysis of the 1976 election (Miller and Miller, 1977) finds that for 1976 a better predictor of the vote is provided by party proximity measures, based on how close the citizen was to the two parties on the issues. We can make use of all of this information from an uncertainty standpoint. The citizen might feel that McGovern has one position but that the Democratic party has a different position. If McGovern were elected, the policy that would be enacted could be expected to fall somewhere in the interval between McGovern's position and the Democratic position. That interval provides the type of range we require to test between the different models. In fact, we would regard this range as smaller than the actual uncertainty range, given that the voter might actually feel that McGovern and the Democrats both fall in regions around the positions to which he ascribes them.

Zechman (1978) employs this information in a Bayesian analysis, where the citizen's placement of the candidate modifies his prior notion of the placement of the party to yield a posterior distribution. We, instead, will use it to develop a series of uncertainty models in addition to the conventional candidate proximity and party proximity measures. In particular, we have the defensive voting model in which the citizen votes against the party *or* candidate furthest from him on the issue, the credulous voting model in which the citizen votes for the party *or* candidate closest to him on the issue, and an average model in which the citizen votes for the side for which the average of the candidate's and party's position is closest to him.

The CPS surveys included both candidate and party placements on the 7-point scales only since 1972. Recalling our earlier discussion, we would

TABLE 12.1 Rates of Successful Prediction of Votes From Different Rational Choice Models, 1972 and 1976*

Issue	1972 Party Proximity	1972 Candidate Proximity	1972 Average	1972 Credulous Voting	1972 Defensive Voting	1976 Party Proximity	1976 Candidate Proximity	1976 Average	1976 Credulous Voting	1976 Defensive Voting
Jobs**	80.8%	83.1%	81.6%	82.1%	83.5%	73.8%	75.4%	73.2%	75.5%	75.5%
						76.9	78.4	77.0	77.8	78.3
Taxes	72.6	73.7	72.5	72.3	76.4	69.9	69.3	68.2	69.5	71.0
Marijuana	79.3	77.7	78.3	79.6	79.2	75.7	76.9	74.8	75.5	77.7
Busing	76.8	78.9	78.1	78.6	80.0	75.8	72.9	74.0	72.9	77.1
Women	71.7	76.2	73.3	75.5	76.2	66.1	70.1	67.3	69.5	69.8
Accused	83.4	83.7	81.8	84.1	86.2	78.0	76.8	77.1	77.8	79.2
Aid to Minorities	78.3	83.5	78.3	80.5	83.2	78.9	78.8	78.2	79.7	80.3
Ideology	81.0	85.9	82.1	83.3	85.8	81.8	83.5	81.8	84.6	82.4
Vietnam	82.5	83.6	82.6	83.1	85.1					
Inflation	75.9	79.9	79.0	78.9	80.3					
Health Insurance						75.5	79.2	77.9	78.3	78.5
Urban Unrest						75.1	77.9	75.5	76.2	77.7
Average	78.2	80.6	78.8	79.8	81.6	75.2	76.2	75.0	76.1	77.0

*Only those issues asked of the entire sample are included. Individuals for whom the model provides no prediction (since they are equally close to each party or candidate) are not included in these calculations.

**The jobs item was included in both the pre-election and postelection surveys. Both results are given here, and their average is included in the "average" row at the bottom of this table.

expect the 1972 campaign to be viewed defensively, while the 1976 campaign might be viewed more ambiguously—Carter campaigned on a credulous basis while Ford tried to shift to a defensive basis. Table 12.1 shows the proportion of respondents who located both candidates and both parties on an issue who voted in accord with each model for the issues asked of the full sample in 1972 and 1976. The differences are not substantial, but the defensive voting prediction has the highest accuracy rate in 1972. On 6 of the 10 issues, the defensive model yields the best predictions, while it comes very close to the best prediction rate with the remaining issues. While the defensive model still has the highest average accuracy rate in 1976, a finer inspection indicates that the defensive and candidate-only models perform best on an approximately equal number of issues. This evidence suggests that the Carter-Ford contest was not viewed primarily in defensive terms, but that the McGovern-Nixon election was—an empirical instance in which a model based on uncertainty predicts the vote better than one based on certainty.

CONCLUSIONS

Uncertainty pervades voting, but previous studies have not made sufficient allowance for its effects. Uncertainty results from the limitations of the citizen, from the conscious actions of the candidate, and from the nature of the electoral process itself. As a result, spatial theories that require precise candidate locations are oversimplified. Zechman (1978) and Shepsle (1972) introduced uncertainty into the formal model of voting, but both employed (subjective) expected utility theory, whereas there are other reasonable theories of decision-making under uncertainty. Of particular interest as alternate theories are defensive voting, where the citizen attempts to defend himself against the potential candidate positions he likes least; and credulous voting, where the citizen is willing to believe that the candidate will adopt the possible positions he likes most. Under defensive voting, the candidate strategies converge to a single point at the median of the voter distribution; or, if candidate positions are inevitably perceived as ranges, then the candidate whose entire range is closest to the median wins. In contrast, under credulous voting, the optimal candidate strategy is to cover the entire policy dimension, or (if candidate's strategies cannot be subsets of one another's) at least to cover the median. This analysis suggests that candidates should attempt to manipulate the uncertainty environment in particular ways. Centrist candidates should foster defensive voting, while candidates with vague issue positions should attempt to be viewed credulously. An election campaign could become a conflict over the uncertainty environment as much as over issue positions.

In sum, once uncertainty is taken into account, rational voting encompasses a wider variety of behavior than usually believed, partisanship and candidate orientation become rational parts of the decision on how to vote, survey research attempts to operationalize the rational model appear too limited, and candidate competition will include competition over how the citizenry should react to the existing uncertainty. If all of this seems to make the study of voting less tidy, it also makes the study of voting more realistic.[16]

NOTES

1. Our emphasis is on candidate preference rather than on the final voting decision. Previous analyses have incorporated uncertainty into the turnout decision but not candidate preference. See also the emphasis on uncertainty in Popkin et al. (1976).

2. Downs did not discriminate between a party and its candidate, treating the two as fully equivalent by regarding parties as "teams."

3. This is explicitly the one form of uncertainty which Downs (1957: 80) permits in his model.

4. The relation of the candidates to uncertainty in voting is discussed in Page (1978). Uncertainty associated with the candidate is dealt with in Shepsle's (1972) formal analysis of uncertainty effects in voting.

5. A standard argument against viewing the candidate as a range is that the citizen might think there is *some* slight probability of *every* candidate taking *any* possible position on *any* issue. Rather than adopt that extreme position, we would instead assume that the citizens construct a region in which they expect there is a very high chance that the candidate's position falls. This is analogous to the notion of a 95% confidence interval and might even be modeled as a two standard deviation range around the citizen's stated estimate of the candidate's position.

6. This conclusion would also hold if the judgmental distributions were viewed as continuous distributions uniform over the range 2 to 4 for candidate A and over the range 1 to 7 for candidate B.

7. Consider the prescriptive flavor of Raiffa (1968).

8. This is in the spirit of the minimax-regret criterion that has been applied to the turnout decision in Ferejohn and Fiorina (1974).

9. Formally this is a "maximax" strategy of determining the maximum benefit that might be derived from each candidate and choosing the candidate who might provide the greater maximum benefit. It is also related to "sincere voting" since the citizen chooses the alternative which contains his more preferred outcome.

10. Two mixed models have received formal attention. Hurwicz's pessimism-optimism index weights the best- and worst-case analyses (Luce and Raiffa, 1957: 282–284). Ellsberg (1961) instead suggests that people weight their expected utilities and the minimax possibility.

11. While we have presented the models in the unidimensional case, the multidimensional generalizations are direct. When dealing with a set of issues, the citizen can view the candidate's position as a region in the space rather than as a single point. The citizen might consider the mean position in the region to calculate the party differential but might instead consider either the point furthest from his own or closest point or some mix of those points.

12. This way of looking at the vote decision is advocated by Popkin et al. (1976).

13. This expectation is bolstered by the agenda experiments of Plott and Levine (1978). Some subjects followed each of these decision rules.

14. The best strategy for B is not to "bracket" A, but to sneak up one side or the other and take all the voters on that side (though he still loses).

15. In accord with Shepsle's (1972) suggestion, competition against an incumbent can be modeled by portraying the incumbent as a certain point while the challenger is a range on an issue. Our results apply to this case. If the incumbent is perceived as the certain status quo, then the incumbent would win in the defensive voting situation (unless the *entire* range of the challenger is closer to the median) but would lose under credulous voting (unless *any* part of the challenger's distribution is closer to the median).

16. We have restricted our attention to models of candidate preference, but there are a number of interesting questions about how these results would generalize to models of the voting decision for multi-party races and for the turnout decision. A minimax regret analysis of turnout has been provided by Ferejohn and Fiorina (1974). They suggest that the turnout question is: "My God, what if I didn't vote and the candidate who could screw me worse won by one vote and then completely screwed me? I'd feel like killing myself." The credulous voter would instead ask: "My God, what if I didn't vote and the candidate who would have helped me most lost by one vote? I'd feel like killing myself." In each case, turnout to vote is fully rational in these models. A consideration of defensive voting also adds a new rational reason for abstention: abstention due to satisfaction when the citizen feels secure that neither candidate could really screw him (Weisberg, 1977).

13

CONTEXTUAL SOURCES OF VOTING BEHAVIOR: THE CHANGEABLE AMERICAN VOTER

John R. Petrocik

Election study followed election study; each portrayed an electorate in which politics was a peripheral concern, something which, in turn, encouraged an uninformed and unsophisticated—but satisfied—view of politics and the political system by the majority of Americans. When called to exercise their oversight function at election time, voters overcame these shortcomings by invoking an unalloyed attachment to one of the parties; those who failed to partake of this crutch displayed their indifference by failing to vote even if they felt an obligation to turn out at the polls. Personalities and situational idiosyncracies were the stuff of political decisions for most citizens (Campbell, et al., 1960; Converse, 1964, 1975). These findings were so consistent that students of mass behavior became extremely reluctant to credit discoveries of new patterns. Elaborations that provided nuances to the broadstrokes painted by the first three or four election studies were eagerly sought (Cf: Repass, 1971; Stimpson, 1975); reformulations of the core generalizations have usually met indifference or derision.

THE DEBATE

Revisions there have nonetheless been. One revision has questioned the accuracy of the original portrait, arguing that various kinds of errors of

AUTHOR'S NOTE: Some of the data used in this paper were supplied by the Inter-University Consortium for Political and Social Research. Neither the Consortium nor the principal investigators are responsible for the uses to which the data were put.

measurement and poorly specified research questions exaggerated the basic characteristics of the electorate. Key (1966), Repass (1971), Boyd (1972), Kessel (1972), Pierce and Rose (1974), Dobson and St. Angelo (1975), and Achen (1975) have portrayed either a less partisan, more issue conscious, or more rational electorate than the original paradigm. An alternate revisionist approach has not argued that the original conclusions are in error but that the electorate has simply undergone a change.[1] Field and Andersen (1969), Pierce (1970), Pomper (1971, 1972), Nie and Andersen (1974), Miller et al., (1976), and Nie et al. (1979) illustrate this reformulation of the dynamics of the American electorate.

Numerous palpable objections, however, have been raised to almost all of the changes that the electorate is thought to have undergone during the last fifteen years; and revising the revisionists has become almost as much of a growth industry in the late 1970s as revision was in the early 1970s. Our conceptions and theories of mass behavior are not sufficiently robust for us to be certain that we have asked the correct questions and reached tenable conclusions; and a host of methodological critiques have not been resolved.

This chapter has two goals: To rebut some of the rebuttals and to change the terms of the debate by concentrating on how changeable the voter is and upon what might be responsible for the shifts. Two of the more controversial changes—in issue consistency and partisanship—will provide the focus.

THE ISSUE CONSISTENCY CHANGES: A METHODOLOGICAL ARTIFACT?

The American Voter (Campbell, et al., 1960) and especially Converse (1964) convincingly documented the ideological confusion of the electorate. In their early studies, only a miniscule proportion of their samples (less than 3%) could be categorized as ideological, and responses to issue questions displayed little consistency. Liberal answers followed conservative answers, and, lest we assume that the average person simply understood politics according to different principles than those used by elites, Converse was able to show that voters did not even respond consistently over time to the same question. The work of Field and Anderson (1969), Pierce (1970), Pomper (1972), and Nie and Andersen (1974), which portrayed the population as more informed, ideological, and issue consistent (at least by the 1960s), represented a serious attack on a widely held model of the electorate. But this later work has not been completely persuasive, and the thesis that voters are now more consistent, in a liberal-conservative sense, than they were in the 1950s, has drawn considerable dissent. Critics have pointed out that the surveys that provide evidence of greater issue consistency used a question and coding format different from those used in the early studies

(Bishop et al., 1978; LeBlanc and Merrin, 1977; Sullivan, et al., 1978; Brunk, 1978). Instrument change, therefore, not a change in voters, has been held responsible for the larger correlations among the opinion questions in 1964 and after.

THE QUESTION EFFECTS

Some of the correlation analyses that have yielded data inconsistent with that reported by Nie and Andersen (1974) and Nie, et al. (1979) offer a serious challenge to the thesis of greater issue consistency after 1960. Bishop et al. (1978), Sullivan et al. (1978), and Brunk (1978) find that the differences reflect the type of question asked of the respondents, although Brunk's data are inconsistent with similar student data.[2] On closer inspection, however, the rival methodological explanation of the greater correlations has some defects of its own.

There are three things that must be examined: First, there is reason to believe that the data used to establish the methodological argument are also polluted with measurement problems. Second, even if the critics' data are taken at face value, the data they present do not support their unqualified conclusions. Third, there is a post-1972 decline in issue consistency which undercuts the foundation of the artifact argument.

First, the 1950s format of the Likert questions used by Bishop, et al. (1978) to refute the thesis of greater issue consistency after 1960 are inadequate for the task.[3] A combination of coding effects, agreement biases, and positivity biases made it almost impossible to obtain clear measures of opinion from the Likert type of items in the 1974 study. Consider the weak correlation between school integration and black welfare: Bishop et al., used this correlation to indicate how poorly the Likert items correlate with each other compared to the 1964-format questions. But what is more striking about the .25 gamma correlation between these Likert measures of opinion on school integration and black welfare in 1974 is that it is *half* of the .50 correlation obtained from the 1956–1958–1960 data. This decline is completely serendipitous, until one realizes that this particularly low correlation reflects the inability of the Likert school integration item to adequately identify racial liberals and conservatives in the 1970s. Several of the Likert items in 1974 produced virtually no variance despite the fact that there are reasons to believe that opinions on these issues are more dispersed than the Likert marginals indicate. The fact that there is so little dispersion in these measures insures that many nonconservatives on the school integration issue, for exampie, are coded as conservatives, while many nonliberals on other items, such as medical care and black welfare, are categorized as liberal. When a question that discriminates poorly is compared to one which does a better job assessing the underlying attitude, the correlation is attenuated because of error, not because the attitudes are unrelated (Schuman and Duncan, 1974; Achen, 1975).[4] This degenerate variance problem plagues the NORC data Bishop and colleagues use to question the increased consistency finding. Furthermore, although the gamma correlation measure treats tied data generously in computing the degree of association in a crosstabulation, such severely skewed data will lower the upper limit of the correlation. In simple 2 × 2 tables, skewed marginals do not normally cause problems. In larger tables, such as the 3 × 3 size used for this analysis, degenerate measures do limit the maximum value of the coefficient (Bruner, 1976).[5]

Second, even if the measurement problem is ignored (although there is no reason for doing so) the data that have been used to refute the thesis of greater consistency can, in fact, be used to lend it support. Consider the following.

Table 13.1 presents gamma correlations among the several issue domains analyzed in Nie and Andersen (1974) and Nie, et al. (1979). The first column in the table presents the gamma coefficients used to measure the level of opinion consistency in the 1956 and 1960 election studies (the Likert style of questions used in those studies are hereafter also referred to as the "1950s-format" questions). Column 2 presents, for the same issue domains, gammas computed with the SRC/CPS 1964 data (these essentially dichotomous questions are hereafter referred to as "1964-format" questions). The coefficients in column 3 are computed among 1950s-format questions that were asked of a subset of respondents interviewed in the 1974 survey that was fielded to test the question effects. The fourth column presents gamma consistency measures on a subset of the 1974 respondents who were asked the 1964-format questions.

If the increased consistency were as robust as the revisionists would prefer, the average gamma of column 3 should be greater than the average of column 1 (it is), and equal to columns 2 and 4 (it is not). There seems to be some greater consistency in the 1970s compared to the 1950s (column 3 *is* greater than column 1), but there also seems to be some question effect (column 3 is smaller than column 4).

At worst, the increase in issue consistency has been exaggerated; there is no warrant in these data for concluding that the increase in the correlation among the issue preferences is *only* a measurement artifact.[6] Moreover, there are data which indicate that even the possible exaggeration is smaller than the critics would like to believe.

Third, the lower level of issue consistency that appears in the data presented by Bishop, et al. (1978), Sullivan et al. (1978), and Brunk (1978) may reflect the fact that their data were collected in the middle 1970s after the high levels of issue consistency had begun to recede. Put differently, their data may not refute the findings of the revisionists; but they may indicate that the greater issue consistency of the mid-1960s to early 1970s was transient. The lower levels of consistency in 1974 and 1976 may reflect changes in the

TABLE 13.1 A Comparison of the Impact of Question Format on Gamma Correlation Coefficients

| | Election Studies | | NORC Study | |
	1956 & 1960	1964	1950s Format	1964 Format
Social welfare by Black welfare	.38	.48	.48	.63
Social welfare by school integration	.16	.26	.07	.52
Social welfare by size of government	.16	.52	.30	.28
Social welfare by cold war	−.09	.26	.12	.06
Black welfare by school integration	.50	.71	.25	.77
Black welfare by size of government	.08	.51	.16	.22
Black welfare by cold war	−.14	.29	.02	.09
School integration by size of government	.20	.46	.37	.25
School integration by cold war	.00	.20	.14	.22
Size of government by cold war	.03	.42	.25	.16
Mean Gamma	.13	.41	.22	.32*

*If the size-of-government item is deleted from the mean for this column, the adjusted mean is .35. Although such an adjustment does not seem essential, it could, in light of the discussion of the changed meaning of the size-of-government question, seem to be an appropriate thing to do.

same variables that the revisionists offered as explanations for the heightened consistency of the electorate after 1964; to wit, a change in the character of American politics.

The post-1972 national studies are especially relevant to this debate. They not only offer more evidence for the impact of the political context on the consistency with which voters respond to political debates, but they also present a direct challenge to the artifact explanation of the increase in issue consistency.

Virtually all of the data used to refute the thesis of greater issue consistency were collected after 1972. Consider the following: First, the average gamma among the 1964-format questions asked in 1974 (column 4 of Table 13.1) is lower than the average gamma for the same questions when they were asked as a part of the 1964 election study (column 2). In fact, issue consistency was lower in 1974 than it was in 1964, irrespective of question format (the averages of both column 3 and column 4 are less than column 2). The average 1974 gamma, however, fits nicely into a trend of declining opinion consistency since 1968. It is entirely possible that the average of the gammas in column 3 of Table 13.1 would have been larger if the study had been done before early 1974.

This, of course, is an almost impossible speculation to prove, but some data lend it more than circumstantial support.

Figure 13.1 presents the average gammas for the entire period. The leap from 1960 to 1964 became a slight decline in 1972, followed by a much larger erosion from early 1974 to the presidential election in late 1976 (even with the size of government question excluded in 1976). A factor analysis, which also was used to trace changes in issue consistency, yields an identical

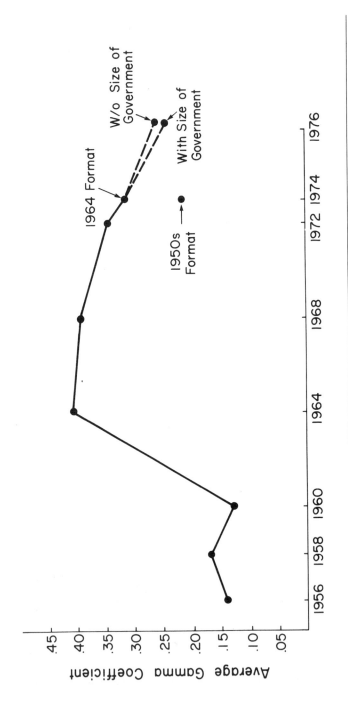

FIGURE 13.1   Average Gamma Coefficient among Five Issue Domains: 1956–1976

pattern (Petrocik, 1978). A summary issue index based on this factor analysis also shows a decline from 1972. About 27% of the population gave relatively consistent answers to the five basic issues in the 1950s. This proportion increased to an average of about 40% for the period from 1964 through 1973 (see Figure 8.4 of Nie et al., 1979). In 1976 the highly consistent had declined to about 27% again, and the proportion of centrists and inconsistents rose to 39%—their 1956 proportion. In short, the trimodal distribution of 1972/1973 had, by 1976, again become a bimodal pattern of the sort found with the 1956 data.[7]

These data are difficult to square with the artifact explanation of issue consistency changes in the 1960s. The artifact thesis is a plausible account of the 1950s to 1960s increase; it cannot explain the 1976 decline, *since the 1976 questions are identical to those used in 1972.*

Moreover, there are some additional changes, unrelated to issue consistency, which also reflect changes in the political context.

The Changing American Voter pointed to the reinterpretation of the size-of-government question as another indicator of the influence of the prevailing context on mass attitudes. The size-of-government question had, up to 1970, captured the classical Republican and conservative concern with "big government." However, by 1970, as Nie et al. (1979) indicated, the question underwent a substantive reinterpretation. Liberals began to see the question as a probe about government spying and the erosion of civil liberties, a change that coincided with the rise of the "social issue" (Scammon and Wattenberg, 1970) and a heightened concern with domestic disorder. As a result, the proportion of liberals agreeing that the government was "too big for the good of the country and the individual citizen" exceed the proportion of conservatives making this response in 1972 (Nie et al., 1979: 125–128).

But as this tide of concern with civil liberties has ebbed, the size-of-government question began to reacquire its initial interpretation. The same question asked of the 1976 electorate yielded relations reminiscent of the middle and later 1960s. The recovery of the size of government item to the point where conservatives once again are more likely than liberals to agree that the government is too big is striking (Nie et al., 1979: 371). Liberals still cast a more baleful eye toward the government than they did in the middle 1960s, but the 1976 relation between the relative thermometer ratings of liberals and conservatives and the size of government question looks much more like it did in 1968 than it did in 1972.

CHANGING LEVELS OF ISSUE CONSISTENCY: AN EXPLANATION

The revisionists have accepted this apparent variability in levels of issue consistency, because their explanation of its origin has emphasized the social and political context within which the individual experiences politics and not his or her cognitive ability and conceptual skills.

The original explanation of the low level of issue consistency within the electorate emphasized the limitations of the average voter (Converse, 1964), although a lack of attention to issues by candidates and others was also mentioned (Campbell et al., 1960: 186–187). In the "limitations explanation," the logic that ties issues into a liberal-conservative dimension becomes weaker and more blurred as less politicized citizens are encountered, because they possess few of the political conceptualization skills that characterize elites. Since these cognitive skills are learned very slowly, the lack of a belief system within the mass public was regarded as a nearly immutable trait over the short term.

But the alternate revisionist model of political issue consistency, which treats constraint as a social, as well as a logical or psychological, phenomenon, only requires some oscillation in the character of the political context for levels of issue consistency to change.

This social context model of issue consistency pivots on the degree of involvement by the individual in the prevailing conflict about issues. As there is an increase in the population's level of involvement in the conflict, the revisionists expect an unavoidable increase in the issue consistency of the population. Consistency should increase not because the population becomes ideological in an intellectual sense (although this may happen) but because individuals can be expected to "strive for consistency within their socio-political environment or because they react against the attitudes of those who belong to . . . undesirable political categories" (Bennett, 1975: 123–124).

Proving that issue consistency varies with the character or salience of politics is difficult, although the coincidence of the surge in 1964 with domestic turmoil, war, and contentious candidates, and its decline with a return to pre-Vietnam quiescense is too close a coincidence to dismiss. And it is this coincidence, if nothing else, which lends credibility to the revisionist's emphasis on the "nature of the times" as the source of greater issue consistency in the late 1960s.

What should be concluded? Clearly, issue consistency is a variable phenomenon. It is, as the revisionists have argued, responsive to the political environment (although the chain of evidence here is incomplete, see Nie et al., 1979: Ch. 20; Petrocik, 1979); its higher level between 1964 and 1972 was not completely artifactual; its decline after 1972 reflects a return to a pre-1964 environment in which politics is less salient.

THE DYNAMICS OF VOTING
THE RISE OF INDEPENDENCE

Virtually everybody is familiar with the post 1960 increase in the proportion of the electorate that eschews any attachment to the parties. Throughout the 1950s less than a quarter of the electorate defined itself as independent, but by 1976 the proportion of independents had climbed to about 38%. As straightforward as this change seems to be, it too has acquired doubters who question whether these are real independents within the meaning of the original formulation. The measure has not changed, but there is some suspicion that a large fraction of the increase has been contributed by "closet partisans," self-styled independents who, because party loyalties have gone out of style, refuse to describe themselves as Democrats or Republicans despite a strong preference for one of the parties and a record of support at the polls (Greeley, 1975; Miller and Miller, 1977).

The genesis of this concern with the intransitivity in the index of party identification (that is, the tendency of leaning independents to be more partisan in their presidential vote choices, among other things) is difficult to explain from the data alone. The intransitivity was visible in the earliest election studies, as Figure 13.2 demonstrates and familiar to most students of mass politics long before it was subject to any systematic analysis (Petrocik, 1974). In addition closet partisanship is limited to presidential contests; the vote in House, and gubernatorial races is monotonically related to party preference; and the intransitivity in the 1976 presidential election is no larger than it was in the 1950s or the 1960s. For all offices, defection is a bit higher after 1960, but the pattern of the relation between identification and voting behavior has not shifted.

More direct measures of party affect also distinguish leaning independents from weak identifiers. Figure 13.3 plots two indicators of party affect, both derived from a comparison of the thermometer ratings given to the Democrats and Republicans. The dashed line is simply the percentage whose ranking of the Republican party is within 10 degrees of their ranking of the Democratic party: The solid line is the percentage who rank their party within 5 degrees of the neutral point (50 degrees). In neither line is there the kind of intransitivity that would argue for treating leaners as more partisan than weak identifiers. The difference between weak and leaning identifiers is not as large as the difference between strong and weak identifiers, but the index was never represented to be an interval scale. In short, the rise in independence seems genuine.[9]

THE DECLINE OF PARTY VOTING

As the expressed partisanship of the electorate has declined so too has the role of partisanship in shaping the vote. The evidence for this is so overwhelming and widely recognized that the point is easily belabored (Nie et al., 1979; Petrocik, 1978). Through 1960, party preference accounted for about 50% of the variance of the voter for various offices, by the late 1960s it was down to about 36% of the variance, and in the 1976 election, party

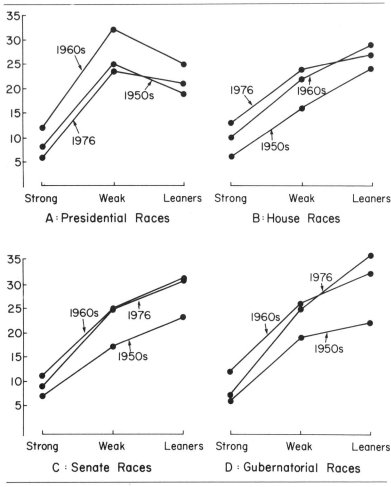

FIGURE 13.2   Defection Rates by Strength of Identification

identification accounted for barely a third of the variance in the vote for the different offices.[8]

THE RISE OF ISSUE VOTING

There is, however, substantially less agreement about a change in the relation of issue preferences to the vote choice.

   (1) Whether there is greater issue voting after the early 1960s depends on the acceptability of defining issue voting by the correlation between liberal-conservative issue preferences and vote choices (see Popkin et al., 1976; Repass, 1976; Margolis, 1977). The very stringent preconditions for issue voting laid down in *The American Voter* (Campbell et al., 1960) and by Campbell and Stokes (1959)—that voters have opinions, that they have some

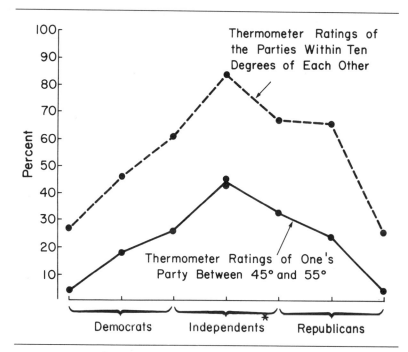

FIGURE 13.3   Party Identification and Ratings on the Feeling Thermometers

*Note that there are two points for the Independents. The larger percentage is the proportion of Independents who rate the Republicans at 50° ± 5°. The smaller number is the percentage who rate the Democrats within this range.

information about governmental policy on the matters in question, that they discriminate between the parties or candidates in terms of the issues, and that they have some concern about the issues—have not figured in the recent estimates of changes in the level of issue voting. The size of the correlation between the vote and issue indices has been the focus of research, and the relevant question is whether this design is sufficient to conclude that issue voting has increased since 1960. The simple correlation is intuitively appealing since it indexes the basic pattern expected with issue voting—a Republican vote among conservatives and a Democratic vote among liberals. Unless there are reasons to believe that the correlation approach does not accurately assess the underlying relation between issue preference and the vote, the evidence for greater issue voting appears to be sound.

(2) Varying definitions of a candidate evaluation, as opposed to a mention of an issue, appears to be responsible for the conclusion by some that the determinant of the vote which has changed the most since 1960 is candidate evaluations, not issue preferences. Evaluations of a candidate can refer to his person, his party or his issue positions. Changes in the overall correlation between the mentions made about candidates and the vote reflect changes in the relation of the vote to one of these facets of the candidate, any two of them, or all three. Declercq et al. (1975), Kirkpatrick et al. (1975), and Popkin (1976) do not distinguish the substance of the mention, and they find a much

larger correlation between a simple number-of-mentions index and the vote. Nie et al. (1979) treat person, party, and issue comments about the candidates as substantively different with only the first representing evaluations of the *candidate*. Decomposed in this way, they find a larger correlation between the vote and issue mentions about the candidate, a decline of the correlation of the vote with party mentions about the candidate, and virtual stability in the relation between mentions of the candidate's personality and the presidential vote.

If the latter approach has greater merit, these open-ended candidate evaluations also point to an increase in issue voting after 1960.

THE DECLINE OF ISSUES AND THE RISE OF PARTY IN 1976

In the 1976 contest, however, party identification was more important and issues less important than in any election since 1960, and the decline between 1972 and 1976 is immune to a methodological interpretation since the same measures are used in each year.

The proportion voting their party identification in 1976 is virtually identical to the rates of party voting in the Eisenhower and Kennedy elections. In fact, the similarity of the three slopes is striking. While the correlation of party preference and presidential vote is lower in 1976 than it was in the other three contests (a change that reflects a shift in the variance of the party identification measure), the relation for all four elections is virtually identical. The results of the regression of party preference on the vote yields indistinguishable slope coefficients. The popularity of Eisenhower surfaces in a much smaller intercept for the 1952–1956 elections, compared to its values in 1960 and 1976, but the regressions are otherwise identical; the 1960 and 1976 regressions cannot be distinguished; all show more party voting than occurred in 1964, 1968, and 1972.

Figure 13.4, which graphs the contribution of party preference and issue preference to the presidential vote from the 1950s through 1960s, illustrates the decline in issues. The graph presents three lines. The solid line is an estimate of the portion of the variance in the presidential vote that is correlated with party preference; the dashed line is an estimate of the vote variance that is correlated with a summary index of issue preference. Both lines are a conservative estimate of the explained variance. The dotted line graphs the variance of the vote that cannot be prudently assigned to either issue or party preference because of the correlation of party and issue preference with each other.[10]

According to Figure 13.4, the 1976 election was more similar to the elections of 1956 and 1960 than it was to the elections of 1964, 1968, or 1972. The unique variance component assigned to issues dropped to 1950s levels; and while the unique impact of party identification was not as great in 1976 as it was twenty years ago (the greater ideological homogeneity of Democrats and Republicans limits the portion of the explained variance that can be prudently ascribed to party), it is much larger than it was in the three most recent presidential contests.

Even more complex models which attempt to assess the variance of the vote that might be embedded in interactions based on especially strong issue effects among Democrats and Republicans or models which partition the shared variance between partisanship and issue preference show a weaker issue component in 1976 compared to recent elections and especially 1972.

ISSUES IN THE 1976 ELECTION: A DIGRESSION

Symbolic political beliefs, in summary, were not a major factor in the outcome of the 1976 election—something which seems to simply reflect the fact that these kinds of issues were not emphasized by candidates in their campaigns; at least they were not emphasized to the exclusion of other items: the state of the economy in general, unemployment and inflation in particular, Ford's pardon of Richard Nixon, and the need to restore trust in govern-

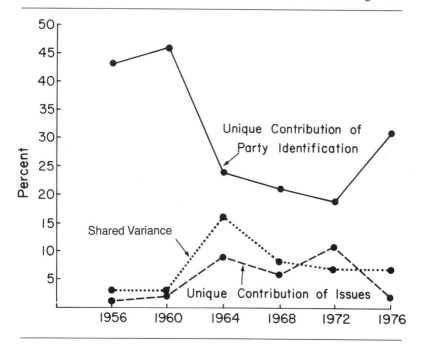

FIGURE 13.4   Percentage of Variance in the Presidential Vote Uniquely Attributable to Party Identification, Issue Preference, and Their Shared Component: 1956–1976

ment. If voters respond to the political context as the preceding data seem to indicate, we might expect the correlation of issues with the vote to reflect the emphasis placed on them by the candidates.

Table 13.2 presents several measures of the individual's vote. The first column of the table uses the reported vote as the dependent variable; the second column excludes partisans who cast a vote for the candidate of the party with which they identify; the third column excludes independents and partisans who cast a party vote. Because the variance in the vote variable changes dramatically from one measure to another, the specific coefficients vary as does the portion of the variance that can be safely attributed to any particular independent variable. Further, since each is measuring slightly different facets of the vote, the role of the variables changes slightly, but the overall pattern is quite consistent.

Column 1, which is based on a nonhierarchical treatment of party identification, shows party identification to be the largest determinant of the vote; all of the issues are markedly less influential. But, of the unique variance components that can be identified, respondents' feelings about Ford's pardon of Richard Nixon, the unemployment rate, and the rate of inflation have a higher unique correlation with the vote than symbolic issue preferences. The pardon and policy satisfaction measures uniquely predict over three times as much of the variance in the vote as the latter item. The second column, which attempts to predict the vote choices of independents and defectors with these same variables, shows a similar pattern. Less than one-fourth of the explained variance (which is admittedly not great in this limited model) is correlated with symbolic political beliefs; the pardon and economic conditions and policy were more influential. If only defectors are examined, as in column 3, basically the same results are obtained. Symbolic issue preferences account for less than one-sixth of the explained variance.

THE CONTEXTUAL SOURCES OF VOTING PATTERNS

Individual demographic and psychological traits are as overstretched when they are used to explain the oscillation in issue voting as when they are used to account for differences in issue consistency. Other variables must be considered. If the voters had been choosing between the same candidates from 1952 through 1976 it would be reasonable to attribute longitudinal differences to an increase in issue consistency, the growth of independence, or some similar change caused by the voters' long exposure to the same candidates. The voters would have "matured" (as Campbell and Stanley [1966] use the term) and this maturation might be held responsible for the changes.

But the situations are not the same; at least they do not appear to be. Several recent presidential elections have been marked by (apparently) strident and ideological candidates; and it is reasonable to question whether the longitudinal differences presented in Figure 13.2 result from the candidate

TABLE 13.2 Predicting the Vote in 1976

	PRESIDENTIAL VOTE		VOTE OF INDEPENDENTS & DEFECTORS		VOTE OF DEFECTORS	
	STANDARDIZED REGRESSION COEFFICIENT	VARIANCE UNIQUELY EXPLAINED	STANDARDIZED REGRESSION COEFFICIENT	VARIANCE UNIQUELY EXPLAINED	STANDARDIZED REGRESSION COEFFICIENT	VARIANCE UNIQUELY EXPLAINED
PARTY IDENTIFICATION	.43	14%				
STATE OF THE ECONOMY	.08	1	−.08	1%	−.15	2%
OPINION OF GOVERNMENT HANDLING OF:						
UNEMPLOYMENT	.07	2	−.07	2	−.11	3
INFLATION	.13		−.10		−.13	
NIXON's PARDON	.24	5	−.15	2	−.04	1
SUMMARY ISSUE MEASURE	.13	1	.10	2	.09	2
UNIQUE EFFECTS		23		6		8
CORRELATED EFFECTS		29		3		5
TOTAL R²		52		9		13

differences more than (or as much as) characteristically different patterns of voter behavior. It is possible that shifts in the level of issue voting reflect not a change in the "demands" of the electorate, but the varying stimuli of the candidates (Steeper and Teeter, 1976).

TYPES OF CANDIDATE-PAIRS AND THEIR EFFECTS ON VOTERS

The following typology of elections assumes that every candidate pairing can be categorized by whether it involves an ideological or popular candidate and by the "balance" of the election.[11] An election with ideological candidates is one in which at least one candidate is distant from the center point of the index that measures issue preference. A balanced election is one in which both candidates are alike in their popularity or alike in their ideological extremity. An election would be ideologically balanced if both candidates are substantially centrist or if one is perceived as well left of center and the other is seen as well right of center.

Four types of contest are possible. The first is an election that is ideological and balanced: Candidates are perceived representing the left and right of popular opinion. A second is an election in which one candidate is seen representing the center while the other is viewed as far from the center either to the left or right. Nonideological elections also fall into two categories. They are considered balanced if there is no difference in the popularity of the candidates and unbalanced if one candidate is substantially more popular than the other.

In a balanced ideological election there should be a steep slope relating issue preferences to the vote even with the effects of partisanship removed.[12] In an unbalanced ideological election, there will be a steep slope but it will be skewed left or right depending on whether the ideological candidate is Republican or Democratic. The hallmark of a nonideological election is a weak slope relating the vote to issue positions. If neither candidate is particularly popular, the slope should cross at the mid-point. When one candidate is notably more popular than the other, the slope should cross to the left or right of the mid-point for popular Democrats and Republicans.

The following table classifies 6 real and 5 mock presidential elections according to the degree to which the contest could be characterized as balanced and ideological. If the candidate-pair is a significant source of variation in issue voting, the slope of the deviations from the normal vote should be similar within any cell of Table 13.3 and different from contests that are in different cells. There should also be differences between the intercepts according to the cells of the typology.

The effect of the candidate-pair on the relation between issue preference and the vote appears in Tables 13.4 and 13.5. As Table 13.4 indicates, the character of the regression of the Democratic vote residual on issue preferences varies with the presence of ideological candidates in the election.[13]

TABLE 13.3   Using the Typology to Classify the Eleven Elections

		IDEOLOGICAL CANDIDATE	
		YES	NO
BALANCED ELECTION	YES	McGovern-Goldwater	1960, 1976 Humphrey-Percy
	NO	1964, 1972 Humphrey-Reagan Kennedy-Reagan	1952, 1956 Kennedy-Percy

When there is at least one ideologically extreme candidate, the regression coefficient tends to be large; when neither candidate is distant from the "center," the coefficient tends to be small. The slope is greatest where there are 2 ideologically extreme candidates opposing each other, slightly less steep where there is only 1 ideological candidate in the election (though the exact shapes differ; see Petrocik, 1979 for a more complex analysis), and the most shallow when neither candidate is far from the political center. The value of the intercept also varies with whether the Democrat or Republican is popular or ideologically extreme. In a balanced, nonideological election (the closest thing to a pure party contest), the Democratic candidate enjoys about a 10-point percentage excess vote among the most liberal fraction of the electorate. The value of the intercept tends to be greater if both candidates are ideologically extreme, or if the Republicans run an "outlier" against a centrist (Nie et al., 1979: Ch. 18). It is less than the pure party value if the Republicans nominate the centrist and the Democrats select an outlier. Similarly, the intercept for popular Democrats is well above the 10 percentage point mark.

The impact of the political context (the candidates in these data) on the level of issue voting is particularly apparent from a more detailed comparison of the 1960 and 1976 contests. The candidate-pairs were very similar in these elections; neither candidate-pair was especially popular and neither was notably ideological. (See Stokes, 1966 for some warrant for this description of the popularity of the candidates and Page, 1978 for information on their ideological distinctiveness.) The response of the voters to this similarity is illustrated in Figure 13.5, which presents a comparison of the normal vote residuals for the 1960 and 1976 elections. The points in Figure 13.5 are the deviations of the Carter vote from the normal vote estimate. The slope in the figure is a polynomial drawn to fit the residuals *for the 1960 election* (Petrocik, 1979). The fit of the 1960s slope to the 1976 data is nothing short of astonishing. While Figure 13.5 is more dramatic than the data in Tables 13.4 and 13.5, they all substantiate the hypothesis that variation in issue voting is closely tied to the ideological balance of the candidate-pair.

Issue voting, like consistency, may be extremely sensitive to the political contest. Except in the most ideological electorate, essentially centrist candidates will not provide enough clues for voters to sort them on any grounds

TABLE 13.4 Unstandardized Regression Coefficients for the Relationship of Issue Preference and the Democratic Vote Residual by Categories of the Candidate-Pair Typology

| | | IDEOLOGICAL CANDIDATE** | |
		YES	NO
	YES	−5.03	−2.58, −2.44 −1.97
BALANCED			
	NO	−3.68, −4.54 −3.58, −3.28	−2.31, −1.33 −2.51

**The numbers in Tables 13.4 & 13.5 are presented in the order the elections are listed in Table 13.3.

TABLE 13.5 Intercepts Associated with the Regression of Issue Preference on the Democratic Vote Residual by Categories of the Candidate-Pair Typology

| | | IDEOLOGICAL CANDIDATE | |
		YES	NO
	YES	23.6	9.7, 10.3 10.5
BALANCED			
	NO	27.1, 7.5 22.8, 28.7	−1.6, −6.4 18.7

other than their party and their personal appeal. So every increase in the issue distance between candidates increases the proportion of the electorate that perceives issue distances and is able, as a result, to make issue-based selections. In sum, more ideologically distinctive candidates in the late 1960s and in 1972, and not only a more ideological electorate, played a role in the increased correlation between the vote choice and political attitudes. The absence of such ideological competition in 1976 seems to be responsible for the decline in the relation.

CONCLUSION: THE CHANGEABLE AMERICAN VOTER

It is not an equivocation to conclude that the American voter has and has not changed over the last two and one-half decades. The preceding data portray an electorate that has oscillated in the character of its political attitudes and behavior. Voters have appeared more issue conscious and less partisan than they were in early portraits; and while the size of some of the

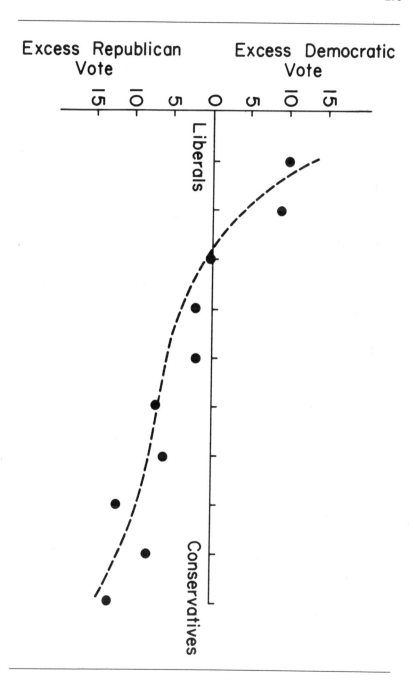

FIGURE 13.5   Fit of the 1976 Carter Vote Residual to the Regression of Issue
Position on the 1960 Kennedy Vote Residual

differences are inflated by measurement problems, not all of them can be traced to methodological variables.

But there is probably *not* a new American voter. It is unlikely that the voter has changed from one stable and normal state to a new stable and normal state. Rather, our image of the voter as a stable creature with a limited repertoire of responses to political events has been undermined. The original emphasis on inherent psychological characteristics in modeling the voter produced a caricature. The inherent psychological properties, while real enough, were overemphasized. It has taken some time for us to explicitly introduce more dynamic political processes.

Voters are probably not dramatically more ideological now than they were in the recent past. The increase in issue consistency and in the portion who used ideology to evaluate political stimuli reflect the intrusion of politics during the 1960s and a widespread use of ideological labels. Similarly, the surge of issue voting in the late 1960s and early 1970s, while not wholly independent of the greater politicization of the population, largely reflected a change in the types of candidates presented to the electorate. The presidential elections of 1952, 1956, and 1960 presented few burning issues to the public, and the candidates went out of their way to emphasize the person or the party they represented. Distinctive issues around which controversy, rather than consensus, reigned were more the stuff of the 1960s. The limited data from the 1930s that were presented in *The Changing American Voter* (Nie et al., 1979) give good reason to believe that an analysis of voting in earlier periods would have prevented us from painting portraits of voters that contained such soporific hues.

In short, the model behaviors of voters are strongly influenced by the prevailing political context. The lower levels of issue consistency, the weaker correlation of issue preferences with the vote, and the resurgency of the correlation of partisanship and the vote in 1976 point to the variable nature of mass behavior and attitudes.

NOTES

1. The character of these disagreements can be caricatured by reducing them to conflicts between traditionalists, revisionists, and neorevisionists. The use of such words here is not meant to imply the existence of formal, contending schools of thought. However, since there is no word more convenient than "revisionist" to describe the recent research that disputes some of the conclusions of the early election studies, it has been adopted here.

2. Petrocik (1978a) reports interitem correlations based on student data collected as Brunk's data were. The Likert questions in that study yielded a smaller average gamma (.34) than the dichotomous questions (.44), but the question effects were much smaller than those reported by Brunk.

3. The data used by Bishop were originally collected by the National Opinion Research Center for Norman Nie, Sidney Verba, and the author in late 1973 and early 1974. We commissioned that study to test the possible confounding effects of post-1960 changes in question wording, something we were concerned about long before the Schuman and Duncan (1974)

work appeared in print. Different thirds of the NORC sample were asked the Likert format, the 1964 format, and the post-1968 format questions. Our analysis of those data led us to believe in the basic soundness of the thesis of greater issue consistency. The following pages recapitulate that work.

4. There is some evidence of a severe skew in the marginals for these Likert style of questions in the 1960 study, leading to the possibility that the low correlations for the 1956 through 1960 period are underestimating the real relation among opinions in the 1950s. Indeed, this possibility is the operative assumption of Achen's paper (1975) on mass belief systems and survey data responses. Unfortunately, there is no acceptable way to investigate this possibility. Achen's analysis illustrates measurement error or nonattitudes; there is no warrant for choosing either possibility from the data presented in his paper. The post-1972 decline in issue consistency that is documented below may be the best evidence, albeit indirect, that issue consistency was low in the 1950s, although it may not have been as low as it appears to be when the Likert-format questions are used to measure it.

5. Different techniques for assessing the level of issue consistency have their own peculiarities. LeBlanc and Merrin's (1977) "absolute" measure of issue consistency shows no change, because their rule for counting consistent responses is insensitive to the off-diagonal changes that contribute to an increased correlation. This discrepancy is especially prominent when their results are compared to correlation analyses that use a generous coefficient like gamma. However, other, more conservative, measures of association such as Pearson's r, while showing less of a change from the 1950s to the 1960s, do indicate greater consistency in the latter decade.

6. So far unpublished work by Kristi Andersen and Stuart Thornson of Ohio State University have led to an estimate that perhaps as much as 50% of the change is a direct result of changes in question format and codes.

7. This summary measure of opinion is based on a factor analysis that is fully described in *The Changing American Voter*. The same principal components analysis was replicated with the 1976 data to build a measure that could be compared with the earlier data.

8. The felt partisanship of the electorate also seems susceptible to political tides. The Watergate-related revelations caused a sharp drop in the proportion of Republicans according to many surveys in 1974. The decline was so abrupt that many observers felt they were witnessing the demise of the Republican party. By 1976, however, the Republicans had rebounded to a 22% rate of identification—the same proportion they enjoyed in 1968 and 1972. The only visible erosion from the 1968–1972 period is in the proportion of Democrats. The fraction describing themselves as Democrats has actually declined about 3 percentage points since 1972.

9. The rise in issue voting has not been confined to presidential elections. The relation of issue preference to the House vote, controlling for partisanship, has also increased. The slope is steeper in the 1966 data than it is in the 1958 data, and the pattern for 1970 shows a stronger relation yet. See Petrocik (1978b) for the relevant data.

10. This "flip-flop" regression technique for decomposing the unique contribution of different variables to the variance in a dependent variable is explained in Nie et al. (1979: 303).

11. The typology of candidate-pairs was developed in Nie, et al. (1979: 319–325). It has been slightly reformulated in Petrocik (1979), who also presented some empirical warrant for the candidate categorization that appears in Table 13.4.

12. There are several ways one might want to remove the effects of partisanship, but they can be reduced to two basic approaches: simultaneous equations or residuals. This analysis uses residuals. Although there are various ways of computing the residuals also, this chapter uses the normal vote (Converse, 1966). Statistical arguments have been raised against this type of residuals analysis, but, for conceptual reasons, I do not find them persuasive. For a brief note on this see Petrocik (1979).

13. The summary issue index is briefly described in n. 7, above, and in Nie et al. (1979).

REFERENCES

ABELSON, R. P. (1975) "Concepts for representing mundane reality in plans." in D. G. Bobrow and A. Collins (eds.) *Representations and Understanding: Studies in Cognitive Science.* New York: Academic Press.

ABRAMSON, P. R. (1979) "Developing party identification: a further examination of life-cycle, generational, and period effect." American Journal of Political Science 23: 78–96.

———— (1976) "Generational change and the decline of party identification in America: 1952–1974." American Political Science Review 70: 469–478.

———— (1974) "Generational change in the American electorate." American Political Science Review 68: 93–105.

ACHEN, C. H. (1975) "Mass political attitudes and the survey response," American Political Science Review 69: 1218–1231.

ADORNO, T. W., E. FRENKEL-BRUNSWICK, D. J. LEVINSON, and R. N. SANFORD (1950) The Authoritarian Personality. New York: Harper Row.

AJZEN, I. (1977) "Intuitive theories of events and the effects of baserate information on prediction." Journal of Personality and Social Psychology. 35: 303–314.

ALLPORT, G. W. (1966) "Traits revisited." American Psychologist 21 (January): 1–10.

ALMOND, G. A., and S. VERBA (1963) The Civic Culture. Princeton, NJ: Princeton University Press.

ALMQUIST, E. M. (1975) "Untangling the effects of race and sex: the disadvantaged status of black women." Social Science Quarterly 56: 129–142.

ALTROCCHI, J. (1961) "Interpersonal perceptions of repressors and sensitizers and component analysis of assumed dissimilarity scores," Journal of Abnormal and Social Psychology 62: 528–534.

ANDERSEN, K. (1979), The Creation of a Democratic Majority 1928–1936. Chicago: University of Chicago Press.

———— (1976) "Generation, partisan shift and realignment: a glance back to the new deal," in N. H. Nie, S. Verba and J. R. Petrocik (eds.) *The Changing American Voter.* Cambridge: Harvard University Press.

ARMOR, D. J. (1974) "Theta reliability and factor scaling," pp. 17–50 in H. L. Costner, (ed.) Sociological Methodology 1973–74. San Francisco: Jossey-Bass.

ARTERTON, C. F. (1974) "The impact of Watergate on children's attitudes toward political authority." Political Science Quarterly 89: 269–288.

ASHER, H. (1976) Presidential Elections and American Politics. Homewood, IL: Dorsey.

———— (1974) "Some consequences of measurement error in survey data." American Journal of Political Science 18: 469–485.

AXELROD, R. (1973) "Schema theory: an information processing model of perception and cognition." American Political Science Review 67: 1248–1266.

———— (1972) "Where the voters come from: an analysis of electoral coalitions, 1952–1968." American Political Science Review 66: 11–20.

BAKER, K. L. (1978) "Generational differences in the role of party identification in German political behavior." American Journal of Political Science 22: 106–129.

BALL-ROKEACH, S. J. and M. L. DeFLEUR (1976) "A dependency model of mass-media effects." Communication Research 3: 3–21.

BARBER, J. D. (1972) Presidential Character: Predicting Performance in the White House. Englewood Cliffs, NJ: Prentice-Hall.

BARTLETT, F. C. (1932) Remembering. London: Cambridge University Press.

BARTON, A. H. and R. W. PARSONS (1977) "Measuring belief system structure." Public Opinion Quarterly, 41: 159–180.

BAYER, A. E. (1975), "Sexist students in American colleges: a descriptive note," Journal of Marriage and the Family 37, 391–397.

BECK, P. A. (1974) "A socialization theory of partisan realignment," in Niemi and Associates (eds.) The Politics of Future Citizens. Washington, DC: Jossey-Bass.

BECKER, L. B., M. E. McCOMBS, and J. M. McLEOD (1977) "The development of political cognitions," pp. 21–63 in Steven H. Chaffee (ed.), Political Communication. Beverly Hills: Sage.

BEM, D. (1970), Beliefs, Attitudes and Human Affairs, Belmont, CA: Brooks/Cole.

BEM, S. L. (1974) "The measurement of psychological androgyny." Journal of Consulting and Clinical Psychology 42: 155–162.

BENNETT, S. (1973) "Consistency among the public's social welfare policy attitudes in the 1960s." American Journal of Political Science 17: 544–570.

BENNETT, S. E., R. OLDENDICK, A. J. TUCHFARBER, and G. F. BISHOP (1979) "Education and mass belief systems: an extension and some new questions." Political Behavior, 1: (Spring): 53–71.

BENNETT, W. L. (1977) "The growth of knowledge in mass belief systems: an epistemological critique." American Journal of Political Science 21: 465–500.

_____ (1976) The Political Mind and The Political Environment. Lexington: Lexington Books.

_____ (1975) "Public opinion: problems of description and inference," in S. Welch and J. Comer (eds.) Public Opinion, San Francisco: Mayfield.

BEREITER, C. (1963) "Some persisting dilemmas in the measurement of change." in Chester W. Harris (ed.) Problems in Measuring Change, Madison, WI: University of Wisconsin Press.

BERELSON, B. R., P. F. LAZARSFELD, and W. N. McPHEE (1954) Voting, Chicago: The University of Chicago Press.

BIERI, J. (1961) "Complexity-simplicity as a personality variable in cognitive and preferential behavior," in D. W. Fiske, S. R. Maddi (eds.) Functions of Varied Experience. Homewood, IL: Dorsey.

_____ A.L. ATKINS, S. BRIAR, R. L. LEAMAN, H. MILLER, and T. TRIPODI (1966) Clinical and Social Judgment: The Discrimination of Behavioral Information. New York: John Wiley.

BISHOP, G. F., R. W. OLDENDICK, and A. J. TUCHFARBER (1978) "Effects of question wording and format on political attitude consistency." Public Opinion Quarterly, 42: 81–92.

_____ and S. E. BENNETT (1978) "Change in the structure of American political attitudes: the nagging question of question wording," American Journal of Political Science 22: 250–269.

_____ (1979) "Questions about question wording: a rejoinder to revisiting mass belief systems revisited." American Journal of Political Science 23: 187–193.

_____ (1978b) "The changing structure of mass belief systems: fact or artifact?" Journal of Politics 40: 781–787.

BLACK, B. (1958) The Theory of Committees and Elections. Cambridge (England): Cambridge University Press.

BLALOCK, Jr., H. M. (1970a) "Estimating measurement error using multiple indicators and several points in time," American Sociological Review 35: 101–111.

_____ (1970b) "A causal approach to non-random measurement errors." American Political Science Review 64: 1099–1111.

_____ (1963) "Making causal inferences for unmeasured variables from correlations among indicators," American Journal of Sociology 69: 53–62.

BLAU, F. D. (1979) "Women in the labor force: an overview," in J. Freeman (ed.) Women: A Feminist Perspective, 2nd edition. Palo Alto, CA: Mayfield.

BLUMLER, J. G. and E. KATZ (1974) The Uses of Mass Communication. Beverly Hills: Sage.

BLUMLER, J. G. and D. McQUAIL (1969) Television in Politics: Its Uses and Influence. Chicago: University of Chicago Press.

BOBROW, D. G. and D. A. NORMAN (1975) "Some principles of memory schemata" in D. G. Bobrow and A. Collins (eds.) Representation and Understanding: Studies in Cognitive Science. New York: Academic Press.

BOHRNSTEDT, G. (1969) "Observations on the measurement of change," in E. F. Borgatta and G. W. Bohrnstedt (eds.) Sociological Methodology. San Francisco: Jossey-Bass.

BOYD, R. W. (1972) "Popular control of public policy: a normal vote analysis of the 1968 election." American Political Science Review 66: 429–449.

————— (1969) "Presidential elections: an explanation of voting defection." American Political Science Review 63: 489–514.

BRODY, R. A. (1978) "Change and stability in the components of partisan identification." Delivered at NSF conference on party identification, Tallahassee, Florida.

————— (1977) "Stability and change in party identification: presidential to off-years." Presented at the 1977 annual meeting of the American Political Science Association, Washington, DC.

BROWN, S. R. (1970) "Consistency and the persistence of ideology: some experimental results." Public Opinion Quarterly 34: 60–68.

BROWNSTEIN, C. N. (1971), "Communication strategies and the electoral decision-making process." Experimental Study of Politics 1: 37–50.

BRUNER, J. (1976), "What's the question to that answer: measures and marginals in crosstabulation," American Journal of Political Science 20 (November): 781–804.

BRUNER, J. S. (1964) "Going beyond the information given" in J. Bruner (ed.) Contemporary Approaches to Cognition. Cambridge, MA: Harvard University Press.

————— and R. TAGUIRI (1954) "Perception of people," in G. LINDZEY (ed.) Handbook of Social Psychology vol. 2. Reading, MA: Addison-Wesley.

BRUNK, G. G. (1978) "The 1964 attitude consistency leap reconsidered." Political Methodology 5: 347–360.

BUDGE, I. et al. (1976) Party Identification and Beyond. New York: John Wiley.

BURNHAM, W. D. (1970) Critical Elections and the Mainsprings of American Politics. New York: Norton.

CAMPBELL, A. (1960) "Surge and decline: a study of electoral change." Public Opinion Quarterly 24: 397–418.

————— et al. (1966) Elections and the Political Order New York: John Wiley.

————— et al. (1954) The Voter Decides, Evanston, IL: Row, Peterson.

CAMPBELL, A. and D. E. STOKES (1959) "Partisan attitudes and the presidential vote," in E. Burdick and A. J. Brodbeck (eds.) American Voting Behavior, New York: Free Press.

CAMPBELL, A., P. E. CONVERSE, W. E. MILLER, and D. E. STOKES (1960) The American Voter. New York: John Wiley.

CAMPBELL, B. A. (1979) The American Electorate: Attitudes and Action. New York: Holt, Rinehart & Winston.

CAMPBELL, D. T. (1969) "Reforms as experiments." American Psychologist 24: 409–429.

————— and J. C. Stanley (1963) Experimental and Quasi-Experimental Designs for Research. Chicago: Rand McNally.

CARMINES, E. G. and D. GOPOIAN (1978) "Issue coalitions, issueless campaigns: the paradox of rationality in American presidential elections." Presented at the annual meeting of the Southern Political Science Association.

CARMINES, E. G. and J. A. STIMSON (forthcoming), "The two faces of issue voting." American Political Science Review.

CHAFFEE, S. H. with M. JACKSON-BEECK, J. DURALL, and D. WILSON (1977) "Mass communication in political socialization," in Stanley Renshon (ed.) Handbook of Political Socialization. New York: Free Press.

CHAFFEE, S. H. and M. J. PATRICK (1975) Using the Mass Media. New York: McGraw-Hill.

CHRISTIE, R. and F. L. GEIS [eds.] (1970) Studies in Machiavellianism. New York: Academic Press.

CHUBB, J. E. (1978) "Multiple indicators and measurement error in panel data: an evaluation of summated scales, path analysis, and confirmatory maximum likelihood factor analysis." Political Methodology 5: 413–444.

CITRIN, J. (1974) "Comment: the political relevance of trust in government." American Political Science Review, 68: 973–988.

——— H. McCLOSKY, J. M. SHANKS, and P. M. SNIDERMAN (1975) "Personal and political sources of political alienation." British Journal of Political Science, 5: 1–31.

CLAGGETT, W. (1979) The Development of Party Attachments in the American Electorate: 1872–1972. Ph. D. dissertation, University of Minnesota.

CONNELL, R. W. (1971) The Child's Construction of Politics. Carlton (Australia): Melbourne University Press.

CONOVER, P. J. (1980) "The perception of political figures: an application of attribution theory," Chapter 5, this volume.

CONVERSE, P. E. (1979) "Rejoinder to Abramson." American Journal of Political Science 23: 97–100.

——— (1976) The Dynamics of Party Support. Beverly Hills: Sage.

——— (1975) "Public opinion and voting behavior," pp. 75–169 in F. Greenstein and N. Polsby (eds.) Handbook of Political Science Vol. 4. Reading, MA: Addison-Wesley.

——— (1974) "Comment: the status of non-attitudes." American Political Science Review 68: 650–660.

——— (1972) "Change in the American electorate," pp. 263–337 in A. Campbell and P. E. Converse (eds.) The Human Meaning of Social Change. New York: Russell Sage.

——— (1970) "Attitudes and non-attitudes: continuation of a dialogue," pp. 168–189 in R. R. Tufte (ed.) The Quantitative Analysis of Social Problems, Reading, MA: Addison-Wesley.

——— (1969) "Of time and partisan stability." Comparative Political Studies 2: 139–171.

——— (1966) "The concept of a normal vote," pp. 9–39 in A. Campbell et al. Elections and the Political Order. New York: John Wiley.

——— (1964) "The nature of belief systems in mass publics," pp. 202–261 in David E. Apter (ed.) Ideology and Discontent. New York: Free Press.

——— and GREGORY MARKUS (1979) "Plus ca change . . .: the new CPS election study panel." American Political Science Review 73: 32–49.

CONVERSE, P. E. and G. DUPEUX (1962) "Politicization of the electorate in France and the United States." Public Opinion Quarterly 26: 23–45.

COVEYOU, M. R. and J. PIERESON (1977) "Ideological perceptions and political judgment: some problems of concept and measurement." Political Methodology 4: 77–102.

CRICK, B. (1973) Political Theory and Practice. New York: Basic Books.

CROCKETT, W. H. and T. MEIDINGER (1956) "Authoritarianism and interpersonal perception." Journal of Abnormal and Social Psychology 53: 378–380.

CRONBACH, L. (1960) Essentials of Scientific Testing. New York: Harper & Row.

CUTLER, S. and R. L. KAUFMAN (1975) "Cohort changes in political attitudes: tolerance and ideological non-conformity." Public Opinion Quarterly, 39: 69–81.

DAHL, R. A. (1961) "The behavioral approach in political science: epitaph for a monument to a successful protest." American Political Science Review 55: 763–772.

DALTON, R.J. (1977) "Was there a revolution? a note on generational versus life cycle explanations of value differences." Comparative Political Studies 9: 459–473.

DARCY, R. and SCHRAMM, S.S. (1977) "When women run against men." Public Opinion Quarterly 41: 1–12.

DAVIES, J.C. (1965) "The family's role in political socialization." Annals of American Academy of Political and Social Science, 361: 11–19.

DAVIS, D.F., J.W. DYSON, and F.P. SCIOLI, Jr. (1975) "The interaction of cognitive structure, political attitudes and information." Delivered at the Southern Political Science Association meetings.

DAVIS, O.A., M.J. HINICH, and P.C. ORDESHOOK (1970) "An expository development of a mathematical model of the electoral process." American Political Science Review 64: 426–428.

DAWSON, R.E. (1973) Public Opinion and Contemporary Disarray. New York: Harper & Row.

DeCHARMS, R.C. (1968) Personal Causation: The Internal Affective Determinants of Behavior. New York: Acadmic Press.

DECLERQ, E., T. HURLEY, and N.R. LUTTBEG (1975) "Voting in American presidential elections: 1956–72." American Politics Quarterly, 3: 222–246.

DeFLEUR, M.L. and F.R. WESTIE (1959) "The interpretation of interracial situations: an experiment in social perception." Social Forces 38: 17–23.

DENNIS, J. (1975) "Trends in support for the American party system." British Journal of Political Science 5: 187–230.

——————— and C. WEBSTER (1975) "Children's images of the president and of government in 1962 and 1974." American Politics Quarterly 3: 386–405.

DeSOTO, C., J.L. KEUTHE, and R. WUNDERLICH (1960) "Social perception and self-perception of high and low authoritarians." Journal of Social Psychology 52: 149–155.

DeVRIES, W. and V.L. TARRANCE (1972) The Ticket-Splitter. Grand Rapids, MI: Eerdmans.

DIAMOND, I. (1977) Sex Roles in the State House. New Haven: Yale University Press.

DOBSON, D. and D.A. MEETER (1974) "Alternative Markov models for describing change in party identification." American Journal of Political Science 18: 487–500.

DOBSON, D. and D. ST. ANGELO (1975) "Party identification and the floating vote: some dynamics." American Political Science Review 69: 481–490.

DOWNS, A. (1957) An Economic Theory of Democracy. New York: Harper & Row.

DREYER, E.C. (1973) "Change and stability in party identification." Journal of Politics 35: 712–722.

EASTON, D. and J. DENNIS (1969) Children in the Political System. New York: McGraw-Hill.

——————— (1965) "The child's image of government.' Annals of American Academy of Political and Social Science 361: 40–57.

ELLSBERG, D. (1961) "Risk, ambiguity, and the savage axioms." Quarterly Journal of Economics 75: 643–669.

ENGSTROM, R.L. (1970), "Race and compliance: differential political socialization." Polity, 3: 101–111.

EPSTEIN, C.F. (1973) "Positive effects of the multiple negative: explaining the success of black professional women," American Journal of Sociology 78: 912–935.

ERIKSON, E.H. (1950) Childhood and Society. New York: Norton.

ERIKSON, R.S. (1979) "The SRC panel data and mass political attitudes." British Journal of Political Science 9: 89–114.

——————— (1978) "Analyzing one variable-three wave panel data: a comparison of two methods." Political Methodology 5: 151–166.

ERSKINE, H. and R. L. SIEGEL (1975) "Civil liberties and the American public." Journal of Social Issues 31: 13–29.

EULAU, H. (1963) The Behavioral Persuasion in Politics. New York: Random House.

FEE, J. (1980) "Symbols in survey questions: solving the problem of multiple word meanings." Political Methodology 7 (forthcoming).

FEREJOHN, J. A. and M. P. FIORINA (1975) "Closeness counts only in horseshoes and dancing." American Political Science Review 69: 920–925.

——————— (1974) "The paradox of not voting." American Political Science Review 68: 525–536.

FERREE, M. M. (1974) "A woman for president? changing responses: 1958–1972." Public Opinion Quarterly 38: 390–399.

FIELD, J. O. and R. E. ANDERSON (1969) "Ideology in the public's conceptualization of the 1964 election." Public Opinion Quarterly, 33: 380–398.

FIORINA, M. (1977) "An outline for a model of party choice." American Journal of Political Science 21: 601–625.

FISHBEIN, M. and I. AJZEN (1975) Belief, Attitude, Intention and Behavior: An Introduction to Theory and Research. Reading, MA: Addison-Wesley.

FLANIGAN, W. H. and D. RePASS (1969) Electoral Behavior. Boston: Little-Brown.

FLANIGAN, W. H. and N. H. ZINGALE (1975, 1979) The Political Behavior of the American Electorate. Boston: Allyn & Bacon.

FRANKLAND, E. G., M. CORBETT, and D. RUDONI (1979) "Is there a 'silent counter-revolution' on campus? a longitudinal study of post-materialist/materialist values." Delivered at the 1979 Annual Meeting of the Midwest Political Science Association, Chicago, April 19–21.

GALTUNG, J. and M. H. RUGE (1965) "The structure of foreign news," Journal of Peace Research. 1: 68–70.

GARCIA, F. C. (1973) Political Socialization of Chicano Children. New York: Praeger.

GILMOUR R. S. and R. B. LAMB (1975) Political Alienation in Contemporary America. New York: St. Martin's Press.

GRABER, D. A. (1976) Verbal Behavior and Politics. Urbana, IL: University of Illinois Press.

GRANBERG, D. and E. E. BRENT (1974) "Dove-hawk placements in the 1968 election: application of social judgment and balance theories." Journal of Personality and Social Psychology 29: 687–695.

GREELEY, A. (1975) "Postscript: plus ca change, plus la meme chose." (Unpublished, National Opinion Research Center.

GREENE, V. (1978) "Simultaneous optimization of factor assessibility and representativeness." Psychometrika 43: 273–275.

——————— and E. CARMINES (1978) "Assessing the reliability of linear composites." Unpublished.

GREENSTEIN, F. I. (1975) "The benevolent leader revisited: children's images of political leaders in three democracies." American Political Science Review 69: 1371–1398.

——————— (1974), "What the president means to Americans: presidential choice between elections." in J. D. Barber (ed.) Choosing the President. Englewood Cliffs, NJ: Prentice-Hall.

——————— (1965) Children and Politics. New Haven, CN: Yale University Press.

——————— (1960) "The benevolent leader: children's images of political authority." American Political Science Review 54: 934–943.

GRETHER, D. and C. R. PLOTT (1977) "Economic theory of choice and the preference reversal phenomenon." American Economic Review, 69: 623–638.

GOLDBERG, A. S. (1969) "Social determinism and rationality as bases of party identification." American Political Science Review 63: 5–25.

HAGNER, P. R. and L. N. RIESELBACH (1978) "The impact of the 1976 presidential debates: conversion or reinforcement?" in G. F. Bishop, R. C. Meadow and M. Jackson-Beeck (eds.) The Presidential Debates. New York: Praeger Publishers.

HAMILTON, D. L. (1976) "Cognitive biases in the perception of social groups," in J. S. Carroll and J. W. Payne (eds.) Cognition and Social Behavior, Potomac, MD: Lawrence Erhlbaum Associates.

HANNAN, M. T., R. RUBINSON and J. T. WARREN (1974) "The causal approach to measurement error in panel analysis: some further contingencies," pp. 293–324 in R. M. Blalock, Jr. (ed.) Measurement in the Social Sciences. Chicago: Aldine Publishing Company.

HARRIS, C. H. [ed.] (1963) Problems in Measuring Change. Madison, WI: University of Wisconsin Press.

HARVEY, J., W. ICKES, and R. F. KIDD (1976) New Directions in Attribution Research Vol. 1, Hillsdale, NJ: Lawrence Erlbaum Assoc.

HARVEY, O. J. [ed.] (1963) Motivation and Social Interaction: Cognitive Determinants. New York: Ronald Press.

——————— D. E. HUNT, and H. M. SCHROEDER (1961) Conceptual System and Personality Organization. New York: John Wiley.

HARVEY, S. K. and T. G. HARVEY (1970) "Adolescent political outlooks: the effects of intelligence as an independent variable." Midwest Journal of Political Science, 14: 565–595.

HASTORF, A. H., D. J. SCHNEIDER, and J. POLEFKA (1970) Person Perception. Reading, MA: Addison-Wesley.

HEIDER, F. (1958) The Psychology of Interpersonal Relations. New York: John Wiley.

HEILBRUN, C. G. (1973) Toward A Recognition of Androgyny. New York: Harper & Row.

HEISE, D. R. (1970) "Comment on 'the estimation of measurement error in panel data'." American Sociological Review 35: 117.

——————— (1969) "Separating reliability and stability in test-retest correlation." American Sociological Review 34: 93–101.

——————— and G. W. BOHRNSTEDT (1971) "Validity, invalidity, and reliability," pp. 104–129 in E. F. Borgatta and G. W. Bohrnstedt (eds.) Sociological Methodology 1970. San Francisco: Jossey-Bass.

HERSHEY, M. R. (1978) "Racial differences in sex-role identities and sex stereotyping: evidence against a common assumption." Social Science Quarterly 58: 583–596.

——————— (1977) "The politics of androgyny? sex roles and attitudes toward women in politics." American Politics Quarterly 5: 261–287.

——————— and J. L. SULLIVAN (1977) "Sex role attitudes, identities, and political ideology." Sex Roles 3: 37–57.

HICKS, J. M. and J. H. WRIGHT (1970) "Convergent-discriminant validation and factor analysis of five scales of liberalism-conservatism." Journal of Personality and Social Psychology 14: 114–120.

HILDEBRAND, D. K. (1977) Analysis of Ordinal Data. Beverly Hills, CA: Sage.

HOCHSCHILD, A. R. (1973) "A review of sex role research." American Journal of Sociology 78: 1011–1029.

HUGHES, C. A. and J. S. WESTERN (1966) The Prime Minister's Policy Speech: A Case Study in Televised Politics. Canberra: Australian National University Press.

HYMAN, H. H. (1959) Political Socialization. New York: Free Press.

——————— and J. S. REED (1969) "'Black matriarchy' reconsidered: evidence from secondary analysis of sample surveys," Public Opinion Quarterly 33: 346–354.

INGLEHART, R. (1977) The Silent Revolution. Princeton, NJ: Princeton University Press.

——————— (1976) "The nature of value change in postindustrial societies," in Leon Lindberg (ed.), Politics and the Future of Industrial Society, New York: David McKay, pp. 57–99.

INSKO, C. A. and J. SCHOPLER (1972) Experimental Social Psychology. New York: Academic Press.

IYENGAR, S. (1973) "The problem of response stability: some correlates and consequences." American Journal of Political Science 17: 797–808.

JACKMAN, R. (1972) "Political elites, mass publics, and support for democratic principles." Journal of Politics 34: 753–773.

JACKSON, J. E. (1975) "Modeling and measuring political attitudes: a question of unobservable variables." Presented at the 1976 Meeting of the American Political Science Association.

JACKSON, T. H. and G. E. MARCUS (1975) "Political competence and ideological constraint." Social Science Research, 4: 93–111.

JAROS, D., H. HIRSCH, and F. J. FLERON, Jr. (1968) "The malevolent leader: political socialization in an American subculture," American Political Science Review, 62: 564–575.

JENNINGS, M. K. and R. G. NIEMI (1978) "The persistence of political orientations: an overtime analysis of two generations." British Journal of Political Science 8: 333–364.

——— (1975) "Continuity and change in political orientations: a longitudinal study of two generations." American Political Science Review 69: 1316–1335.

——— (1974) The Political Character of Adolescence: The Influence of Families and Schools. Princeton, NJ: Princeton University Press.

JOHNSON, M. and S. CARROLL with K. STANWICK and L. KORENBLIT (1978) Profile of Women Holding Office II. New Brunswick, NJ: Center for American Woman and Politics, Rutgers.

JONES, E. E. and K. E. DAVIS (1965) "From acts to dispositions: the attribution process in person perception." in L. Berkowitz (ed.) Advances in Experimental Social Psychology Vol. 1. New York: Acadmic Press.

JONES, E. E. and D. McGILLIS (1976) "Correspondent inferences and the attribution cube: a comparative reappraisal." in J. Harvey, W. Ickes, and R. F. Kidd (eds.) New Directions in Attribution Research Vol. 1. Hillsdale, NJ: Lawrence Erlbaum Assoc.

JONES, W. H. and W. W. RAMBO (1973) "Information and the level of constraint in a system of social attitudes." Experimental Study of Politics 2: 25–38.

KANDEL, D. B. (1971) "Race, maternal authority, and adolescent aspiration." American Journal of Sociology 76: 999–1020.

KARNIG, A. K. and B. O. WALTER (1976) "Election of women to city councils." Social Science Quarterly 56: 605–613.

KATZ, E. and P. F. LAZARSFELD (1955) Personal Influence. New York: Free Press.

KATZ, R. S. (1979) "The dimensionality of party identification: cross-national perspectives." Comparative Politics 11: 147–164.

KELLEY, H. H. (1973) "The processes of causal attribution." American Psychologist, 28: 107–128.

——— (1972) "Causal schemata and the attribution process." in E. E. Jones, D. E. Kanouse, H. H. Kelley, R. E. Nisbett, S. Valins, and B. Weiner (eds.) Attribution: Perceiving the Causes of Behavior. Morristown, NJ: General Learning Press.

——— (1967) "Attribution theory in social psychology." in D. Levine (ed.) Nebraska Symposium on Motivation Vol. 15. Lincoln, NB: University of Nebraska Press.

KELLEY, S., Jr., and T. W. MIRER (1974) "The simple act of voting." American Political Science Review 68: 572–591.

KELLY, G. A. (1963) A Theory of Personality: The Psychology of Personal Constructs. New York: W W. Norton.

——— (1955) The Psychology of Personal Constructs. New York: W. W. Norton.

KERLINGER, F. N. (1972) "The structure and content of social attitude referents: a preliminary study." Educational and Psychological Measurement 32: 613–630.

————— (1967) "Social attitudes and their criterial referents: a structural theory." Psychological Review 74: 110–122.

KERNELL, S., P. SPERLICH, and A. WILDAVSKY (1973) "Public support for presidents," pp. 148–181 in Perspectives on the Presidency, Wildavsky (ed.) Boston: Little, Brown and Co.

KESSEL, J. (1972) "Comment: the issues in issue voting." American Political Science Review 66: 459–465.

KEY, V. O., Jr. (1966) The Responsible Electorate. New York: Vintage Books.

————— (1955) "A theory of critical elections." Journal of Politics 17: 3–18.

————— and F. MUNGER (1959) "Social determinism and electoral decision: the case of Indiana," in E. Burdick and A. J. Brodbeck (eds.) American Voting Behavior. Glencoe, IL: Free Press.

KIESLER, C. A., B. E. COLLINS, and N. MILLER (1969) Attitude Change: A Critical Analysis of Theoretical Approaches. New York: John Wiley.

KINDER, D. R. (1978) "Political person perception: the asymmetrical influence of sentiment and choice on perceptions of presidential candidates." Journal of Personality and Social Psychology 36: 859–871.

KIRKPATRICK, J. (1974) Political Woman. New York: Basic Books.

KIRKPATRICK, S. A., W. LYONS, and M. R. FITZGERALD (1975) "Candidates, parties and issues in the American electorate: two decades of change." American Politics Quarterly 3: 247–283.

KLAPPER, J. T. (1961) The Effects of Mass Communication. Glencoe, IL: Free Press.

KNUTSON, J. N. (1974) "Prepolitical ideologies: the basis of political learning," pp. 7–40 in R. G. Niemi (ed.) The Politics of Future Citizens. San Francisco: Jossey-Bass.

————— (1972) The Human Basis of the Polity. Chicago: Aldine-Atherton.

KRAUSS, W. R. (1974) "Political implications of gender roles: a review of the literature." American Political Science Review 68: 1706–1723.

LADD, E. C., Jr. with C. D. HADLEY (1978) Transformations of the American Party System. New York: W. W. Norton.

LADNER, J. A. (1972) Tomorrow's Tomorrow: The Black Woman. Garden City, NJ: Doubleday.

LANE, R. E. (1973) "Patterns of political belief," in Jeanne Knutson (ed.) Handbook of Political Psychology. San Francisco: Jossey-Bass.

————— (1962) Political Ideology. New York: The Free Press.

LANSING, M. (1974) "The American woman: voter and activist," pp. 5–24 in J. S. Jaquette (ed.) in Women in Politics. New York: Wiley.

LAWRENCE, D. G. (1976) "Procedural norms and tolerance: a reassessment. American Political Science Review 58: 80–100.

LAZARSFELD, P. F. and N. W. HENRY (1968) Latent Structure Analysis. Boston: Houghton-Mifflin.

LeBLANC, H. L. and M. B. MERRIN (1977) "Mass belief systems revisited." Journal of Politics 39: 1082–1087.

LEVANTHAL, H., R. L. JACOBS, and N. Z. KUDIRKA (1964) "Authoritarianism, ideology, and political candidate choice." Journal of Abnormal and Social Psychology 5: 539–549.

LIEBERT, R. M. and M. D. SPIEGLER (1974) Personality: Strategies for the Study of Man. Homewood, IL: Dorsey Press.

LICHTENSTEIN, S. and P. SLOVIC (1971) "Reversals of preferences between bids and choices in gambling decisions." Journal of Experimental Psychology 89: 46–55.

LIPSET, S. M. (1960) Political Man. Garden City, NJ: Doubleday.

LIPSITZ, L. (1970) "On political belief: the grievances of the poor," pp. 142–172 in P. Green and S. LEVINSON (eds.) Power and Community: Dissenting Essays in Political Science. New York: Random House.

LODGE, M., D. V. CROSS, B. TURSKY, and J. TANENHAUS (1975) "The psychophysical scaling and validation of a political support scale." American Journal of Political Science, 19: 611–649.

———— and R. REEDER (1976) "The psychophysical scaling of political support in the 'real world.'" Political Methodology, 3: 159–182.

LORD, F. M. (1963) "Elementary models for measuring change," in C. W. Harris (ed.) Problems in Measuring Change. Madison, WI: University of Wisconsin Press.

———— and M. R. NOVICK (1968) Statistical Theories of Mental Test Scores. Reading: Addison-Wesley.

LUCE, R. and H. RAIFFA (1957) Games and Decisions. New York: John Wiley.

LUTTBEG, N. R. (1968) "The structure of beliefs among leaders and the public." Public Opinion Quarterly 32: 388–409.

LYNN, N. B. (1979) "American women and the political process," pp. 404–429 in J. Freeman (ed.) Women: A Feminist Perspective 2nd Edition. Palo Alto, CA: Mayfield.

McCLEOD, J. M. and G. J. O'KEEFE, Jr. (1972) "The socialization perspective and communication behavior," pp. 121–168 in F. G. Kline and P. J. Tichenor (eds.) Current Perspectives in Mass Communications Research, Beverly Hills, CA: Sage.

McCLOSKY, H. (1958) "Conservatism and personality." American Political Science Review 52: 27–45.

———— (1964) "Consensus and ideology in American politics, American Political Science Review 58: 361–382.

———— P. J. HOFFMAN, and R. O'HARA (1960) "Issue conflict and consensus among party leaders and followers." American Political Science Review, 54: 406–429.

McCOMBS, M. E. and D. L. SHAW (1972) "The agenda-setting function of the mass media." Public Opinion Quarterly 36: 176–187.

McGRATH, J. E. and M. F. McGRATH (1962) "Effects of partisanship on perceptions of political figures." Public Opinion Quarterly 26: 236–248.

McGUIRE, W. J. (1968) "Personality and susceptibility to social influence," in E. F. Borgatta and W. W. Lambert (eds.) Handbook of Personality Theory and Research. Chicago: Rand McNally.

MAGGIOTTO, M. and J. E. PIERESON (1977) "Partisan identification and electoral choice: the hostility hypothesis." American Journal of Political Science 21: 745–768.

MALBIN, M. J. (1975) "Party system approaching crossroads in 1976 election." National Journal 7: 799–814.

MARCUS, G. E., D. TABB., and J. L. SULLIVAN (1974) "The application of individual differences scaling to the measurement of political ideologies." American Journal of Political Science 18: 405–420.

MARGOLIS, M. (1977) "From confusion to confusion: issues and the American voter, 1956–1972." American Political Science Review 71: 32–43.

MARKUS, G. B. (1979) "The political environment and the dynamics of public attitudes: a panel study." American Journal of Political Science 23: 338–359.

MARKUS, H. (1977) "Self-schemata and the processing of information about the self." Journal of Personality and Social Psychology 35: 63–78.

MASLOW, A. H. (1970) Motivation and Personality. New York: Harper & Brothers.

MASON, K. O., J. L. CZAJKA, and S. ARBER (1976) "Change in U. S. women's sex-role attitudes, 1964–1974." American Sociological Review 41: 573–596.

MASON, K. O., W. M. MASON, H. H. WINSBOROUGH, and W. K. POOLE (1973) "Some methodological issues in cohort analysis of archival data," American Sociological Review 38: 242–258.

MATTHEWS, D. R. and J. A. STIMSON (1975) Yeas and Nays: Normal Decision-Making in the U. S. House of Representatives. New York: Wiley Interscience.

MEZEY, S. G. (1978) "Women and representation: the case of Hawaii." Journal of Politics 40: 369–385.

MILBRATH, L. W., and W. W. KLEIN (1962) "Personality correlates of political participation." Acta Sociologica 6 (Fasc. 1–2): 53–66.

MILLER, A. H., P. GURIN, and G. GURIN (1978) "Electoral implications of group identification and consciousness: the reintroduction of a concept." Presented at American Political Science Association meetings, New York.

MILLER, A. H. (1974), "Political issues and trust in government: 1964–1970." American Political Science Review, 68: 951–972.

———— and W. E. MILLER (1977) "Partisan and performance: 'rational' choice in the 1976 presidential election." Presented at the 1977 annual meeting of the American Political Science Association, Washington, DC.

———— A. S. PAINE, and T. A. BROWN (1976) "A majority party in disarray: policy polarization in the 1972 election." American Political Science Review 70: 753–778.

MILLER, W. E. and T. E. LEVITIN (1976) Leadership and Change. Cambridge, MA: Winthrop.

MILLER, W. E. and D. E. STOKES (1963) "Constituency influence in Congress." American Political Science Review 53: 45–56.

MISCHEL, W. (1968) Personality and Assessment. New York: John Wiley.

MUELLER, J. E. (1973) War, Presidents, and Public Opinion. New York: John Wiley.

MUELLER, W. J. (1966) "Need structure and the projection of traits onto parents." Journal of Personality and Social Psychology 3: 63–72.

National Center for Education Statistics (1976) Changes in Political Knowledge and Attitudes, 1969–76. Denver, CO: Education Commission of the States.

NEIER, A. (1978) "Response to George Will." American Civil Liberties Union, internal memo, February 9.

NEISSER, U. (1976) Cognition and Reality: Principles and Implications of Cognitive Psychology. San Francisco: W. H. Freeman.

NEWCOMB, T. M. (1961) The Acquaintance Process, New York: Holt, Rinehart, & Winston.

Newsweek (1979) "The Golden Passport." May 14.

New York Times (1978) "Most college freshmen in poll shun liberal label." January 22.

NIE, N. H. and K. ANDERSON (1974) "Mass belief systems revisited: political change and attitude structure." Journal of Politics, 36: 540–591.

NIE, N. H. and J. N. RABJOHN (1979) "Revisiting mass belief systems revisited." American Journal of Political Science, 23: 139–175.

NIE, N. H., S. VERBA, and J. R. PETROCIK (1976) The Changing American Voter. Cambridge, MA: Harvard University Press.

NIE, N. H., C. H. HULL, J. G. JENKINS, K. STEINBRENNER and D. H. BENT (1975) Statistical Package for the Social Sciences, 2nd Edition. New York: McGraw-Hill.

NIMMO, D. (1978) Political Communication and Public Opinion in America. Santa Monica, CA: Goodyear.

———— and R. L. SAVAGE (1976) Candidates and Their Images: Concepts Methods and Findings. Santa Monica, CA: Goodyear.

———— (1974) "Effects of victory or defeat upon the images of political candidates." Experimental Study of Politics 3: 1–30.

———— (1971) "Political images and political perceptions." Experimental Study of Politics 1: 1–36.

NISBETT, R. E., E. BORGIDA, R. CRANDALL, and H. REED (1976) "Popular induction: information is not always informative," in J. Carroll and J. Payne (eds.) Cognition and Social Behavior. Potomac, MD: Lawrence Ehrlbaum.

NOVICK, M. R. and C. LEWIS (1967) "Coefficient alpha and the reliability of composite measurements." Psychometrika 32: 1–13.

NUNN, C. Z., H. J. CROCKETT, Jr., and J. A. WILLIAMS, Jr. (1978) Tolerance for Noncon-
formity. San Francisco: Jossey-Bass.
NUNNALLY, J. C. (1967) Psychometric Theory. New York: McGraw-Hill.
NYGREN, T. E. and L. E. JONES (1977) "Individual differences in perceptions and preferences for political candidates." Journal of Experimental Social Psychology 13: 182–197.
ORUM, A., R. S. COHEN, S. GRASMUCK and A. W. ORUM (1974) "Sex, socialization and
politics." American Sociological Review 39: 197–209.
PAGE, B. I. (1978) Choices and Echoes in Presidential Elections: Rational Man and Electoral
Democracy, Chicago: University of Chicago Press.
————— (1976) "The theory of political ambiguity." American Political Science Review 70:
742–752.
————— and R. A. BRODY (1972) "Policy voting and the electoral process: the Vietnam
war issue." American Political Science Review 66: 979–995.
PEABODY, D. A. (1967), "Trait inferences: evaluative and descriptive aspects," Journal of
Personality and Social Psychology Monograph 7 whole no. 644.
PETROCIK, J. R. (1979) "Level of issue voting: the effect of candidate-pairs on presidential
elections." American Politics Quarterly 23: 303–327.
————— (1978a) "Comment: reconsidering the reconsiderations of the 1964 change in attitude consistency." Political Methodology 5: 361–368.
————— (1978b) "The changeable American voter: some revisions of the revision." Pre-
sented at the Annual Meeting of the American Political Science Association, New York.
————— (1974) "An analysis of intransitivities in the index of party identification." Political
Methodology 1: 31–48.
PETTIGREW, T. F. (1972) "When a black candidate runs for mayor: race and voting behavior,"
pp. 95–118 in H. Hahn (ed.) in Urban Affairs Annual Review. Vol. 6. Beverly Hills, CA:
Sage.
PHILLIPS, K. (1969) The Emerging Republican Majority. New Rochelle, NY: Arlington
House.
PIAGET, J. (1929,1951) The Child's Conception of the World. New York: Humanities Press.
PIERCE, J. C. (1979) "Water resource preservation: personal values and public support,"
Environment and Behavior (June): 147–161.
————— (1975) "The relationship between linkage salience and linkage organization in mass
belief systems." Public Opinion Quarterly 39: 102–110.
————— (1970) "Party identification and the changing role of ideology in American poli-
tics." Midwest Journal of Political Science 14: 25–42.
————— and D. D. ROSE (1974) "Nonattitudes and American public opinion: the examination of a thesis." American Political Science Review, 68: 626–666.
PIERCE, J. C., W. P. AVERY and A. CAREY, Jr. (1973) "Sex differences in black political
beliefs and behavior." American Journal of Political Science 17: 422–430.
PLOTT, C. R. and M. E. LEVINE (1978) "On using the agenda to influence group decisions."
American Economic Review 68: 146–160.
POMPER, G. M. (1975) Voters' Choice. New York: Dodd, Mead & Company.
————— (1972) "From confusion to clarity: issues and American voters, 1956–1968."
American Political Science Review 62: 415–428.
————— (1971) "Toward a more responsible two-party system, what, again?" Journal of
Politics 33: 916–940.
POPKIN, S. L., J. W. GORMAN, C. PHILLIPS, and J. A. SMITH (1976) "What have you
done for me lately?" American Political Science Review 70: 779–805.
PROTHRO, J. W. and C. M. GRIGG (1960) "Fundamental principles of democracy: bases of
agreement and disagreement." Journal of Politics 22: 276–294.
RABINOWITZ, W. (1956) "A note on the social perception of authoritarians and non-
authoritarians." Journal of Abnormal and Social Psychology 53: 384–386.

RAIFFA, H. (1968) Decision Analysis. Reading, MA: Addison-Wesley.

RAINE, A. S. (1975) "Change in the political agenda: social and cultural conflict in the American electorate." Sage Professional Papers in American Politics 3. Beverly Hills, CA: Sage.

RePASS, D. E. (1976) "Comment: political methodologies in disarray: some alternative interpretations of the 1972 election." American Political Science Review 70: 814–831.

————— (1971) "Issue salience and party choice." American Political Science Review 65: 389–400.

REYNOLDS, H. T. (1977) Analysis of Nominal Data. Beverly Hills, CA: Sage.

————— (1974) Politics and the Common Man. Homewood, IL: Dorsey Press.

ROKEACH, M. (1968) Beliefs, Attitudes and Values. San Francisco: Jossey-Bass.

————— (1960) The Open and Closed Mind. New York: Basic Books.

ROSE, D. D. and J. C. PIERCE (1974) "Rejoinder to 'comment' by Philip E. Converse." American Political Science Review 68: 661–666.

ROTTER, J. B. (1966) "Generalized expectancies for internal versus external locus of control of reinforcement." Psychological Monographs 80: 1–28.

RUSK, J. G. and H. F. WEISBERG (1972) "Perceptions of presidential candidates: implications for electoral change." Midwest Journal of Political Science 16: 338–410.

SANDAY, P. R. (1973) "Toward a theory of the status of women." American Anthropologist 75: 1682–1700.

SARASON, I. G. and G. H. WINKEL (1966) "Individual differences among subjects and experimenters and subjects' self-descriptions." Journal of Personality and Social Psychology 3: 448–457.

SCAMMON, R. and B. WATTENBERG (1970) The Real Majority. New York: Coward-McCann.

SCHNEIDER, D. J. (1973) "Implicit personality theory: a review." Psychological Bulletin, 79: 294–309.

SCHREIBER, E. M. (1978) "Education and change in American opinions on a women for president." Public Opinion Quarterly 42: 171–182.

SCHUMAN, H. and O. D. DUNCAN (1975) "Questions about attitude survey questions." in H. L. Costner (ed.) Sociological Methodology: 1973–1974. San Francisco: Jossey Bass.

SCHUMAN, H. and S. PRESSER (1977) "Question wording as an independent variable in survey analysis," Sociological Methods and Research 6: 151–171.

SCODEL, A. and M. L. FRIEDMAN (1956) "Additional observation on the social perceptions of authoritarians and non-authoritarians." Journal of Abnormal and Social Psychology 52: 92–95.

SCODEL, A. and P. MUSSEN (1953) "Social perceptions of authoritarians and non-authoritarians." Journal of Abnormal and Social Psychology 48: 181–184.

SEARS, D. O. (1975) "Political socialization." in F. I. Greenstein and N. W. Polsby (eds.) Handbook of Political Science, Vol. 2: Theoretical Aspects of Micropolitics. Reading, MA: Addison-Wesley.

————— and R. E. WHITNEY (1973) Political Persuasion. Morristown, NJ: General Learning Press.

SEARS, D. O. and R. P. ABELES (1969) "Attitudes and opinions," pp. 253–288 in P. H. Mussen and M. R. Rosenzweig (eds.) Annual Review of Psychology 20. Palo Alto, CA: Annual Reviews.

SEARING, D. O., J. SCHWARTZ, and A. LIND (1973) "The structuring principle: political socialization and belief systems." American Political Science Review 67: 415–432.

SHAFFER, S. D. (1978) "Balance theory and political cognitions: 1972–1976." Presented at the 1978 Annual Meeting of the Southern Political Science Association, Atlanta, GA.

SHAVER, K. (1975) An Introduction to Attribution Processes. Cambridge, MA: Winthrop.

SHEPSLE, K. A. (1972) "Parties, voters, and the risk environment," in R. G. Niemi and H. F. Weisberg (eds.) Probability Models of Collective Decision Making. Columbus, OH: Charles E. Merrill.

SHERROD, D. (1971) "Selective perceptions of political candidates." Public Opinion Quarterly 35: 554–562.

SHIKIAR, R., N. WIGGENS and M. FISHBEIN (1976) "The prediction of political evaluation and voting preference: a multidimensional analysis." Journal of Research in Personality 10: 424–436.

SHIVELY, W. P. (1979a) "The relationship between age and party identification: a cohort analysis." Political Methodology 6: forthcoming.

————— (1979b) "The development of party identification among adults: exploration of a functional model." American Political Science Review 73: forthcoming.

SHRANGER, S. and J. ALTROCCHI (1964) "The personality of the perceiver as a factor in person perception." Psychological Bulletin 62: 289–308.

SIGEL, R. (ed.) (1970) Learning About Politics. New York: Random House.

————— (1964) "Effect of partisanship on the perception of political candidates." Public Opinion Quarterly 28: 483–496.

————— and M. B. HOSKIN (1977) "Affect for government and its relation to policy output among adolescents." American Journal of Political Science 21: 111–134.

SIMONS, H. W. (1966) "Authoritarianism and social perceptiveness." Journal of Social Psychology 68: 291–297.

SLOVIC, P. and A. TVERSKY (1974) "Who accepts Savage's axiom?" Behavioral Science 19: 368–373.

SNIDERMAN, P. M. (1975) Personality and Democratic Politics. Berkeley, CA: University of California Press.

————— and J. CITRIN (1971) "Psychological sources of political belief: self-esteem and isolationist attitudes." American Political Science Review 65: 401–417.

STEEPER, F. and R. M. TEETER (1976) "Comment on 'a majority party' in disarray." American Political Science Review 70: 806–813.

STEINER, I. D. and H. H. JOHNSON (1963) "Authoritarianism and tolerance of trait inconsistency." Journal of Abnormal and Social Psychology 67: 388–391.

STEPHENS, S. V. (1976) "Communication: a reanalysis of Achen's critique of the Converse model of mass political belief." American Political Science Review 70: 1224–1226.

STERN, R. N., W. R. GOVE and O. R. GALLE (1976) "Equality for blacks and women: an essay on relative progress." Social Science Quarterly 56: 664–672.

STIMSON, J. A. (1975) "Belief systems: constraint, complexity, and the 1972 election." American Journal of Political Science 19: 393–418.

————— and E. G. CARMINES (1977) "The continuing issue in American politics." Presented at the annual meeting of the Southern Political Science Association.

STOTLAND, E. and L. K. CANON (1972) Social Psychology: A Cognitive Approach. Philadelphia, PA: Saunders.

STOUFFER, S. A. (1955) Communism, Conformity, and Civil Liberties. Garden City, NJ: Doubleday.

SULLIVAN, J. L., J. PIERESON, and G. E. MARCUS (forthcoming) Political Tolerance in the United States.

————— (1979) "An alternative conceptualization of political tolerance: illusory increases, 1950s–1970s." American Political Science Review, 73: 781–794.

————— (1978) "Ideological constraint in the mass public: a methodological critique and some new findings." American Journal of Political Science, 22: 233–249.

————— and S. FELDMAN (1979a) "The development of political tolerance: the impact of social class, personality, and cognition." International Journal of Political Education, 2: 115–139.

——————— (1979b) "The more things change, the more they stay the same: the stability of mass belief systems." American Journal of Political Science 23: 176–186.

SUNDQUIST, J. (1973) Dynamics of the Party System. Washington, DC: Brookings Institution.

TAFT, R. (1955) "The ability to judge people.' Psychological Bulletin 52: 1–23.

TAGIURI, R. (1968) "Person perception," pp. 345–449 in G. Lindzey and E. Aaronson (eds.) in Handbook of Social Psychology 2nd ed., vol. 3. Cambridge, MA: Addison-Wesley.

TAVRIS, C. (1973) "Who likes women's liberation—and why." Journal of Social Issues 29: 175–198.

TESSER, A. and C. LEONE (1977) "Cognitive schemas and thought as determinants of attitude change." Journal of Experimental Social Psychology 13: 340–356.

TESSER, A. and M.C. CONLEE (1975) "Some effects of time and thought on attitude polarization." Journal of Personality and Social Psychology 32: 637–644.

THOMASSEN, J. (1976) "Party identification as a cross-cultural concept: its meaning in the Netherlands." in Budge et al. (eds.) Party Identification and Beyond. New York: John Wiley.

THOMIS, D.B. (1978) "Political belief systems and ideo-affective resonance: the structuring principle revisited." Experimental Study of Politics 6: 34–89.

THOMPSON, D. (1970) The Democratic Citizen. New York: Cambridge University Press.

TURNER, B.F. and C.B. TURNER (1974) "The political implications of social stereotyping of women and men among black and white college students." Sociology and Social Research 58: 155–162.

WARR, P.B. and C. KNAPPER (1968) The Perception of People and Events. London: John Wiley.

WATTS, M.W. (1974) "Semantic convergence in the measurement of political attitudes." Political Methodology 1: 133–148.

WEISBERG, H.F. (1978) "Towards a reconceptualization of party identification." Presented at the 1978 annual meeting of the Midwest Political Science Association, Chicago.

——————— (1977) "Rational abstention due to satisfaction." Mimeo.

——————— (1974) "Models of statistical relationship." American Political Science Review 68: 1638–1655.

——————— and J. Rusk (1970) "Dimensions of candidate evaluation." American Political Science Review (December): 1167–1185.

WHITE, R.W. (1959) "Motivation reconsidered: the concept of competence." Psychological Review 66: 297–333.

WILEY, D.E. and J.A. WILEY (1970) "The estimation of measurements error in panel data." American Sociological Review 35: 112–117.

WILEY, J.A. and M.G. WILEY (1974) "A note on correlated errors in repeated measurements." Sociological Methods and Research 3: 172–188.

WILL, G. (1978) "Nazis: outside the constitution." Washington Post, February 2.

WITCOVER, J. (1978) Marathon: The Pursuit of the Presidency, 1972–1976. New York: Signet, New American Library.

ZADNEY, J. and H.B. GERARD (1974) "Attributed intentions and informational selectivity." Journal of Experimental Social Psychology 10: 34–52.

ZECHMAN, M. (1978) Dynamic Models of Voting Behavior and Spatial Models of Party Competition. Chapel Hill: Institute for Research in Social Science. University of North Carolina.